What's Next

What's Next

Countering Satan's Deceptions and Reclaiming God's Word in a Confused World

Scott & Sandy Boyd

Carpenter's Son Publishing

What's Next

Published by Carpenter's Son Publishing, Franklin, TN
Christianbookservices.com

Cover and Interior Design by Suzanne Lawing

Printed in the United States of America

ISBN: (print) 978-1-956370-79-9

Table of Contents

Introduction

For decades now, there has been a war against God's Holy Word. There has been a move of the enemy to discredit and ban the Bible. Satan would love to have the Bible labeled "hate speech" and removed from the internet and shelves of stores. Unfortunately, I believe this will eventually happen before Jesus returns. Satan knows that without the Bible, we would all float off into a black sea of deception and confusion. Everyone would simply do what is right in their own eyes, and spiritual chaos would take over. Satan has even caused strange hybrid forms of the Bible to be introduced to society that have muddied the waters of people's understanding.

So what is the Bible? The Bible is the infallible Word of God. It was originally written in Hebrew, Aramaic, and Greek. It was written over a 1,500-year period by the Holy Spirit, through forty authors who were holy men of God. Incredibly, it has perfect accuracy and continuity throughout, and it is the only book to write history in advance with 100% accuracy. God did not have trouble writing the Bible through His holy servants, but sometimes people have trouble understanding it. It is my desire that this book will help you understand the Bible, answer some of your questions, and help establish you in your faith. This book will not only equip you, but it will enable you to disciple and equip others as well.

I believe persecution is on the rise. With that said, the Bible will continue to be attacked and marginalized. We do plan on putting out a Bible through our ministry one day soon. I do believe the Bible will eventually be so persecuted, it will be removed from the internet and smart devices completely. So it is important to purchase a good physical Bible that you can take to church with you and study at home. I love the Modern English Version (MEV) as a great reading Bible. This book you hold in your hands will contain scriptures from the MEV throughout.

Additionally, I highly recommend the 1995 version of the New American Standard Bible (NASB 1995) as one of the most accurate Bible translations I have used. Finally, I recommend the 1987 Classic Amplified Bible (AMPC 1987). The Amplified will be especially helpful in studying the prophets and the poetic books of the Bible, and it brings more depth of meaning from the original Hebrew, Aramaic, and Greek throughout the entire Bible. I would avoid purchasing the newer NASB that came out in 2020, and the Amplified that was reissued in 2015, as they have made changes I do not care for. I believe the NASB 1995, the AMPC 1987, and the MEV Bibles will be a huge blessing to you as you read and study God's Holy Word.

I will discuss some of this in the last chapter of this book, but you will need to really know the Bible for yourself so you will not be deceived in these last days. The Bible predicts great deception in the end times right before Jesus returns. You are living in these times! The Bible, and the Holy Spirit, are the only true sources of truth that everything must be judged by.

Go through this study slowly and get everything out of it that you can. Learn to look up and find the scriptures for yourself. As you are reading *What's Next*, you can listen to the recommended sermons to help bring a depth to your understanding. As you go through the 56-week Bible study, it will help lay a strong foundation in your life.

If you will use this book to its potential, I believe it will help you develop a powerful prayer life, know the Bible for yourself, and be an effective witness for the Lord.

BIBLE TRANSLATIONS

Why are we using the MEV in this book? The MEV is derived from the original King James Version. In 1982 the King James Version was revisited and made into the New King James Version to be easier to read, but still retain the integrity of the translation. Around thirty years later, the King James Version was revisited again for the twenty-first century. In the MEV, the King James Version was made easy to read in our modern vernacular without compromising the translation in any way. It is a very accurate literal translation from the original Hebrew, Aramaic, and Greek. This is a wonderful translation that in every way exemplifies excellence in the literal translation. The syntax from the original King James Version is obvious, and it is very comfortable for either a new believer or seasoned saint to sit and enjoy reading.

I believe if you follow the suggested Bible studies in this book, it will be the equivalent of two years of Bible school that will help you get established in your faith. You will then be able to teach and help others. I suggest that you give yourself at least two to three years to complete the recommended reading, personal research, and complete all the studies in this book. If that is moving too quickly, feel free to go at a slower pace. The goal should not be how fast you can complete the suggested reading, but rather, it should be getting all that you can out of the program. Be consistent and diligent to finish the program from beginning to end. I know it will transform your life.

The recommended sermon series throughout this book are able to be watched or listened to for free on our website www.fnirevival.com and have corresponding notes uploaded with each sermon. Just go to the media page of our website, then click on the playlists tab of the media player, and find the recommended series.

You will need to purchase your own personal journal to document everything you are learning as you go through this material. Personal journaling is very important. Not only can you document what you learn from the book, but also what God is speaking to you at this season of your life. I do not recommend digital journals, but would encourage a physical journal and a physical Bible.

In section two, I will walk you through the entire Bible in 56 weeks. This section has corresponding teaching videos you can view online for free which will deepen your understanding, and it also has scripture memory to get God's Word in your heart.

Section three has a brief teaching on the importance of the Hebrew roots of our Christian faith. Understanding the Hebrew roots from a New Testament perspective will bring great depth to your scriptural understanding and walk with God. We have also added an explanation of Biblical symbolism which many times can be confusing to a new believer.

As you move into section four, there is an outline to follow to have a powerful personal prayer life, how to spiritually cleanse your home and land, powerful spiritual warfare prayers, and finally a father's blessing to impart to your children and grandchildren.

In sections five and six, I have placed a brief description of each book of the Bible to help you understand when it was written, the author, an outline of what is covered, and key points and scriptures. This should help your personal studies of the word of God tremendously.

In section seven of this book we will discuss some challenges of living in these last days. With that said, the most important thing I could tell you in your personal walk with Christ is to grow in a deep meaningful personal prayer life, live righteously in a healthy fear of God, and deeply study the Bible for yourself. This will protect you from deception, and it will prepare you for the coming of the Lord. The Lord is coming for a bride without spot or blemish and those filled with extra oil.

May God richly bless you in Christ Jesus our Lord,
Pastor Scott Boyd

Section One: What's Next

GOD'S PLAN OF SALVATION

I highly recommend watching the New Believers Bible Study teaching videos on our website media player. You can go to the media player on our media page, and click on the playlists tab to view them.

God created hell for Satan and his fallen angels. It was never God's desire or plan for a human being to end up there. In fact, the Bible says it is not God's will that any should perish, but rather that all come unto repentance. God looked down and saw our situation of living in sin, on our way to hell, and created a plan of salvation. The biblical principle is that you are a slave to the one you obey. When Adam and Eve obeyed the voice of Satan and sinned, they opened up the human race to be enslaved by Satan. We are born with a sinful nature, have sinned since our childhood, and we are on a path of spiritual destruction that will ultimately end in hell. God loved us so much that He sent His Son to pay the ultimate price for our salvation. God became a man, entering the human race through Mary's womb. As a human being Jesus is called the "Last Adam" in 1 Corinthians 15:45-47. He lived a perfect life. He never sinned one time. When Adam fell in the garden of Eden, God killed an animal and clothed Adam and Eve with animal skins. He gave them the gospel when He told them that from the seed of the woman one would come who would crush the head of the serpent. You can read this story in Genesis chapter 3. Adam learned that only through the shedding of blood is there forgiveness for sins. From that moment on, every animal sacrificed was pointing to a day that Jesus would come and offer himself as a sacrifice on the cross. This is why John the Baptist called Jesus the "Lamb of God, who takes away the sin of the world (John 1:29)."

We live now on the other side of the cross. Those who died before Christ were offering animal sacrifices while looking for the promised Messiah who would come, but now we have the complete work of Jesus. We look back at the Messiah who came and His death and resurrection.

I give this example in our pamphlets that we give out. I will share it here as well. Let's say you robbed a bank, killed some people in the process, and were caught on video in the act. Then you stood before a judge. You are guilty without a doubt. This judge would have to send you to the electric chair for your crimes. Even if this judge knew you personally and loved you, he would still have to sentence you. Imagine that a stranger came in the back of the courtroom who never committed a crime in his life and offered to take your punishment for you. This individual asked the judge that even your record would die with him in the electric chair so that you would leave the courtroom completely free without even a criminal record. It would be as though you never committed the crime. Then later you saw that man dying for you in the electric chair. This is what Jesus did for you. He took your punishment and criminal record with him on the cross. When you truly accept what He did for you and confess your sins, the Bible teaches that God forgives you and gives you a clean record. Not only are you forgiven, but the Holy Spirit of God enters you, and you are born again. This new birth causes God to see you as His child. Once we become children of God, we must cleanse our lives and homes, and learn the Bible so that we can understand what pleases and displeases the Lord. This is also why attending a good church is so important. We need the teaching and the strength that comes from other believers.

By accepting Jesus Christ, you have made the most important decision of your life! This is much deeper than just agreeing with some beliefs or an emotional experience. Rather, this is a deep spiritual change that will affect the rest of your life. The Bible calls this being born again. The Holy Spirit of God enters the heart of an individual. When this happens, you will become a new creation in Christ. Gradually, all the old things will pass away, and everything will eventually become new.

God leveled the playing field. The gospel is free and so simple that many don't accept it. No matter your social economic status, race, or gender, all have to humble themselves and come to the foot of the cross for salvation.

Jesus took your death, your punishment, and your record of sins upon himself. The blood He shed has the power, like spiritual soap, to wash away all your sins and declare you clean before God. God's justice was satisfied on the cross.

If you are reading this and you are not sure of your salvation, I want you to close your eyes and picture Jesus on the cross dying for your sins. Now as you open your eyes again, you can sincerely pray this prayer to him.

> *Jesus, I believe you are the Son of God and the only way to God. You died for my sins in my place, and then you rose from the dead. I ask you to forgive me of all my sins, transgressions, and iniquity. I thank you for your blood washing me clean from all my sins. Because of your blood, I am entering a covenant with you, and I am now a child of God. I am of the seed of Abraham, and the oath and blessings given to Abraham are my inheritance. I am justified, sanctified as holy unto you, and have become the righteousness of God in Christ Jesus. I thank you that*

I am now born again as your Holy Spirit has entered my heart. I am a new creation, and I will never be the same.

This teaching is written to help you understand what to do next. It will be very important to apply everything you read in this book to your life. The book of James in the Bible warns of those who hear the word but don't put it into practice. Make sure that you are one who will both hear the word and will apply it to your life.

CLEANING HOUSE

We have included our cleansing homes and land prayer in this book to help you pray over your home and property (Page 167).

Now that you have accepted Christ and entered into a covenant with Him, the Bible calls you a child of God. In high school when a young lady breaks up with her boyfriend, she throws his letterman jacket back in his face, and she gives back anything he gave her. In the same way, you need to remove anything out of your life that will cause you to stumble. Anything of the devil needs to be purged from your life. This means you need to go through your home and your car and throw away anything of the occult and/or sexual immorality (pornography). You need to dump the alcohol down the drain, flush the drugs down the toilet, and throw the cigarettes in the trash. If there are videos or music that you know is not pleasing to God, you need to get rid of them. You need to sever any old friendships that would lead you astray and cause you to fall back into the sins you just came out of. You need to start going to church and making new friendships that will replace the old. As you are very young in the Lord, you need to find a good Bible-believing church where the Holy Spirit moves in power. Find a pastor that preaches the truth and speaks against sin. It is a good sign when you sit through a convicting sermon, and you feel you need to go down and ask forgiveness for your sins and get things right with God at the altar. Those are the types of churches God is pleased with, and where you need to go. Anything in your life that could cause you to sin, you need to remove it and separate from it. This process of cleansing your life and home is incredibly important for you to continue to move forward into all that God has for you and not be pulled backwards into your past. It is important to make a list of people you need to forgive and out loud choose to forgive each one by name. It is also so important that you write out a list of all the sins you have ever committed. Then out loud confess them to God and ask His forgiveness. He has promised to forgive you and cleanse you from all unrighteousness.

WATER BAPTISM

Sadly, water baptism in many places is just a dead religious ritual. Water immersion is much more powerful than most Christians in America really understand. In 1 Corinthians 10 the apostle Paul wrote about how Israel was baptized into Moses through the Red Sea. That same water that baptized them then closed behind them and destroyed their pursuing enemies. That water seemed to consecrate them and separate them from their sinful past (their Egypt). I have personally seen people delivered and healed in water immersion. God's presence can be so strong that it breaks through stubborn issues as people are baptized. I would add that the priesthood was consecrated to enter God's manifest presence by the blood, water immersion, and anointing with oil (Exodus 29). This pattern still holds true in the New Testament. In the church I pastor, a couple of times a year we pray and fast for a few weeks. Then we end that fast with a deep consecration service. During this service, we take communion in a special way together, anoint everyone with oil and lay hands on them for a powerful impartation, and then close the service with water immersion for those who want to come. This has been extremely powerful. These seasons of fasting and consecrating ourselves has a lot to do with the incredible presence of God in our midst. I have felt the glory fire of God in the water as we immerse people. God taught

Israel about water immersion after being defiled, and also before entering into His presence. In the same way, I have seen people return to the Lord and get baptized, and it was so powerful. I have seen those under our ministry go deeper in God's presence after immersion. The last thing I would say is that in Jewish tradition, a bride would immerse herself before being married to leave her old life behind and move into her new life. Could it be that God is calling us to a new understanding of water immersion because He is using it to prepare a bride to meet her bridegroom at the marriage supper of the Lamb?

THE IMPORTANCE OF A PERSONAL PRAYER LIFE

I highly recommend that you watch or listen to the sermon series entitle Keys to an Effective Prayer Life. This is one of my most important series I have ever taught, and it will teach you how to have a powerful prayer life. You can go to our media page of our website, scroll down to the media player, and click on the playlists tab to find this series.

When God created man and placed him in the garden, it was for fellowship. When sin entered the world, it brought a separation between God and man. The reason Jesus died on the cross was to remove sin so that fellowship could be restored.

The single most important aspect of your salvation is to develop a living relationship with the Lord. That relationship will be developed primarily through prayer. Your personal prayer life is one of the most important parts of your salvation experience. Prayer is where you will learn to hear from God, learn the Word as you read it, and learn to be led by the Spirit. Romans 8:14-17 states that those that are led by the Spirit of God are sons of God. Sonship implies maturity. In other words, leaving behind spiritual childishness and growing up. So basically those who never learn to be led by the Spirit are remaining babes in Christ.

We must get to know the Bible for ourselves so we are not deceived. It is so important to develop a relationship with the Holy Spirit so we are not led astray by another spirit. We have to have a strong prayer life to be spiritually strong and in tune with the Lord. A praying Christian is a strong Christian just like a praying church is a powerful church.

When God mightily touched my life as a young man, I asked a man of God I respected for advice. He told me, "Learn to pray."

Jesus taught us in Matthew chapter 6 by saying "when you pray, when you fast, and when you give" as He gave instructions concerning these things. In other words, He never said "if" you do these things. It was assumed these would be a normal healthy part of our Christian walk. If you want to know how to have an effective prayer life, I recommend Larry Lea's book *Could You Not Tarry One Hour?* I also recommend Dr. David Yonggi Cho's book *Prayer That Brings Revival.* These are life-changing books that will really help you in your prayer life.

CHURCH ATTENDANCE

Rebellious people come up with a lot of excuses why they can't or won't do certain things. I have found this to be especially true in church attendance. The people that don't want to attend church faithfully come up with all kinds of excuses to not have to do what they are supposed to do. The Bible tells us to not forsake assembling ourselves together in Hebrews 10:25. The people who don't want to attend usually have an issue with submission to authority and accountability that comes with church attendance.

The church is where God has invested His gifts and His authority. Many people who attend our church with a good attitude of submission to authority experience tremendous answers to prayers and miracles in their lives. It is through the local church, and the prayers of God's people, that these miracles come forth.

Find a church that preaches the hardcore truth and calls you to repentance of sin. Find a place that loves the Word. Also, the church you attend needs to be a praying church that seeks the move of the Holy Spirit and the gifts of the Spirit in operation. You should be able to go to church and experience a healing or a breakthrough when going through a spiritual battle. It should be a place you can expect the power of God to show up, and to have answers to prayer take place. Don't look to the size of the building, the number of attendees, the entertainment, or the social club aspects of modern church life. Those things are just an empty, powerless shell of what a church should be. Find a place where God shows up and transforms lives by the power of HIS Word and HIS Spirit.

THE PLAN OF SALVATION

Before you begin to study this lesson, are you wondering why people need to be "saved"? Why does everyone have to be "born again"? Aren't some people just "good people"? Won't God just let them in to heaven? If you are a new Christian you may be wondering about some of these questions even if you have accepted the Lord for yourself and have been born again. So, let's begin with what the Word of God says.

Read Romans 3:23. Who is guilty of sin?

Read Romans 6:23. What is the penalty for sin or disobedience to God?

When Adam and Eve sinned in the Garden of Eden, sin entered the human race, and all people have a sin nature. There is an attitude of rebellion in our hearts that makes us want to rebel against God and His standards. This causes a separation between us and God.

After reading Jeremiah 17:9, write down two conditions of the heart of man:

Read Mark 7:21-23 and list at least 12 evil things that men do. These are things that come out of the heart of man:

Now that you have studied several scriptures about the sins of man, meditate on the following three verses: 1 John 1:8–10. These three verses have three very important points. In 1 John 1:8 if we say we have not sinned, who have we deceived or lied to?

In 1 John 1:10 if we say that we have not sinned, what are we saying about God?

So, it is important to recognize our true condition when we come to Christ. He was perfect, and only He can forgive our sins. We can have hope that if we truly come to Christ with a repentant heart and ask Him to forgive us, He will forgive us and live in our hearts. He died on the cross to take the penalty of our sin from us. But, we must receive this forgiveness by truly repenting from the heart and turning from our old ways to our new life in Christ.

MEMORY WORK: MEMORIZE ROMANS 3:23; ROMANS 6:23; AND 1 JOHN 1:9

To continue our study of salvation, let's look at what happens when someone truly is "born again." First, admit that you are a sinner. Second, you must believe that Jesus is the Son of God and that He is perfect and that He died for our sins on the cross and that He rose again. And you receive Christ by faith, not of your works. After truly surrendering your life to Christ, make a public confession of your faith to other people. All of these steps are important, and your spirit will bear witness with His Spirit that you are truly a child of God.

So, let's look closer at a few things. Ephesians 2:8-9 "For by grace you have been saved through faith, and this is not of yourselves. It is the gift of God, [9]not of works, so that no one should boast." So, after reading this, can you say that you can work your way to heaven by doing good works?

Read Romans 10:9-10. After reading this, explain what you must do to be saved.

Read and then memorize John 1:12-13: "Yet to all who received Him, He gave the power to become sons of God, to those who believed in His name, [13]who were born not of blood, nor of the will of the flesh, nor of the will of man, but of God."

After reading the above scriptures, can you have assurance of your salvation?

Write down any other reflections you have about the above scriptures.

What happens after you receive Christ? Read 2 Corinthians 5:17-18. After accepting Christ, how are we different?

If we have truly been changed, should we want to live in sin?

It is time to let go of the old things, the old way of doing things and let Christ wash you and cleanse you and make you a completely new person in Christ with His desires in your heart.

As you pray every day, let this verse be a part of your life: Galatians 2:20. Explain what this verse means to you.

Read Philippians 4:13 and explain how you can live an overcoming life.

THE BIBLE AND SCRIPTURE MEMORY

In this book we have included a Bible reading plan to take you through the entire Bible in 56 weeks. There are specific scriptures to read, and I have some corresponding teaching videos to help you understand what you are reading. You can find this in section two of this book.

King David taught us in the Psalms to hide God's Word in our hearts that we might not sin against the Lord. I would add that scripture memory will increase your faith and keep you in times of trouble. One of the more important aspects in our walk with God is to begin studying and memorizing scripture. When Jesus was directly confronted with Satan in the wilderness, He rebuked Satan by quoting scripture. The Bible is even described as a sword, and it is the only offensive weapon in our armor listed in Ephesians chapter 6. I know from Bible prophecy that the Bible itself will continue to be attacked and eventually scrubbed from the internet and society before Jesus comes. I would strongly recommend that you get a really good physical copy of the Bible that you can use and not just depend on your phone or the internet to be the source of your Bible. Other than the Modern English Version you hold in your hands, the two other versions of the Bible that I personally love are the NASB 1995 and the AMPC 1987. These three translations are very pure from the original Greek and Hebrew text and are easy to read.

As you study each of the lessons in this study course, it will help you grow spiritually so that you can be a strong Christian. Study each lesson carefully and memorize some scriptures that will benefit you as you continue to grow as a Christian.

The Word of God gives us understanding and will build us up. It is how we take a stand against the devil. When the devil was tempting Jesus in the wilderness, he quoted scripture to the devil which made Satan leave Him alone. This is the example for us to follow.

Hebrews 4:12 is an excellent scripture to memorize this week as you study this lesson:

"For the word of God is alive, and active, and sharper than any two-edged sword, piercing even to the division of soul and spirit, of joints and marrow, and able to judge the thoughts and intents of the heart." It's important to know how the scriptures were originally given. Read the two verses below and then write out what it says about how the scriptures were given.

2 Timothy 3:16

2 Peter 1:20-21

Why is it important to know that the scriptures were inspired by God and not just of man?

The Bible, Word of God, is profitable or beneficial for Christians in four ways. What four things does it say in 2 Timothy 3:16 that the Word of God is used for?

Read Psalm 119 all the way through as it will encourage your heart concerning God's Word.

How can a young person live a holy life? (Psalm 119:9)

Why should people hide God's Word in their hearts or memorize scriptures? (Psalm 119:11)

When young men hide God's Word in their heart, what two results are produced? (1 John 2:14)

When God speaks about the sword that Christians are to take up as part of their armor (Ephesians 6:17), what is He referring to?

What does Psalm 119:105 say about the Word of God and how it helps people live in this world?

Psalm 119:30 states two things that the Word of God gives to our thoughts. List them.

What did God send to help the sick as stated in Psalm 107:20?

What does the Lord want us to do with the Word of God? How do we prove our love for Him? (John 14:21)

Read the following verses and list the things they say the Scriptures do for us.

John 15:3

John 17:17

Acts 20:32

After studying this lesson and realizing the importance of the Word of God in your life, memorize the scriptures at the beginning of the lesson before moving on to the next lesson.

SUMMARY

We have gone over some key things in the previous lessons of this Bible study. When you truly come to Christ and surrender your life to Him, you must admit that you have sinned, ask Jesus to completely wash you of all sins and accept Him into your life as Savior and Lord. This is the time when you will really turn away from your past life of sin and surrender everything to Christ. Remember that sin separates you from God as stated in Isaiah 59:2: "But your iniquities have made a separation between you and your God, and your sins have hidden His face from you so that He does not hear" (NASB). The only way to be able to go to heaven is to accept what Christ did on the cross. He took your sins on Himself and gave His life in your place because He was sinless. Once you have accepted Christ into your life, you have become a new creation as is stated in 2 Corinthians 5:17: "Therefore, if any man is in Christ, he is a new creature. Old things have passed away. Look, all things have become new."

The other thing we talked about was the importance of the Bible and how it is perfect, complete, and inspired by God. The Word of God will bring correction, reproof, teaching (doctrine), and instruction in righteousness as found in 2 Timothy 3:16. The Bible also offers comfort to the hurting and gives you guidelines in your everyday life. It's important to read the Bible every day and to memorize scriptures. Never be ashamed of the Word of God or of your relationship with the Lord Jesus Christ. Romans 1:16 states, "For I am not ashamed of the gospel of Christ. For it is the power of God for salvation to everyone who believes, to the Jew first, and also to the Greek."

FORGIVENESS

It is recommended to listen to or watch the sermon series entitled Broken on the media player on our website.

In Mark 11:20-26, Jesus teaches us that if we do not forgive others, our sins are not forgiven and our prayers are not answered. In fact, Jesus teaches us if we hold unforgiveness, we will be given over to tormentors and put in a spiritual prison (Matt. 18:21-34). Even though you can't see the prison or tormentors, I have known bitter people, and I assure you, they are in a spiritual prison and live tormented.

Forgiveness is an act of the will, not an emotion. It is something we choose to do. Once we choose to forgive people, we may still feel hurt, and that is okay. The choice to forgive needs to be made very quickly, but it may take time for the hurt to heal. Once we start obeying the Bible and pray for them, and bless them, we will notice over time that we will feel differently toward them. God helps us forgive from the heart and move into emotional healing and wholeness.

Forgiveness does not mean you have to have them become a part of your life or trust them. Some people are simply toxic. A good example of trust is this. Someone asked me for $100 and told me they would pay me back in a month, so I gave them the money. They never paid me back, so I FORGAVE the debt, but if they came and asked me to borrow money again, I would not lend it to them because I don't trust them. We have to set healthy boundaries in our lives for people. Holding unforgiveness is simply an act of stubborn pride. If we will admit it, we have made mistakes and hurt others also. We want God to forgive us for all that we have done, and He expects us to also forgive others as He has forgiven us.

I encourage you to make a list of everyone you have unforgiveness toward, and out loud, pray to the Lord and choose to forgive each one by name. Then make a list of all the sins you have ever committed, and confess each one to the Lord as sin. As you have forgiven others, you can stand on the promise that the Lord is faithful and just to forgive you of all your sins and cleanse you from all unrighteousness. This will be the beginning of a great personal revival in your life.

THE IMPORTANCE OF FORGIVENESS

There are a lot of things that a new Christian needs to learn about, but this issue of forgiveness is so important, I decided to put it here. As you go through life, you will be offended or hurt by people because people are imperfect. But Jesus said we are to forgive people completely and keep forgiving them even if they keep hurting us. We need to forgive quickly. I always pray before going to sleep at night and make sure I have forgiven everyone and confessed any sins. Many things are very minor, such as someone forgetting to call you back or not shaking your hand at church. You shouldn't even consider these things as offenses. But other things are more serious such as someone gossiping about you or telling your boss negative things about you that will affect your job. Even more serious things have happened to people, such as being robbed, having their identity stolen, getting beaten up and left with a permanent injury, or having a family member who has been killed or raped. These are serious things that happen and require God's help to forgive. Yet, Jesus said that we must forgive these people who have done these things to us. The only way to be able to forgive these serious things is for Jesus to help you do it. And remember that Jesus was betrayed by one of His disciples—one of the 12 men who walked closely with Him for three years. Judas decided to betray Jesus with a kiss. Then he received 30 pieces of silver for betraying Him. The people who can hurt us the most are those who are the closest to us such as our parents, siblings, best friends. Many pastors have been hurt by the people that are the closest to them in their church. It's what we do with this betrayal and hurt that determines our walk with God and our future.

I wanted to begin this section with the Parable of the Unmerciful Servant found in Matthew 18:21-35:

> Then Peter came to Him and said, "Lord, how often shall I
> forgive my brother who sins against me? Up to seven times?"
> [22]Jesus said to him, "I do not say to you up to seven times, but
> up to seventy times seven. [23]Therefore the kingdom of heav-
> en is like a certain king who wanted to settle accounts with
> his servants. [24]When he began to settle the accounts, one was
> brought to him who owed him ten thousand talents. [25]But
> since he was not able to pay, his master ordered that he be
> sold with his wife, their children, and all that he had, and pay-
> ment to be made. [26]So the servant fell on his knees, pleading
> with him, saying, 'Master, have patience with me, and I will
> pay you everything.' [27]Then the master of that servant was
> moved with compassion, released him, and forgave him the
> debt. [28]But that same servant went out and found one of his
> fellow servants who owed him a hundred denarii. He laid
> hands on him and took him by the throat, saying, 'Pay me
> what you owe.' [29]So his fellow servant fell down at his feet and
> entreated him, saying, 'Have patience with me, and I will pay
> you everything.' [30]But he would not and went and threw him
> in prison until he should pay the debt. [31]So when his fellow

servants saw what took place, they were very sorry and went and told their master all that had taken place. [32]Then his master, after he had summoned him, said to him, 'O you wicked servant! I forgave you all that debt because you pleaded with me. [33]Should you not also have had compassion on your fellow servant, even as I had pity on you?' [34]His master was angry and delivered him to the jailers until he should pay all his debt. [35]So also My heavenly Father will do to each of you, if from your heart you do not forgive your brother for his trespasses."

1. When Jesus said that we should forgive others seventy times seven times, what does He mean by this?
2. Is it optional that we forgive people?
3. In your opinion is it difficult for you to forgive people?
4. Why do you think Jesus told this story about the unforgiving/unmerciful servant?
5. What did you learn from the story?
6. In the last verse it says we must "forgive your brother or sister from your heart." What does that mean to you?
7. Why do you think it is harder to forgive some offenses than others?

In this section I would like to continue the topic of forgiveness by discussing what happened to Joseph in the Bible. When you have time, please read Genesis 37-48, which is the story of Joseph. There is a lot that can be learned from his story. I will summarize it here.

Joseph was the favorite son of Jacob. Because of this, his father made him a coat of many colors. His other brothers became jealous of him because it seemed like his father favored him. Joseph was also very close to God and received some prophetic dreams from the Lord. He decided to tell his father and his brothers these dreams. They had to do with the fact that they would one day all bow down to him. Well, that really bothered his older brothers. One day they all were walking along and decided they wanted to kill Joseph but his oldest brother said to just put him in a pit instead. He planned to get him out later. Some Midianites came by and so the brothers sold Joseph to them and took his special coat and dipped it in blood and took it back to his father so that he would think he was dead. So we can say right here that Joseph was mistreated badly by his brothers. But, God was with Joseph as he worked in Potiphar's house in Egypt as the head man there. But, Potiphar's wife wanted Joseph to sleep with her, but he refused, because he was a righteous man. So, she lied about him and said that he tried to rape her, and consequently he was thrown in prison. Okay, second point. Not only was he betrayed by his brothers and sold into slavery but he was lied about and thrown into prison.

Once he was in prison for several years, he interpreted the dreams of the baker and the butler, and what he interpreted came to pass. But they forgot to tell the pharaoh about this, so he remained in prison for another two years. The point is that he was terribly mistreated once again. He had a choice. Should he not forgive his brothers and this woman that lied about him or should he forgive and release them? If he did not forgive them, roots of bitterness would go deep into his spirit. In prison, God was refining him and he did forgive people. And God raised him up to be second-in-command in Egypt during a famine. He was able to help save his whole family and was reunited with his brothers and father.

In this last section, I wanted to share a few comments that John Bevere made in his book The Bait of Satan. In chapter one on page 4 he discusses the fact that many times we don't know that we are offended by someone because it's hidden, sometimes in pride. Sometimes we don't admit that we are hurt, which keeps us from dealing with it. God will purify your heart like pure gold if you let Him turn up the heat and get out the impurities.

"God refines with afflictions, trials, and tribulations, the heat of which separates impurities such as unforgiveness, strife, bitterness, anger, envy, and so forth from the character of God in our lives."[1] One time John Bevere went through intense trials, and he was angry with and rude to his family. He prayed about where this anger was coming from. God had to show him that he needed to get the dross of sin out of his life. As it says in Revelations 3:18, "Anoint your eyes with eye salve, that you may see." Don't act like a victim or blame other people. Just allow God to heal your hurts and forgive and release those who have hurt you. With God you can do this. God forgives sin, not blame-shifting or excuses. If we will humble ourselves and confess our sins, God will forgive us and heal us. You will not be able to truly do all that God has called you to do, truly fulfilling your destiny, until this is dealt with. With God's help we can do all things. (Phil. 4:13). Be quick to forgive and quick to repent and you will see God move mightily on your behalf.

8. Is there anyone that you are having trouble forgiving?
9. Do you need to go to someone and talk to them about this?
10. Give God permission to show you things that are in your heart daily so that you can walk in love and forgiveness continually.

SUBMISSION TO AUTHORITY

The Bible predicts right before Jesus comes there would be a tremendous amount of rebellion. We have seen a huge increase of rebellion in America in the last couple of decades. How we respond to authority will be a great test for everyone. God cannot trust someone with authority if they themselves cannot submit to authority. You will never really know if someone is rebellious until they are told NO. A submissive person will handle things well when they don't get their

---

1 John Bevere, *The Bait of Satan* (Lake Mary FL: Charisma House, 2014), 6.

way. The minute someone wants something and is told NO, then you will see quickly if they are a submissive person or a rebel. It will show up in their attitude. There are always going to be rules. Sometimes we don't understand the reason for the rules, but we have to humble ourselves and be submissive.

The root of rebellion is pride. God has placed all of us under authority. This begins first in the family dynamic. The husband is the head of the home, the wife submits to him in everything as unto the Lord, and children are to honor and obey their parents (Ephesians 5-6). Children growing up in a biblical home will understand and be comfortable with submitting to authority. Then outside the home, we have church leaders we are to submit to and obey. We also see secular authority in our workplaces and government. The Bible never says to submit to authority only if they are perfect, or only if we agree with everything. The only time we should go against secular authority is when they are trying to cause us to go against God and His Word. An example could be if it is illegal to witness for Christ. The Bible commands us to be a witness, so now we have a conflict between obeying God or obeying man. In such a case, we must obey God.

Rebellion is seen most frequently in one's attitude toward authority. This attitude will be expressed in little left-handed comments or unnecessary negativity. People with submission issues will usually have cocky, disrespectful attitudes when talking to authority. In many cases rebellion and witchcraft go together. Rebellion and witchcraft are placed together in the Bible. Most of the time, where you see rebellion, you will also find a Jezebel spirit at work manipulating. I would encourage everyone here to read John Paul Jackson's book, *Unmasking the Jezebel Spirit,* and also gain some knowledge about the Leviathan spirit. These two spirits will be very strong in the last days before Jesus comes, and we must know how to live free from their influence.

Guard yourself from the evil of rebellion. It will continue to increase in these last days we are living in. Keep your heart very pure and humble before the Lord.

The kingdom of God is not set up like a democracy. We do not vote on things or have public opinion sway the way things go. Things are set up in accordance with spiritual authority. And, as it was with the lesson on forgiveness, your attitude toward authority and your ability to submit to leadership even when you don't really understand why they are doing things that way will determine your destiny. So, we will discuss this issue now so that you will understand how important it is to your future walk with God and your happiness and any future ministries you will be involved in.

The very first thing I wanted to go over with you is an example of how David dealt with his spiritual authority in the Bible. His story is found in 1 Samuel 17 through 1 Samuel 24. To set the stage for this story, I will summarize what happened in David and Saul's life before chapter 24. Saul was anointed king over Israel but really did not obey the Lord or the prophet Samuel. Because of this, he really lost the kingdom, and the Spirit of God departed from him. But he was still the king over Israel; he just didn't have the Spirit of God helping him. In the meantime, Samuel the prophet went and anointed the young shepherd boy, David, as the future king of Israel. Shortly after this, the army of King Saul was afraid to fight the giant Goliath, but David came and slew him with a sling shot. Because of this huge victory, people were singing about how great David was, and Saul became jealous of David and fearful he would take his kingdom from him. Whenever the evil spirit came upon Saul, he asked David to play the harp for him. But, then Saul would throw javelins at him to kill him. The only way he survived was to get out of the way and run from Saul's presence. Saul's son, Jonathan, helped him escape when he realized that his father was planning on killing David. This began many years (probably around 14 years) of David hiding in caves to avoid being killed by King Saul. Yet during all of this time, David never wanted to go against Saul, disrespect him, or hurt him. David pleaded with Saul, asking him what he had done to make him hunt him and try to kill him. But during all of this time, he never lifted a hand to hurt Saul, nor did he speak disrespectfully of him, because he was the Lord's anointed.

Below I have included the full text of 1 Samuel 24 because there are several points to cover for discussion. Be ready to take notes and discuss how David showed honor to Saul and how this applies to our lives today:

> When Saul had returned from following the Philistines, it was reported to him, saying, "David is in the Wilderness of En Gedi." [2]Then Saul took three thousand chosen men out of all Israel and went to seek David and his men in front of the rocks of the wild goats. [3]He came to the sheep pens by the way and a cave was there. And Saul went in to relieve himself. Now David and his men were sitting in the rear of the cave. [4]The men of David said to him, "This is the day of which the Lord said to you, 'I am giving your enemy into your hand. You may do with him as seems good in your eyes.'" Then David arose and secretly cut off the corner of Saul's robe.
>
> [5]Afterward David's heart troubled him because he had cut off a corner of Saul's robe. [6]He said to his men, "The Lord forbid that I should do this thing to my lord, the Lord's anointed, to stretch out my hand against him. For he is anointed of the Lord." [7]So David dispersed his men by these words and did not let them rise against Saul. And Saul arose from the cave and went on his way. [8]David arose afterward and went out from the cave. And he called after Saul saying, "My lord the king!" And when Saul looked behind him, David had bowed down with his face to the ground and paid homage. [9]David said to Saul, "Why do you listen to the words of men saying, 'David seeks your harm'? [10]This day you have seen with your own eyes that the Lord delivered you today into my hand in the cave. So that some said to kill you, but my eye had compassion on you. And I said, 'I will not put forth my hand against my lord,

for he is anointed of the Lord.' 11See, my father! Look at the
corner of your robe in my hand. Indeed, I cut off the corner of
your robe, but I did not kill you. Observe and see that there is
no evil or rebellion in my hand. I have not sinned against you,
but you are lying in wait for my life to take it. 12The Lord will
judge between me and you, and the Lord will avenge me on
you, but my hand will not be against you. 13As the proverb of
the ancients says, 'From the wicked comes forth wickedness,'
but my hand will not be against you.

14"After whom has the king of Israel come out? After whom
are you pursuing? After a dead dog? A single flea? 15May
the Lord be judge, and decide between me and you. And may
He see and plead my case, and deliver me out of your hand."

16When David finished speaking these words to Saul, Saul
said, "Is this your voice, my son David?" And Saul lifted up
his voice and wept. 17And he said to David, "You are more
righteous than I. For you have rewarded me with good, while
I have rewarded you with evil. 18And you have shown today
that you have dealt well with me, when the Lord delivered
me into your hand and you did not kill me. 19For if a man
finds his enemy, will he let him safely go away? Therefore
may the Lord reward you well for what you have done for
me this day. 20Now, listen, I know that you will surely be king
and that the kingdom of Israel will be established in your
hand. 21Therefore swear to me now by the Lord that you will
not cut off my descendants after me and that you will not destroy my name out of my father's household."

22So David swore to Saul and Saul went home. But David and
his men went up to the stronghold.

1. What have you learned about David in this passage of scripture?
2. What are some examples of how he showed respect for Saul?
3. Do you think King Saul is regretting how he treated David? Give an example to show that.

4. How does this passage of scripture apply to you today?
5. What are some things you learned from how David treated King Saul?

To continue with this story, Saul is eventually killed by someone else and David becomes king. He helps any survivors from Saul's family out of respect for Saul. We have to show proper honor to pastors and leaders in the body of Christ. The Bible says, "Do not touch my anointed ones, and do no harm to my prophets" (Psalm 105:15). Our attitude toward authority will determine our destiny.

6. Do you think that David's story would have ended differently if he had not honored Saul? In what way?
7. Do you think God was developing character in David as he hid in caves for many years trying to avoid being killed by King Saul?

Now, I would like to focus on a few modern-day examples of how people should submit to the spiritual authority over them. As we study this, consider how this might apply to you now or in the future. Here is an example from my mother Diane Boyd:

> "One example is when I went on a mission trip to Santiago, Chile. I had gone through training, as had the others on the trip. I think I might have understood spiritual authority pretty well. We were working with a missionary who had actually planned for us to go on a national TV show to share testimonies. We were there for a long time and we kept waiting for our turn. Finally, the missionary said we needed to go. He had a lot of ministry for us to do anyway. This was just wasting too much time. Well, I had always been told on mission trips to listen to the missionary and be flexible. Things change a lot. So, I was fine with the change. I knew that we would still minister to lots of people. I was not disappointed. But this is an example of being in submission to the authority over you. What if 20 of the people on the trip had an attitude about the change or were saying negative things about the leader? If

people had had a bad attitude, it might have affected the unity of the group and hindered our effectiveness."

If God's people will remain in unity and under authority, it is very hard for the enemy to hinder us.

8. What would have happened if everyone wanted to go a different direction?
9. Why is it important that I stay submitted to authority, in unity with other believers, and walking in forgiveness?

Here is a final example from John Bevere's book Under Cover Participant's Guide, pages 17–19.

In the 1980s John Bevere was a youth pastor at a really nice church. Because he wanted to grow, he visited a very successful church in another city. They preached the Word of God and had a wonderful youth ministry. But they said their success was in having home cell groups or "parties" to help get the unbelievers there. Then, a leader would preach to them the gospel and many kids were getting saved. It was an awesome way to get his youth group to grow and was spiritually sound. The pastor seemed to be in favor of it. John worked with leadership groups and they planned this out for eight months. They were just about to launch the home cell groups when all the associate pastors met with the pastor. The pastor had been praying, and the Holy Spirit told him their church was not to have the home cell groups. Well, at first John was very upset. He had been working on this for eight months! He was very angry. Now, he could have gone to his youth leaders and told them that the pastor was not supporting him and didn't know what was best for the youth, but he didn't do that.

10. What would have happened if John had gone to his youth group and spoke negatively about what his pastor had decided?

What actually happened is that he prayed about all of it and the Lord told him if he were to go forward with the home cell groups, he would be going in one direction and the church in another. It would cause division. So what he actually did was call the pastor and apologize for his attitude and immediately cancel the home cell groups. Then he spoke to his 24 leaders and told them that the pastor had heard from the Lord and they were not to have home cell groups. He made it a positive thing, not a negative. The kids accepted it, and it was not brought up again.

11. Could this have been a test for the youth pastor?
12. Now the question is, how does this apply to you?
13. After studying this lesson, do you think you have a problem submitting to authority?
14. If so, what are you going to do to take care of that?

In conclusion, there is a saying that goes like this: "Your attitude determines your altitude." How far up do you want your ministry to go? How close to God do you want to be? Do you want anything to keep you down? So, when it comes to spiritual authority, your attitude toward authority will affect your destiny either positively or negatively. God can never trust someone with authority who does not know how to submit to authority. This is the time to really examine your heart and commit all of this to prayer.

SPIRITUAL WARFARE AND THE ARMOR OF GOD

It is recommended that you listen to or watch the sermon series entitled Transformed on our website media player. After that, there are other series on this subject under a separate playlist entitled Deliverance and Spiritual Warfare that will help you learn to conquer in spiritual warfare and bring deliverance to others.

Take note that Ephesians 5 was written before Ephesians 6. In Ephesians 5, we see order in the home laid out clearly. Then Ephesians 6 deals with high level spiritual warfare. I believe the message Paul intended is this, you better have your home in order before you enter a spiritual battle. If there is disorder (rebellion) and division, you will get hurt in spiritual warfare.

To have a strong marriage and happy home, it is recommended to listen to the sermon series entitled Love, Family, and Marriage on our website media player.

In this lesson we will discuss the spiritual battle you are in because you have decided to follow Jesus Christ. Because of that decision, the devil is not happy. He still wants to pull you away from Christ and have you fall into sin and end up in hell one day. The devil knows your weaknesses and tries to trick you and pull you away from your devotion to Christ. Because of this battle, you need to put on the armor of God every day as you face the day.

First Peter 5:8 describes what the devil does: "Be sober and watchful, because your adversary the devil walks around as a roaring lion, seeking whom he may devour."

1. After reading the above scripture, what does it say the devil is constantly doing?
2. What does it say that we should do in order to be protected from him?

There is another scripture that talks about our hearts and what is in them:

Jeremiah 17:9 "The heart is more deceitful than all things and desperately wicked; who can understand it?"

3. If our hearts are like this, how does the devil attack us?

But, since we have accepted Christ as our Lord and Savior, we have a new heart and a new desire to live holy before our God. But, the devil will continue to try to tempt us and pull us away from God.

Read James 1:13-15. "Let no man say when he is tempted, 'I am tempted by God,' for God cannot be tempted with evil; neither does

He tempt anyone. [14]But each man is tempted when he is drawn away by his own lust and enticed. [15]Then, when lust has conceived, it brings forth sin; and when sin is finished, it brings forth death."

4. Describe what this is talking about in your own words.
5. Describe what might be going on in someone's mind before they do something like shoplifting.
6. So, does the devil try to tempt everyone?

Let's talk about this situation. If we have been born again, then we are a new creation and have the Holy Spirit living in us. In fact, it says in 1 Corinthians 3:16 that we are the temple of God.

Read 1 Corinthians 3:16-17. "Do you not know that you are the temple of God, and that the Spirit of God dwells in you? [17]If anyone defiles the temple of God, God will destroy him. For the temple of God is holy. And you are His temple."

7. How could a person defile his temple?
8. After studying this lesson so far, what do you think we can do to fight the devil?

The devil is trying to draw you back into sin which will open you up to evil spirits and cause you to fall away from God. And sin leads to spiritual death. Some people have been delivered from evil spirits, and then they were pulled back into sin which caused the evil spirits to come back. But there are definitely things we can do to fight back spiritually. For one thing, let's remember that God is greater than the devil:

First John 4:4 states, "You are from God, little children, and have overcome them; because greater is He who is in you than he who is in the world."

We need to remember that. Also, Jesus is continually interceding for us before the Heavenly Father. Another thing you can do is renew your mind by reading the Bible. In fact, you should memorize key scriptures so that you are prepared and can stand against the devil with scriptures just as Jesus did in the wilderness. You should also pray before starting your day and before facing a difficult situation. Prayer can work miracles in your life.

Read James 4:7. "Therefore submit yourselves to God. Resist the devil, and he will flee from you."

9. What do you think it means to resist the devil?

10. How can you do that?

Okay, now the final and most important thing is that you should always put on your spiritual armor every day so that you are protected from the attacks of the enemy in your life. The pieces of the armor are listed in Ephesians 6. Verse 12 states that we wrestle "against principalities, against powers, against the rulers of the darkness of this world, and against spiritual forces of evil in the heavenly places." Because of this, we can't physically fight these battles. This is a spiritual battle and must be fought in the spirit. The armor of God is found in Ephesians 6:13-18. After reading this, we will discuss it.

"Therefore take up the whole armor of God that you may be able to resist in the evil day, and having done all, to stand. [14]Stand therefore, having your waist girded with truth, having put on the breastplate of righteousness, [15]having your feet fitted with the readiness of the gospel of peace, [16]and above all, taking the shield of faith, with which you will be able to extinguish all the fiery arrows of the evil one. [17]Take the helmet of salvation and the sword of the Spirit, which is the word of God. [18]Pray in the Spirit always with all kinds of prayer and supplication."

11. What are your thoughts on how this spiritual armor might protect you?

If you look at it closely, the armor covers all of your body except your back. We should be moving forward, never running from the enemy. The helmet of salvation should protect our thought life. We should know that we have salvation in Christ and have confidence in this. The breastplate of righteousness, His righteousness, should protect our heart, our emotions, so we can stand steadfast in His righteousness as we crucify the flesh daily. The belt of truth is helpful because we can absolutely count on the truth of His Word and His promises in the Bible. We should always be ready to share the gospel to the nations and walk in peace. This is our protection over our feet. The shield of faith is very important because it is held up to stop the fiery darts of the devil—his lies, his condemnation, his doubts that he is putting in your mind. The sword of the Spirit is extremely important because the Word of God can literally stop Satan in his tracks and drive him away. It is a powerful offensive weapon.

In the mornings before starting your day, you should have a time of prayer, communion, and worship. You also need to definitely put on the spiritual armor. It is very important even though you cannot see it with your eyes. It can be seen in the spiritual realm. You want your thoughts protected. You want to know the truth so you can tell it to the devil. You always want to be ready to witness. So, this is how we handle spiritual warfare. Remember that the devil is going about as a roaring lion, looking for a chink in your armor. Stay spiritually pure, be ready for spiritual warfare, and go forward in faith.

WATER BAPTISM

It is recommended that you listen to the sermons under the playlist entitled Deep Consecration on our website media player.

Let's talk about some background information about water baptism here. First of all, the word "baptize" in the Greek actually means "immerse." So that's why people are actually immersed in water when they are baptized. It is important to not just be sprinkled, but rather immersed completely when being baptized.

Where does it say in the Scriptures that we are to be baptized? Let's look at a few of the passages.

"Go therefore and make disciples of all nations, baptizing them in the name of the Father and of the Son and of the Holy Spirit, [20]teaching them to observe all things I have commanded you. And remember, I am with you always, even to the end of the age." Amen." (Matthew 28:19-20)

What does this verse say about baptizing people? Is it a command of the Lord's?

"He who believes and is baptized will be saved. But he who does not believe will be condemned." (Mark 16:16)

What does this verse indicate about the importance of baptism?

Even Jesus, the Son of God, was baptized in water even though He had never sinned. He is our example. This also shows the importance of water baptism. He is our role model in everything He did.

"Then Jesus came from Galilee to John at the Jordan to be baptized by him. [14]But John prohibited Him, saying, 'I need to be baptized by You, and do You come to me?' [15]But Jesus answered him, 'Let it be so now, for it is fitting for us to fulfill all righteousness.' Then he permitted Him. [16]And when Jesus was baptized, He came up immediately out of the water. And suddenly the heavens were opened to Him, and He saw the Spirit of God descending on Him like a dove. [17]And a voice came from heaven, saying, 'This is My beloved Son, in whom I am well pleased'" (Matthew 3:13-17).

1. According to the above verses, why did Jesus want John the Baptist to baptize Him?
2. How did God the Father show that He was pleased with Jesus when He was baptized in water? Matthew 3:17

So, you can see from the above scriptures that the Lord indicates that water baptism is very important. It actually represents Christ's death, burial, and resurrection. First, a person needs to truly repent and turn away from all of past sins and ask Jesus to come into their heart and surrender fully to Christ. That will result in the experience of being born again. Then one of the next steps is water baptism. When you step into the water it is symbolic of dying to your old carnal self and sins. Then being immersed in water represents being buried—your old life being buried completely. Then, when you come up out of the water, it represents the resurrection of your new life in Christ.

Baptism in water is very powerful. When I was baptized, I felt new and clean. I felt power come over me to live a victorious life. Baptism is also a public confession of your decision to follow Christ. In some countries people are actually killed for believing in Christ, but they decide to follow Christ anyway to the death. Thinking back to when Israel left Egypt, the Israelites crossed the Red Sea on dry ground because God caused the waters to open up for them. And then the sea closed over the entire Egyptian army and killed them. Water baptism has the power to defeat your enemies for you and help separate you spiritually from your past. The most important thing is that the Lord has told us to be water baptized. So, we should follow all of the commands of the Lord.

Look up and read Acts 2:38-39.

In the above verse, what does Peter say about baptism?

1. Did baptism seem important to him?
2. Considering the things that we have touched upon above, wouldn't you want God to defeat your enemies for you?

In Matthew 28:20 what does Jesus promise us?

3. In this Great Commission, what is Jesus telling the disciples to do?
4. Isn't water baptism one of those things that Christ has commanded us to do?
5. Read Acts 2:41. After the people received the Lord as their Savior, what did they do?

When Philip met up with the Ethiopian eunuch on the roadway, he preached Christ to him. Read the following scriptures:

"Then Philip spoke, beginning with the same Scripture, and preached Jesus to him. [36]As they went on their way, they came to some water. And the eunuch said, 'Look, here is water. What hinders me from being baptized?' [37]Philip said, 'If you believe with all your heart, you may.' He answered, 'I believe that Jesus Christ is the Son of God.' [38]And he commanded the chariot to halt. Then both Philip and the eunuch went down into the water, and he baptized him" (Acts 8:35-38).

11. From the above scriptures, do you think it was important to Philip to baptize this new believer?
12. What did the man have to do before he could be baptized in water?
13. Continue reading in the same passage: Acts 8:39. How did the eunuch feel when he came up out of the water?

Look up and read Romans 6:4. What did you learn from this scripture?

14. According to the above verse, how should we live after accepting Jesus as our Savior and being water baptized?

I wanted to conclude this section by saying that water baptism does not save you, but it is extremely important and very powerful. There are some people who accept Jesus Christ on their death bed and have no opportunity to be water baptized. Then, there is the example of the thief on the cross who could not be water baptized, but the Lord told him He would see him in paradise that day. So, it is your belief in the Lord Jesus Christ, and your faith in what he did for you on the cross that brings salvation, but water baptism is a very powerful thing and something the Lord has commanded us to do. If you are physically able to be baptized, you should be baptized. It will powerfully affect your Christian walk.

THE HOLY SPIRIT AND THE BAPTISM IN THE HOLY SPIRIT

Over the last couple of centuries Bible prophecy regarding the end times has been rapidly unfolding. One of the most significant prophecies being fulfilled is that God is pouring out His Spirit on all flesh. This began in the days of John Wesley, and continues to this day. I recommend going through the sermon series entitled Historic Revivals in our media player. This series will help you understand how God moved in revivals like Cane Ridge, Wales, Azusa, and many more. You will also learn about more current revivals, and a great revival in front of us that will usher in the coming of Christ.

One thing we must understand as a new believer is the person and work of the Holy Spirit. The Father is in heaven seated on His throne. The Bible says Jesus is at His right hand, ever living to make intercession for us. So, who is actually dwelling in us and is with us? The Holy Spirit is the person of the Godhead who dwells within us and changes us into Christ's image. He convicts us of sin and leads us. As we learn to pray and be led by the Spirit, we are maturing in our walk with God. When we understand the Holy Spirit properly, our prayer lives can take on a depth and power that could never have been without His presence and power at work.

After salvation (baptism into Christ), we need to get water immersed as quickly as it is possible, but there is more. We also need to be baptized into the Holy Spirit. Matthew 3:11 teaches us that Jesus is the great baptizer into the Holy Spirit. We see this in Acts 2 as the early church was filled and baptized into the Holy Spirit and began to speak in tongues. I would encourage you to turn to Acts 2 and read that chapter. The baptism into the Holy Spirit is the introduction to the supernatural aspect of Christianity. The gifts of the Spirit will begin operating in your life and you will be clothed with power from on high to do the works of Jesus in the earth. We cannot be the effective witnesses we are called to be without the power of the Holy Spirit. Every area of our Christian life and spiritual growth will be tremendously affected by the direct activity of the Holy Spirit. He is the one who surrounds us with protection, empowers us to be effective, teaches us the Bible, and helps us to live a righteous life before God. If we do not have the Holy Spirit in our lives, we are not truly God's child.

I would add that when you accept Christ as your Savior, the Holy Spirit comes to live inside you, and He will change you and teach you. Then when you are baptized into the Holy Spirit, the Holy Spirit fills you and comes upon you to clothe you with power. You will then move into a life of power, revelation, and the supernatural. We desperately need this additional work of grace in our lives to empower us and strengthen us.

This leads me to the importance of tongues. The only reason tongues is a controversial subject is because Satan wants it to be. The New Testament church was born on the Day of Pentecost. Speaking in tongues should simply be a very normal, healthy part of Christian living. The benefits of speaking in tongues are these:

1. You build up your most holy faith. Jude 20
2. You edify yourself. 1 Corinthians 14:4
3. You utter mysteries. 1 Corinthians 14:2
4. You pray the perfect will of God. Romans 8:26-27
5. It sharpens your discernment. Ephesians 6:18

There are many other benefits, but for the purpose of this teaching, these will suffice. We are living in a time that we need to pray in tongues daily. This strengthens (edifies) and builds up our inner spirit man tuning us into the Lord, and sharpening our discernment. Uttering mysteries means God will give us revelation and direction directly from Him. There are times that we have prayed all that we know how to pray, and that is when the Holy Spirit can take over and pray through us in tongues what we simply do not know what/how to pray. The Holy Spirit will pray the perfect will of God. You can feel a strong burden, but after praying a while, the burden will lift and be replaced with joy. When this happens, you know you have prayed the matter all the way through. A great man of God stated before his death that a time would come (we are now in this time) that spiritual warfare would be so severe that it would seem impossible to get on the other side. He stated when that happens, get alone with God and pray in the Spirit until you get your breakthrough.

During times of severe warfare, I have found that taking communion, speaking the Word of God out loud, taking authority over the enemy, and praying in tongues have been very effective in getting on the other side of it.

The Holy Spirit is very important in our walk with God and our new life in Christ. He is part of the Trinity—God the Father, God the Son, and God the Holy Spirit. He is our comforter and teacher. When we are baptized in the Holy Spirit, we have boldness and power to be witnesses for Christ.

Another thing I wanted to point out is that there are three baptisms. When you are baptized into Christ's body that means that you were born again and accepted Christ as your Savior and Lord. The Holy Spirit begins to work in your life at that point. When you were baptized in water, that was a physical act where you were physically baptized in water. The third baptism is the baptism in the Holy Spirit. Jesus is the one who baptizes us into the Holy Spirit. That is when the Holy Spirit fills you to overflowing and clothes you with power. The initial evidence of being baptized in the Holy Spirit is that you begin to speak in another language—or tongue. Once you have experienced this baptism, you will have power to witness and have boldness. I will add that you should continually seek to be refilled and overflowing with His presence continually. The baptism into the Holy Spirit causes us to receive a prayer language so that we can pray in tongues during our personal prayer times. When praying in tongues, we are praying the perfect will of God because it is a heavenly language that the Holy Spirit uses to pray through us.

In John 14:26 Jesus says, “But the Counselor, the Holy Spirit, whom the Father will send in My name, will teach you everything and remind you of all that I told you.”

1. What two things will the Holy Spirit do as stated in John 14:26?

In John 16:13-14 Jesus says, “When the Spirit of truth comes, He will guide you into all truth. For He will not speak on His own authority. But He will speak whatever He hears, and He will tell you things that are to come. 14 He will glorify Me, for He will receive from Me and will declare it to you.”

2. List four things the above scripture teaches about the Holy Spirit and what He will do.

Read Luke 24:49 carefully.

3. What does Jesus tell the disciples to do when He leaves the earth?

Memorize Acts 2:4. “They were all filled with the Holy Spirit and began to speak in other tongues, as the Spirit enabled them to speak.”

Read Acts 2:40-42.

4. After reading this portion of scripture, how many people were saved that day when Peter preached his sermon?
5. What did they do after they were saved and baptized?
6. What do you think gave Peter such boldness to preach the sermon he preached?
7. How is Peter different in this passage than he was a few weeks prior when he denied Christ?

PRAYING IN TONGUES

In 1 Corinthians 14:14-15, Paul gives us some good instruction about the Holy Spirit and praying in tongues: “For if I pray in an unknown tongue, my spirit prays, but my understanding is unfruitful. [15]What is it then? I will pray with the spirit, and I will pray with the understanding. I will sing with the spirit, and I will sing with the understanding."

8. Journal what this means to you.

When you are praying in the Holy Spirit, it is between you and God, but when there is a message in tongues at church, it should be interpreted so the whole body will be edified. These are two different aspects of speaking in tongues. One is personal and the other is for the corporate body. The corporate message in tongues is what Paul is referring to in 1 Corinthians 14:13, 23: "Let him who speaks in an unknown tongue pray that he may interpret… [23]Therefore if the whole church assembles in one place and all speak with tongues, and those who are unlearned or unbelievers come in, will they not say that you are out of your mind?" This is why when giving a corporate message in tongues someone needs to interpret what is being said.

When Peter was preaching, he quoted what the prophet Joel had said in the Old Testament:

Acts 2:17-18: "'In the last days it shall be,' says God, 'that I will pour out My Spirit on all flesh; your sons and your daughters shall prophesy, your young men shall see visions, and your old men shall dream dreams. [18]Even on My menservants and maidservants I will pour out My Spirit in those days; and they shall prophesy."

Journal what happens when people are baptized in the Holy Spirit.

Paul teaches us that tongues is a sign to the unbeliever. Tongues is not something to be ashamed of or keep in secret, but it is a sign that will help people come to know Jesus like we saw on the day of Pentecost.

1 Corinthians 14:22 "So tongues are for a sign, not to believers, but to unbelievers. But prophesying does not serve unbelievers, but believers."

Memorize Acts 1:8: "But you shall receive power when the Holy Spirit has come upon you; and you shall be witnesses to Me in Jerusalem, and in all Judea and Samaria, and to the end of the earth."

GIFTS AND FRUIT

It's important for Christians to exhibit the nine fruits of the Spirit as listed in Galatians 5:22-23. Write them out in your journal:

9. Are you exhibiting these spiritual fruits of the Spirit in your life?

Another thing that you can study on your own are the nine gifts of the Spirit as listed in 1 Corinthians 12:8-10. Write them out in your journal as well.

Read Acts 2:38-39:

10. Who can receive the gift of the baptism in the Holy Spirit?

If you have not been baptized in the Holy Spirit yet, seek this. Pray and ask with faith. He will give you what you are asking for. You are His child and He wants to give you good gifts.

THE PROMISE OF THE HOLY SPIRIT

John 7:38-39 "'He who believes in Me, as the Scripture has said, out of his heart shall flow rivers of living water.' [39]By this He spoke of the Spirit, whom those who believe in Him would receive. For the Holy Spirit was not yet given, because Jesus was not yet glorified."

Luke 11:9-13 "And I tell you, ask, and it will be given to you; seek, and you will find; knock, and it will be opened to you. [10]For everyone who asks receives, and he who seeks finds, and to him who knocks it will be opened. [11]"If a son asks for bread from any of you who is a father, will you give him a stone? Or if he asks for a fish, will you give him a serpent instead of a fish? [12]Or if he asks for an egg, will you offer him a scorpion? [13]If you then, being evil, know how to give good gifts to your children, how much more will your heavenly Father give the Holy Spirit to those who ask Him?"

PRAYER AND CHURCH ATTENDANCE

It is recommended that you listen to the sermon series entitled What Brought Revival under the playlist entitled How Revival Came on our website media player.

All of the things that we have written about so far are important to you as a new Christian, but prayer, and finding a good local church to attend are extremely important for your spiritual growth. As you know, communication is very important in a love relationship. We love Jesus so much that we want to spend all of our time with Him and enjoy fellowship with Him. We can do that by communicating with Him every day, letting Him know we love Him, asking for things that we need, and thanking Him. Prayer is the key to true intimacy and fellowship with the Lord.

Finding a local church to attend where they preach the Word of God is vital. Staying at home and watching a preacher on TV is not the same as going to a local church and worshipping with other believers and fellowshipping with them. When you attend a church, you also receive encouragement, guidance from other believers, and teaching that you need to grow spiritually. The world will get darker and more evil, thus we will need the spiritual strength that comes from faithful church attendance. Remember our only source for truth is the Holy Bible; that will be the basis of good solid preaching.

Consider Hebrews 10:23-25: "Let us firmly hold the profession of our faith without wavering, for He who promised is faithful. [24]And let us consider how to spur one another to love and to good works. [25]Let us not forsake the assembling of ourselves together, as is the manner of some, but let us exhort one another, especially as you see the Day approaching."

And remember that there is no perfect church because there are no perfect people. We are all saved by grace. God is working on all of us to be more like Jesus. Our entire lives will be a work in progress. Be patient with one another. Some are new Christians. Some seem to be more friendly than others. But what we need is more of God's perfect love for each other. The love of Christ will solve a lot of problems. If you get hurt in church, look at it as an opportunity to be more like Jesus. It is an opportunity to forgive someone and show unconditional love.

John 13:34-35 "A new commandment I give to you, that you love one another, even as I have loved you, that you also love one another. [35]By this all men will know that you are My disciples, if you have love for one another."

1. How can you show love to people in your church?

Make sure that your church preaches and adheres to the whole Word of God, you are able to worship freely, and that the Holy Spirit is in control of the service.

Now let's talk about the importance of prayer. Remember that prayer is just talking to God like you would talk to a loving father. Once you have asked Jesus to come into your life and be your Savior, you can talk to God and He will hear you. Your heavenly Father will hear your heart-felt prayers and longs to have a close relationship with you. He longs for you to worship Him and spend time in His presence.

John 4:23 "But an hour is coming, and now is, when the true worshipers will worship the Father in spirit and truth; for such people the Father seeks to be His worshipers."

James 5:13-18 "Is anyone among you afflicted (ill-treated, suffering evil)? He should pray. Is anyone glad at heart? He should sing praise [to God]. [14]Is anyone among you sick? He should call in the church elders (the spiritual guides). And they should pray over him, anointing him with oil in the Lord's name. [15]And the prayer [that is] of faith will save him who is sick, and the Lord will restore him; and if he has committed sins, he will be forgiven. [16]Confess to one another therefore your faults (your slips, your false steps, your offenses, your sins) and pray [also] for one another, that you may be healed and restored [to a spiritual tone of mind and heart]. The earnest (heartfelt, continued) prayer of a righteous man makes tremendous power available [dynamic in its working]. [17]Elijah was a human being with a nature such as we have [with feelings, affections, and a constitution like ours]; and he prayed earnestly for it not to rain, and no rain fell on the earth for three years and six months. [18]And [then] he prayed again and the heavens supplied rain and the land produced its crops [as usual]" (AMPC).

2. What does this tell you about how to approach God?
3. What kind of prayer is effective? (Read James 5:16)
4. By what can we enter boldly into God's presence? (Hebrews 10:19)
5. According to the above verse, what do we have to do in order to receive what we ask for?

LOOK UP AND MEMORIZE JOHN 15:7

Let's just talk generally about prayer and how to have an effective prayer life. Each morning you should go through the blood of Jesus. You could take communion, which is a very powerful way of coming through the blood of Jesus. Taking communion helps you examine yourself, forgive others, and repent of sins. It is also a powerful way to remember we are God's blood covenant people and to confess out loud our covenant promises. Use the Ten Commandments as a basis to examine your heart. After that, you can enter boldly into His presence. You can praise and worship at this point because that definitely draws you into His presence. Then you can talk to Him and listen to what He is speaking to you. It's not a formula or meant to be mechanical. It should be Holy Spirit led. Get to know the Holy Spirit. He will help you have a powerful effective prayer life. The Lord might put some things on your heart to pray specifically about. The Lord's Prayer is a good pattern to follow.

What are some things that can hinder prayer? Having unforgiveness in your heart is one thing. Another thing is doubt, which is discussed in James 1:6-7. Now look at James 4:3 and answer the following question:

6. What might keep us from receiving what we want from God according to James 4:3?
7. What does 1 Peter 3:7 say would hinder a husband's prayers?

LET'S LOOK AT ANOTHER PASSAGE OF SCRIPTURE:

1 John 5:14-15 "This is the confidence which we have before Him, that, if we ask anything according to His will, He hears us. [15]And if we know that He hears us in whatever we ask, we know that we have the requests which we have asked from Him."

8. What do we know about our prayers according to the above verses?

It's good to have a set time to pray every day if you can. I recommend starting your day with prayer every morning. However, the Bible says in 1 Thessalonians 5:17 to "pray without ceasing," so we should be in a continual place of prayer throughout our day as we have opportunity.

In conclusion, it is important to abide in Christ, come to Him through the blood of Jesus, and pray with faith—not doubting. Come humbly before God and worship Him. Make sure there is no sin in your life or unforgiveness toward anyone before you start to pray. And then, just talk to God. He loves you so much and wants to spend time with you.

1 John 1:5-9 "This then is the message which we have heard from Him and declare to you: God is light, and in Him is no darkness at all. [6]If we say that we have fellowship with Him, yet walk in darkness, we lie and do not practice the truth. [7]But if we walk in the light as He

is in the light, we have fellowship one with another, and the blood of Jesus Christ His Son cleanses us from all sin. [8]If we say that we have no sin, we deceive ourselves, and the truth is not in us. [9]If we confess our sins, He is faithful and just to forgive us our sins and cleanse us from all unrighteousness."

James 4:1-10 "Where do wars and fights among you come from? Do they not come from your lusts that war in your body? [2]You lust and do not have, so you kill. You desire to have and cannot obtain. You fight and war. Yet you do not have, because you do not ask. [3]You ask, and do not receive, because you ask amiss, that you may spend it on your passions. [4]You adulterers and adulteresses, do you not know that the friendship with the world is enmity with God? Whoever therefore will be a friend of the world is the enemy of God. [5]Do you think that the Scripture says in vain, 'He yearns jealously for the spirit that lives in us'? [6]But He gives more grace. For this reason it says: 'God resists the proud, but gives grace to the humble.' [7]Therefore submit yourselves to God. Resist the devil, and he will flee from you. [8]Draw near to God, and He will draw near to you. Cleanse your hands, you sinners, and purify your hearts, you double-minded. [9]Grieve and mourn and weep. Let your laughter be turned to mourning, and your joy to dejection. [10]Humble yourselves in the sight of the Lord, and He will lift you up."

9. Have you ever had a prayer not answered? If so, reflect on that and maybe why it was not answered. Sometimes things take a long time. It may take a while longer.
10. What prayers have you seen God answer?

ADDITIONAL REFERENCES FOR PRAYER

THE LORD'S PRAYER

Matthew 6:7-15 "But when you pray, do not use vain repetitions, as the heathen do. For they think that they will be heard for their much speaking. [8]Do not be like them, for your Father knows what things you have need of before you ask Him.

[9]Therefore pray in this manner:

Our Father who is in heaven, hallowed be Your name. [10]Your kingdom come; Your will be done on earth, as it is in heaven. [11]Give us this day our daily bread. [12]And forgive us our debts, as we forgive our debtors. [13]And lead us not into temptation, but deliver us from evil. For Yours is the kingdom and the power and the glory forever. Amen.

[14]For if you forgive men for their sins, your heavenly Father will also forgive you. [15]But if you do not forgive men for their sins, neither will your Father forgive your sins."

THE TEN COMMANDMENTS

1. Do not have other gods before me.
2. Do not worship idols.
3. Do not take the Lord's name in vain.
4. Remember the Sabbath day, and keep it holy.
5. Honor your father and mother.
6. Do not murder.
7. Do not commit adultery.
8. Do not steal.
9. Do not lie.
10. Do not covet.

TWELVE HEBREW NAMES FOR GOD SO THAT YOU CAN GLORIFY HIS NAME:

1. Yahweh (Almighty God or Jehovah) Genesis 2:4
2. Elohei Mishpah (The Lord the righteous judge) Isaiah 30:18
3. Jehovah Nissi (The Lord my Banner, Strong in Battle, Victorious) Exodus 17:15

4. Jehovah Tzevaot (The God of Angel Armies) Isaiah 6:3
5. Jehovah Rohi (The Lord my Shepherd) Psalm 23:1
6. Jehovah Rapha (The Lord my Healer) Exodus 15:26
7. Jehovah Shammah (The Lord the Divine Presence continually with us) Ex. 48:35
8. Jehovah Tsidkenu (The Lord my Righteousness) Jeremiah 23:6
9. Jehovah Makadesh (The Lord my Sanctification) Exodus 31:13
10. Jehovah Jireh (The Lord our Provider) Genesis 22:13-14
11. Jehovah Shalom (The Lord our Peace) Judges 6:24
12. El Elyon (God most high) Genesis 14:18-20

THE IMPORTANCE OF WITNESSING

Jesus taught us that after we are clothed with power, we will be His witnesses. It is the job of the body of Christ to go to the whole world and make disciples. Jesus prophesied the gospel of the kingdom will be preached to all, then the end will come.

It is the responsibility of each believer to be a light and witness to those around them. I pray that each of you reading this truly gets a burden for souls that will cause you to intercede for the lost and spread the gospel to those around you. Your testimony of how Jesus changed your life has power to change the lives of others. Begin to learn how to share your faith effectively.

Pray this simple prayer: "Lord, give me a burden for souls, and help me be the witness you desire for me to be for the lost."

Well, let's talk about witnessing and what it means to all of us. When you witness to someone, you are telling them what God has done in your life and what it says in the Word of God about the need of a Savior. Before Jesus ascended back into heaven, He gave us the Great Commission:

Mark 16:15 "He said to them, 'Go into all the world, and preach the gospel to every creature.'"

1. What did He tell us to do?
2. Where are we supposed to go?

Let's look at Acts 1:8. (Please memorize this scripture.)

"But you shall receive power when the Holy Spirit comes upon you. And you shall be My witnesses in Jerusalem, and in all Judea and Samaria, and to the ends of the earth."

3. Who will help us as we witness?
4. What will we receive from the Holy Spirit?
5. How was Peter changed once he actually was baptized in the Holy Spirit?
6. Where are we commanded to go and witness?
7. When you think about witnessing, do you only think about other countries or places far away, or do you also think about your own family and neighborhood?

If you feel like you don't know what to say when you go out witnessing, just allow the Holy Spirit to give you the words to say. Remember, you have your testimony! How did He change you? What is different in your life now? Share that. People want to hear about that. People are looking for answers, and they haven't found them. Pray for boldness, and then go out in love because you really do not want anyone to go to hell. You want everyone to find salvation and go to heaven. It is the work of the Holy Spirit to convict of sin and draw people to Jesus. We must depend on His leading and power.

1 Peter 3:14-17 "But even if you suffer for the sake of righteousness, you are blessed. 'Do not be afraid of their terror, do not be troubled.'
[15]But sanctify the Lord God in your hearts. Always be ready to give an answer to every man who asks you for a reason for the hope that is in you, with gentleness and fear. [16]Have a good conscience so that evildoers who speak evil of you and falsely accuse your good conduct

in Christ may be ashamed. [17]For it is better, if it is the will of God, that you suffer for doing good than for doing evil."

8. What are some ways you can prepare as you go out to witness?

9. Do you need to learn a little bit more about the salvation message?

10. Are you comfortable actually praying with someone to receive Christ?

Look up and read Acts 22:15.

11. What did the Lord ask Paul to do?

Matthew 5:16 "Let your light so shine before men that they may see your good works and glorify your Father who is in heaven."

12. Why should we let our light shine before others?

Look up and read 2 Timothy 1:8.

13. What are we not supposed to be ashamed of?

14. What can you do if you feel shy or embarrassed about witnessing?

It is good to go out by twos or more so if you are shy, have someone go with you that is bold. Then as they talk, you will be drawn into the conversation and will feel comfortable sharing your faith. Jesus always sent people out in a group of two or more. Some people will gladly receive the message of the gospel while others may say they are not interested. A huge point I want to make is that it is extremely important to pray before going out. Do you want to win souls and have people healed? Pray before going so that their hearts are more prepared to receive the Word of God. I have even gone out ahead of time and prayed over the land and the area I am going to go to and claimed it for Christ. All of this helps to prepare things for the moving of the Lord. There is a very real spiritual battle raging over the lost. We must break the blindness of their minds to help them see the need for a Savior.

2 Corinthians 4:3-4 "But if our gospel is hidden, it is hidden to those who are lost. [4]The god of this world has blinded the minds of those who do not believe, lest the light of the glorious gospel of Christ, who is the image of God, should shine on them."

Let's read Matthew 10:32-33 carefully:

"Therefore everyone who confesses Me before men, I will also confess him before My Father who is in heaven. [33]But whoever denies Me before men, I will also deny him before My Father who is in heaven."

15. Write out what this means to you.

In other countries, people have been persecuted for their faith in a greater way than we have experienced in America. However, persecution seems to be increasing in America. In other countries some have been thrown into prison for years just because they were preaching Christ or own a Bible. Others have been severely beaten and tortured in many ways. In America, we have freedom to preach Christ. So, let's do it with great boldness. When you are witnessing, give a clear presentation of the gospel.

Peter and John were persecuted for preaching about Jesus. In fact, they were beaten and told not to preach anymore about Him, but they had to obey God and continue to testify. They had to obey the Lord.

Read Acts 4:13, 19-20 "When they saw the boldness of Peter and John and perceived that they were illiterate and uneducated men, they marveled. And they recognized that they had been with Jesus… [19]But Peter and John answered them, 'Whether it is right in the sight of God to listen to you more than to God, you judge. [20]For we cannot help but declare what we have seen and heard.'"

I wanted to finish this section by saying that there is no specific formula for the right way to witness. Many times we use "The Way of the Master" pattern which is very effective in showing people that they need a Savior by comparing their lives to the Ten Commandments first. Then, when they realize they are guilty before God, they want to have Jesus forgive their sins and make them righteous before God. But, you can follow the leading of the Lord, just make sure they truly turn away from their sins and ask the Lord to come into their heart and forgive them and help them live a holy life. After asking the Lord to come into their hearts, they need to realize they need to continue to pray and live a holy life. Grace is not a license to sin.

People's names can be erased from the Book of Life as it states in Revelation 3:5: "He who overcomes shall be clothed in white garments. I will not blot his name out of the Book of Life, but I will confess his name before My Father and before His angels."

Some will fall away from the faith by being deceived. 1 Timothy 4:1 "Now the Spirit clearly says that in the last times some will **depart from the faith** and pay attention to seducing spirits and doctrines of devils" (emphasis mine). 2 Thessalonians 2:1-4 "Now, brothers, concerning the coming of our Lord Jesus Christ, and concerning our gathering together unto Him, we ask you [2]not to let your mind be quickly shaken or be troubled, neither in spirit nor by word, nor by letter coming as though from us, as if the day of Christ is already here. [3]Do not let anyone deceive you in any way. For that Day will not come unless a **falling away** comes first, and the man of sin is revealed, the son of destruction, [4]who opposes and exalts himself above all that is called God or is worshipped, so that he sits as God in the temple of God, showing himself as God" (emphasis mine).

So, go on for God and ask Him to help you as you witness for Him. Remember that when Jesus witnessed to people, He usually started right where they were, like the woman at the well. It was logical to talk to her about water and being thirsty which led into a salvation message.

Be bold for Jesus and filled with love. Love casts out fear. If you really love people, you will not want anyone to end up in hell, even the worst sinner.

HEALING FOR OUR BODIES

It is recommended that you watch or listen to the sermon series entitled Faith Comes by Hearing on our website media player.

There are many scriptures on healing in the Bible. In this lesson we will discuss several scriptures and what the Bible says about physical healing. For one thing, you need to understand that it is the devil who puts sickness on people and not God. God wants us to walk in health, life, and vitality. Jesus took the stripes (whipping) on His back for our healing.

Healing the Sick by T.L. Osborn is an amazing book that will help you learn about faith and healing.

3 John 2 "Beloved, I pray that all may go well with you and that you may be in good health, even as your soul is well."

Acts 10:38 "God anointed Jesus of Nazareth with the Holy Spirit and with power, who went about doing good and healing all who were oppressed by the devil, for God was with Him."

The Bible teaches us to view sickness as an oppression from the enemy. It is not something God desires for His children. In fact, that is why Jesus paid such a horrible price at the whipping post for our healing. It is a reward for Christ's suffering when we are healed.

1 Peter 2:24: Memorize this scripture.

"He Himself bore our sins in His own body on the tree, that we, being dead to sins, should live unto righteousness. 'By His wounds you were healed.'"

What does this say about our healing?

Read Exodus 23:25.

1. What does Exodus 23:25 teach you?

2. Explain what Psalm 103:3 means.

Now I think it is important to discuss faith.

3. What is faith according to Hebrews 11:1?

4. Did it take faith for Abraham to believe he was going to have a son when he had to wait 25 years?

5. Did it take faith for Noah to build an ark before it had rained?

Hebrews 11:6 states, "Without faith it is impossible to please God, for he who comes to God must believe that He exists and that He is a rewarder of those who diligently seek Him."

6. How do you think faith fits in to receiving physical healing?

Read Mark 6:5-6. "He could not do any miracles there, except that He laid His hands on a few sick people and healed them. [6]And He was amazed because of their unbelief."

7. What does this tell you about the importance of faith in healing?

8. Can people's lack of faith hinder healings and miracles?

Now, let's look at Galatians 3:13-14. "Christ has redeemed us from the curse of the law by being made a curse for us—as it is written, 'Cursed is everyone who hangs on a tree'—[14]so that the blessing of Abraham might come on the Gentiles through Jesus Christ, that we might receive the promise of the Spirit through faith."

Derek Prince broke down Deuteronomy 28-29 and Leviticus 26. He placed the curse of the law into nine categories and the blessings of obedience in seven categories. The curse included:

- **Curse under the law:** humiliation, barrenness, unfruitfulness, mental or physical breakdown, family breakdown, poverty or famine, defeat, oppression, failure, and God's disfavor.
- **Blessing of Abraham:** exaltation, health, fruitfulness, prosperity, abundance, God's favor, victory over enemies

9. What is the curse of the law?

Part of the curse is referring to the diseases He put on Egyptians, then we have been redeemed from them.

So, then how do we receive healing for ourselves? First of all, it is faith. You need to claim your healing and stand on His promises even if you don't see any changes. Specifically, it is faith in what Jesus accomplished at the cross. Kenneth Hagin stood on the scriptures for a year while his body was healing. He never wavered from believing that he was receiving his total healing. Some people have used healing scriptures, quoting them out loud, listening to them, believing them, and getting them in their spirit. The result was healing in their lives. Kenneth Hagin Sr. has some wonderful teaching on faith and healing that will be a great strength to you.

There are a few other things to mention here. The Bible gives some specific instructions about being healed. One thing we can do as believers is to lay hands on the sick and pray for them. Also, in James 5:14 it says that we can call for the elders in the church and have them anoint the sick with oil in person and pray the prayer of faith in Jesus' name.

In Psalm 107:20 it says, "He sent His word, and healed them, and delivered them from their destruction." This is a reference to words of knowledge being released that bring healing.

In the book of Mark chapter 9 the disciples tried to cast an evil spirit out of a boy, but they could not. They asked Jesus later, and He said in vs. 29, "This kind cannot come out except by prayer and fasting." This shows that adding fasting can bring a powerful breakthrough in healing, especially when deliverance is connected to the healing.

This leads to the point that there are times when healing is directly connected with being delivered from the demonic, as we see in Matthew 17:16-18:

"'I brought him to Your disciples, and they could not cure him.' [17]And Jesus answered and said, 'You unbelieving and perverse generation, how long shall I be with you? How long shall I put up with you? Bring him here to Me.' [18]Jesus rebuked the demon, and he came out of him. And the child was healed instantly."

We can see clearly from this scripture, and many others, that some sickness is caused directly by demons. The healing came when the demon was driven out.

What does Mark 16:17-18 mean to you?

How was the woman healed in Luke 13:16?

How does God provide healing to the church? Read 1 Corinthians 12:1-13 and James 5:14-15 for the answer.

So, in conclusion, we know that God does want to heal us. We must come to God with faith knowing that He can and does heal today. We need to believe. We can meditate on the scriptures and continue to hear them as our bodies heal. We need to believe BEFORE we receive the healing. So, faith is first, then the physical changes occur because of the faith.

DELIVERANCE FOR THE TORMENTED

If you haven't already, it is recommended that you watch or listen to the sermon series entitled Transformed on our website media player.

THREE STEPS IN DELIVERANCE: WRITTEN BY SANDY BOYD

Many Christians have varying degrees of satanic influence in their lives. This can certainly come from past sinful activity in life. Even though the sin is forgiven, the results and bondages of that sin have never fully been dealt with. Unforgiveness is a very big door for satanic torment, fears, demonic health problems, and major bondage to Satan. Generational sin, curses, and spirits are also very serious. They can travel down family bloodlines and torment for generations, if they are not dealt with. Also, people can simply be oppressed by something they are around. The main goal of the demonic is to keep someone from ever accepting Christ as their Savior. After a person accepts Christ, the next big goal of the demonic is to keep them from ever being able to do anything for the Lord. The demonic wants to keep them defeated, struggling with sin, bitter, hurt, so sick they can't be productive, or impoverished and working multiple jobs to makes ends meet.

There are three basic steps to effective deliverance. First, **cancel legal ground to the enemy**. What opened the door in the first place? What legal rights does the enemy have? Confession and repentance of sins, the sins of ancestors, and forgiving others will usually deal with most legal ground. Keep in mind that there might need to be renunciations of past agreements, pacts, oaths, or ceremonies either the individual or their family bloodline participated in. The worship of other gods and the occult are huge doors for demonic entrance. Also, sex outside of marriage is a huge door for demonic entrance and defilement. I have also heard that things from ungodly movies, music, to posters on walls can allow demonic entrance and oppression into someone's life. We see many times in Scripture that we need to confess and repent of our sins. Satan loses his grip when we do this because the blood of Jesus washes us clean. It is incredibly important that we receive forgiveness and cleansing from sin by faith. Don't go by feelings. We may not feel clean or forgiven, but the Bible says God is faithful and just to forgive us of our sins and cleanse us from all unrighteousness if we will confess our sins. This is laid hold of by faith. Faith is a very important component to receive any healing or deliverance of any kind.

The next step in deliverance is **destroying the works of Satan**. As Christians we have authority over all the power of the enemy as we see in Luke 10:19. We must lift up our voice and break every curse and destroy every work of Satan. The words of our mouth spoken in Jesus' name have awesome authority over the enemy. Also, the power of the Holy Spirit is what destroys the bondages! I have learned that God's holy angels are of great help in deliverance. The main point here is to directly and specifically break any and all works of Satan. There needs to be confrontation with faith and boldness! An example of this could be if someone has a curse and spirit in their life because their mother went to a witch for help. So after the person confesses this sin and renounces the witchcraft (canceling legal rights), then the oppressed person or deliverance minister can lift up his/her voice and say something like: "I destroy any curse or work of Satan that has been at work in this person's life because her mother visited a witch—I destroy this right now in the name of Jesus!" It's important to speak with faith and authority and to not rely on feelings. These things are conquered through faith.

The third step to deliverance is **direct confrontation with demons**. ALWAYS start with the strongman or the others won't leave (Mark 3:27). Either the deliverance minister or the person needing deliverance can speak directly to the demon and say: "I bind you in Jesus' name. You no longer have a right to this person's life. The blood of Jesus is against you and has canceled your right. I command you to come out and go from this person now and forever. You will no longer have anything to do with them or their family." And they have to leave. Again, it is important to do all this by faith and not rely on feelings. So we see deliverance takes place through: 1. Canceling legal rights. 2. Destroying the works of Satan. 3. Driving out the demonic.

The final point I would add is this. The Scriptures state that Satan comes to steal, kill, and destroy. So Jesus plainly reveals him as a thief. In Proverbs 6:31, it states that when a thief is caught he must pay back sevenfold, though it costs him all the wealth of his house. I want you to understand that the enemy should have to repair the damage caused, restore sevenfold what is stolen, take out all they have sown in that person's life, and put every disorder they have created back in order upon their departure. This is significant. I know a minister friend who commanded cancer to leave. It was a demon, but he added, you must take all the cancer out of the body as you go. The person went back to the doctor and was reported completely cancer free. Demons would love to just leave a mess when they leave. You can command them to put things back the way they are supposed to be and leave.

REPLACING THE SATANIC

Only God can heal people. People can be wounded in their spirit, soul, or physical body. Only God can truly heal. The first step toward healing is forgiveness. My husband and I have had reports of endless counseling that never really brought change. We need the power of the Holy Spirit to bring true healing.

After driving out the demonic and destroying the enemy's works, it is vital to replace these places with blessings and what Jesus paid for us to have. Many people we have prayed with have many curses and works of Satan destroyed. One of the most powerful things that can happen to someone is for a father to speak (not pray) a blessing over them. This is all throughout Scripture. Even in the New Testament, Jesus blessed (didn't pray for them or prophesy over them) the little children that were brought to him. Even to this day Jewish families will have a father speak a blessing over his wife and children every Sabbath. Usually my husband, or some other male authority figure, will stand in proxy as their biological father and speak a father's blessing over them. This is replacing the curses that were once there. Blessings are extremely powerful. A curse will hold people back, but blessings release them into destiny and God's purposes for them. I heard a true testimony from a man who had a bad heart but was blessing his heart daily. He would lay his hand on his heart and speak something like this: "I bless you, heart, to be healthy and strong and function perfectly." After a year or so he went back to his doctor. To his doctor's amazement, a creative miracle had changed his heart into exactly what he had spoken over it. I have heard of marriages and family relationships restored by speaking blessings. Blessings empower, release life and positive change, and angels enforce blessings. Begin to speak a blessing over your spouse, children, home, and overall life on a regular basis. Things will change! Sometimes because people haven't been taught better, they are very negative in what comes out of their mouths. Without realizing it, they are cursing so much of their lives. This is legal permission for demonic oppression. Derek Prince has some wonderful teaching on deliverance and spiritual warfare that will help you grow in your understanding of how to overcome the enemy.

I am so incredibly thankful that God put me into a full-gospel church right after my salvation! They taught me the truth of the need to fully repent of my sins and have a holy fear of God. I shudder to think where I would be today if I were in a different church teaching me that I could live in sin and still go to heaven! I am also so thankful that right after my salvation, I was baptized in the Holy Spirit and received my prayer language. Where at one time demons were at work in my life, now the Holy Spirit filled those areas and gave me strength. The change was remarkable.

A DEEP CONSECRATION UNTO GOD

There is a much deeper significance to what we call sacraments in church than we sometimes understand. The church for the most part is ignorant of the true power of communion, water baptism, and anointing with oil. We are priests unto God and need to understand the consecration of priests in Scripture. This deep consecration enabled them to be able to enter into the Tabernacle and draw close to God's presence.

Read Matthew 9:1-8. How did Jesus cancel the legal ground in this man's life?

What does the Bible say in regard to destroying Satan's works in these scriptures: Luke 10:17-20; 1 John 3:8; John 14:12?

What does Jesus teach us about driving out demons in these scriptures? Read Mark 3:13-35; Matthew 12:43-45.

What does John 8:34-36 mean to you?

TITHES AND OFFERINGS

It is recommended that you watch or listen to a sermon series entitled Kingdom Finance on our website media player.

Matthew 6:24-34 "No one can serve two masters. For either he will hate the one and love the other, or else he will hold to the one and despise the other. You cannot serve God and money. [25]"Therefore, I say to you, take no thought about your life, what you will eat, or what you will drink, nor about your body, what you will put on. Is not life more than food and the body than clothing? [26]Look at the birds of the air, for they do not sow, nor do they reap, nor gather into barns. Yet your heavenly Father feeds them. Are you not much better than they? [27]Who among you by taking thought can add a cubit to his stature? [28]"Why take thought about clothing? Consider the lilies of the field, how they grow: They neither work, nor do they spin. [29]Yet I say to you that even Solomon in all his glory was not dressed like one of these. [30]Therefore, if God so clothes the grass of the field, which today is here and tomorrow is thrown into the oven, will He not much more clothe you, O you of little faith? [31]Therefore, take no thought, saying, 'What shall we eat?' or 'What shall we drink?' or 'What shall we wear?' [32](For the Gentiles seek after all these things.) For your heavenly Father knows that you have need of all these things. [33]But seek first the kingdom of God and His righteousness, and all these things shall be given to you. [34]Therefore, take no thought about tomorrow, for tomorrow will take thought about the things of itself. Sufficient to the day is the trouble thereof."

It is important as a new believer to realize that when you come to God, you really give Him control over every aspect of your life. If you realize how much He loves and cares about you, financial giving to the Lord is a joy, and God loves a cheerful giver. Understanding all God has done for you, it will be in your heart to want to give back to God. As you start out in this Christian walk, it is important to give God your talents, your time, and your efforts, as well as giving to Him financially. For a deeper study, you can look at the introduction to the book of Deuteronomy; there is teaching on the seven realms of scriptural giving.

One thing that God instituted in the book of Genesis was giving the "tithe" (ten percent) back to God. We will talk about that a little more here with many examples from the Bible. As you obey God in every way, including in giving financially, He will abundantly bless you.

One of the first examples of bringing tithes to God was found in Genesis 14:17-20 when Abram brought a tithe of all he had to Melchizedek who was a priest to the Most High God. When you are giving to your church, or in this case to the priest, you are giving back to God. The book of Hebrews shows us we are sons and daughters of Abraham, and Christ is a priest in the order of Melchizedek.

"After his return from the defeat of Kedorlaomer and the kings who had joined with him, the king of Sodom went out to meet him in the Valley of Shaveh (that is, the King's Valley). [18]Then Melchizedek king of Salem brought out bread and wine. He was the priest of God Most High. [19]And he blessed him and said, 'Blessed be Abram by God Most High, Creator of heaven and earth; [20]and blessed be God Most High, who has delivered your enemies into your hand.' Then Abram gave him a tenth of everything."

1. Why do you think Abram gave a tithe to Melchizedek who is a picture and type of Christ and His eternal priesthood?
2. Was Abram (later Abraham) a blessed man?
3. Do you think Abraham's generosity as a giver caused him to be a blessed man?

It's important for you to realize that God really owns everything in the earth. He wants to provide for all of us. He wants us to be blessed. So He gives us the opportunity to sow financially and reap blessings in our lives.

Read Psalm 24:1.

4. Write out what this verse means to you in your own words.
5. If God owns everything in the earth, what are we expected to do?

Jacob had a wonderful experience in Genesis 28:13-17.

6. After Jacob had this experience with God, how did he feel?

7. What did God promise to do for him in verse 15?

After Jacob had that experience, he set up a pillar, and then he made a vow. Read verses 20-22 and then be able to discuss what he promised God at that point.

"Jacob vowed a vow, saying, 'If God will be with me and will protect me in this way that I go, and will give me bread to eat and clothing to put on, [21]so that I return to my father's house in peace, then the Lord will be my God. [22]Then this stone, which I have set for a pillar, will be the house of God, and from all that You give me I will surely give one-tenth to You.'"

8. Explain what Jacob said to God in your own words.

9. Do you think after studying these examples that God had established giving the tithe to God with Adam?

Remember that even Cain and Abel had brought offerings of the firstfruits of their labor to the Lord.

10. In Proverbs 3:9 it says, "Honor the Lord with your substance, and with the firstfruits of all your increase; 10 then will your barns be filled with plenty, and your vats will overflow with new wine." What do you think "firstfruits" means here?

Giving to God really has a lot to do with **faith** in God and **trust** in His ability to provide for your needs. Many people are just living from paycheck to paycheck and have no extra money. If you will truly give the Lord your first and best, and make sure a tenth of your money is given to God, the Lord promises He will make sure that your needs will be met. We all have to learn to trust God. There are so many stories of how God helped people's money stretch supernaturally. For example, appliances lasted longer than they should have. They received financial miracles when they needed them. It's good to share with others how God has taken care of you to strengthen their faith. God keeps His promises.

I want you to read another passage in the Old Testament to see what God says about tithes and offerings and what He will do for us as we trust Him: Malachi 3:8-12.

"Will a man rob God? Yet you have robbed Me. But you say, 'How have we robbed You?' In tithes and offerings. [9]You are cursed with a curse, your whole nation, for you are robbing Me. [10]Bring all the tithes into the storehouse, that there may be food in My house, and test Me now in this, says the Lord of Hosts, if I will not open for you the windows of heaven and pour out for you a blessing, that there will not be room enough to receive it. [11]I will rebuke the devourer for your sakes, so that it will not destroy the fruit of your ground, and the vines in your field will not fail to bear fruit, says the Lord of Hosts. 12 Then all the nations will call you blessed, for you will be a delightful land, says the Lord of Hosts."

11. According to this passage, why was God angry with the people?
12. What are the blessings promised to us if we give our tithes and offerings?
13. What does it mean that He will "rebuke the devourer"?

Now let's look at some New Testament scriptures about giving financially to God.

2 Corinthians 9:6-8 "But this I say: He who sows sparingly will also reap sparingly, and he who sows bountifully will also reap bountifully. [7]Let every man give according to the purposes in his heart, not grudgingly or out of necessity, for God loves a cheerful giver. [8]God is able to make all grace abound toward you, so that you, always having enough of everything, may abound to every good work."

14. In a previous lesson we have discussed the idea that whatever a man sows, that shall he also reap (Galatians 6:7). According to 2 Corinthians 9:6-8 does this also apply financially?
15. What kind of giver should we be?

There is one other passage I want you to read. Luke 6:38:

"Give, and it will be given to you: Good measure, pressed down, shaken together, and running over will men give unto you. For with the measure you use, it will be measured unto you."

16. After reading the above scriptures, do you think it is God's will to prosper us?

17. What do we have to do to receive God's blessings?

Psalm 35:27 "May those who favor my righteous cause shout for joy and be glad; may they say continually, 'The Lord be magnified, who delights in the prosperity of His servant.'"

Proverbs 10:22 "The blessing of the Lord makes rich, and He adds no sorrow to it" (NASB).

2 Corinthians 8:9 "For you know the grace of our Lord Jesus Christ, that though He was rich, yet for your sakes He became poor, that through His poverty you might be rich."

18. What do these three scriptures mean to you as you read them?

In writing this book I hope to convey that God's will was demonstrated at the cross. Jesus paid a dear price for our sins to be forgiven, but Jesus also paid a dear price for our healing (1 Peter 2:24), deliverance (Galatians 3:13-14), and prosperity (2 Corinthians 8:9). The Bible shows us:

John 10:10 "The thief comes only to steal and kill and destroy; I came so that they may have life, and have it abundantly" (NASB).

GOD'S PLAN FOR ISRAEL

It is recommended that you listen to a sermon series entitled Communion Hebrew Roots on our website media player. It is located under the playlist entitled Understanding our Hebrew Roots. This sermon series will help you understand the entire Word of God more clearly. Christianity grew up out of the soil of the Hebrew faith. Understanding the Hebrew roots will bring the New Testament to life, and help you understand end time prophecy

more clearly. This sermon series will teach you how the feasts of Israel, the Hebrew calendar, and the Tabernacle of Moses apply to us today. You will understand how the Lord's Supper came out of Passover, how Christ has fulfilled the feasts, and much more.

When God called Abram, he was from Ur, a Chaldean (Babylonian) city full of idolatry and paganism under the rulership of Nimrod. History records the capital city Nimrod ruled from was Shinar. Some Bible scholars believe that Abram was targeted for death by Nimrod and fled to live with Shem, the righteous son of Noah. Through his time with Shem, he learned of the one true God and creator of all things. Shem was later known as Melchizedek the king/priest of Salem which later became Jerusalem. This story very well could be true, but regardless, Abram was a man who had found favor with God, had a very special destiny, and was called out of ancient Babylon/Sumer to the land of Canaan. God made a covenant with Abram, changing his name to Abraham. In this covenant, God swore to Abraham that his descendants would inherit the land of Canaan, he would have innumerable descendants, and he would become a blessing to the entire world.

We know that through Abraham, Isaac, then Jacob (whose name was changed to Israel) came King David. Then through the line of David came Jesus Christ. Through Jesus, the entire world has been blessed with salvation. When Jesus comes back to the earth, He will come to Jerusalem, the city of David, and live and rule for 1,000 years on the throne of David. God has a special destiny for both the land of Israel and the Jewish people in end-time prophecy. Because of how much anti-Semitic rhetoric is out there, it is important to include this teaching so that you can stand with God and His plan for Israel. Be careful not to fall into the anti-Israel deception that is so prevalent in this end-time world we are living in. The reason Israel is under constant warfare and threat of annihilation is because the Bible says Jesus Christ will return to Israel. Therefore, Satan is trying to destroy

Israel to stop the second coming of Christ to the earth. In this next section, we will look at God's plan for Israel, how Christ was like another Moses, and how Jesus was born in Israel as the fulfillment of the law and prophets.

Read Genesis 12:1-5.

What did God say to Abram?

Read Genesis 17.

Who did God make an everlasting covenant with and what did God promise him?

Read Genesis 18.

Did God promise Abraham a son? What did you learn from this chapter?

Later, two descendants of Abraham were specifically named to be a part of this covenant. Which two were named? Exodus 6:3-4; Leviticus 26:42

How many people did God promise would be blessed through his seed, and what two pictures did God use to illustrate this to Abraham? Genesis 22:17-18. Also, what did God change Jacob's name to? Genesis 35:10

Once God established His covenant with Abraham, He told Abraham his descendants would be in a foreign land for 400 years where they would be persecuted, but they would eventually come back to the land of Canaan. Jacob, whose name was changed to Israel, moved his family of 70 people into Egypt during a great famine. Joseph took good care of them while he was alive. They became a mighty, populous nation while living in Egypt. So the Egyptians treated them harshly and made slaves of them. When 400 years were up, God called Moses and his older brother Aaron to go bring deliverance to Israel. You can read about the great deliverance of Israel out of Egypt by reading Exodus chapters 1-12.

Read Deuteronomy 18:18-19 and Acts 3:22-26.

What promise does God give to Moses?

Jesus was like unto Moses in the fact he was almost killed at his birth, had great authority, operated in signs and wonders, and spoke the very words of God Himself. The Lord knew that Israel would be led astray into idolatry and paganism. Later, we see in scripture that God promised to send a Messiah through the line of David, and this Messiah's rule would be eternal.

Read Isaiah 11:1-5; Matthew 1:1.

To whom does this passage refer, and what ancestral line was Jesus prophesied to come through?

In this section we have discovered Israel's special calling and purpose before God. Not only did God use them to bring the Bible into the world, but also Jesus Christ the Messiah of the world came through Israel as a Jew. Jesus was the foretold prophet like unto Moses, He was the direct descendant prophesied to come in the line of David, and in the future, He is coming to Israel to rule over the world for 1,000 years on the throne of David as prophesied by Gabriel in Luke 1:32. Make sure you stand with Israel and have a proper attitude of honor and love for Israel and the Jewish people.

Read Romans chapters 9-11.

This passage shows us that God has a family tree that is described as an olive tree. The root system of the tree goes back to the faith of Abraham, Isaac, and Jacob. Jesus is the trunk of the tree, or the centerpiece. The unbelieving Jews have become broken-off branches, while the believing gentiles replaced them as wild olive shoots that were grafted in. Both Jew and gentile make up God's family tree together. Neither is better than the other. We are all recipients of God's abundant grace and mercy. Let's love one another and live in harmony together in Christ.

> Therefore remember that formerly you, the Gentiles in the flesh, who are called the "uncircumcision" by the so-called "circumcision" in the flesh by human hands, [12]were at that time apart from Christ, alienated from the citizenship of Israel and strangers to the covenants of promise, without

hope and without God in the world. [13]But now in Christ Jesus you who were formerly far away have been brought near by the blood of Christ. [14]For He is our peace, who has made both groups one and has broken down the barrier of the dividing wall, [15]by abolishing in His flesh the enmity, that is, the law of the commandments contained in ordinances, that in Himself He might make the two into one new man, thus making peace, [16]and that He might reconcile both to God into one body through the cross, thereby slaying the enmity. [17]And He came and preached peace to you who were far away and peace to those who were near. [18]For through Him we both have access by one Spirit to the Father.

[19]Now, therefore, you are no longer strangers and foreigners, but are fellow citizens with the saints and members of the household of God, [20]having been built upon the foundation of the apostles and prophets, Jesus Christ Himself being the chief cornerstone, [21]in whom the entire building, tightly framed together, grows into a holy temple in the Lord, [22]in whom you also are being built together into a dwelling place of God through the Spirit. Ephesians 2:11-22

THE LAST DAYS AND THE RAPTURE OF THE CHURCH

It is recommended that you watch or listen to the two-sermon series Spine of Prophecy and Revelation: The Final Days, which can be accessed on our website media player under the playlist entitled End Time Prophecy. These two series will give you a depth of understanding about what the Bible predicts will happen in the last days. This series covers the entire Bible, shows Israel's significance in prophecy, and what lies ahead for Israel, the church, and sinful world.

Jesus gave us warnings of what to look for in the Last Days so we would not be caught by surprise, and so that we would be ready for

His coming. It is apparent that we are living in the Last Days. The good news is that those who keep themselves unblemished by the world, and are looking for the Lord's return, will be caught up with Him in heaven when He returns. The Bible seems to indicate a special promise for those who would be spiritually pure, walk close with the Lord, and be filled with extra oil. That promise is the sudden catching away. This is commonly called the rapture. This catching away will happen before the world is thrust into what is called the Tribulation time or the Days of Jacob's Trouble. Jacob's name was changed to Israel. So the Tribulation time is intended to get the nation of Israel ready for the return of Christ. It is not intended for the Bride of Christ who has made herself ready. So how can we be ready?

1. PURIFY OUR LIVES

Revelation 19:6-8 "Alleluia! For the Lord God Omnipotent reigns! [7]Let us be glad and rejoice and give Him glory, for the marriage of the Lamb has come, and His wife has made herself ready. [8]It was granted her to be arrayed in fine linen, clean and white."

Ephesians 5:26-27 "He might sanctify and cleanse it with the washing of water by the word, [27]and that He might present to Himself a glorious church, not having spot, or wrinkle, or any such thing, but that it should be holy and without blemish."

How can you get your life pure before God? Are there things in your life or relationships that are a spiritual hindrance to you?

2. BE FILLED WITH EXTRA OIL

Matthew 25:1-13 "Then the kingdom of heaven shall be like ten virgins, who took their lamps and went out to meet the bridegroom. [2]Five of them were wise and five were foolish. [3]Those who were foolish took their lamps, but took no oil with them. [4]But the wise took jars of oil with their lamps. [5]While the bridegroom delayed, they all rested and slept. [6]But at midnight there was a cry, 'Look, the bridegroom is coming! Come out to meet him!' [7]"Then all those virgins rose and trimmed their lamps. [8]But the foolish said to the wise, 'Give us some of your oil, for our lamps have gone out.' [9]The wise answered, 'No, lest there not be enough for us and you. Go rather to those who sell it, and buy some for yourselves.' [10]But while they went to buy some, the bridegroom came, and those who were ready went in with him to the wedding banquet. And the door was shut. [11]Afterward, the other virgins came also, saying, 'Lord, Lord, open the door for us.' [12]But he answered, 'Truly I say to you, I do not know you.' [13]Watch therefore, for you know neither the day nor the hour in which the Son of Man is coming."

The only difference between the wise and foolish virgins was the extra oil. When we understand that sleeping is prayerlessness in Scripture and being awake and alert has to do with being a prayerful watchmen, we can gain significant insight into this parable. We obtain extra oil through personal prayer and intimacy with the Lord. Also we see Enoch walked with God continually in prayer, and God raptured him out of the world. He is a picture of the end-time bride that will live holy in an evil generation and walk with God. Also, the Bible promises us help. God said He would pour out His Spirit in the last days. We have been seeing great outpourings of the Holy Spirit. These outpourings are meant to usher in a harvest of souls, and also intended to fill the bride with extra oil, thus preparing us for Christ's return.

Let's look at some more scriptures concerning the end times. We are promised an escape.

Luke 21:36 "Therefore watch always and pray that you may be counted worthy to escape all these things that will happen and to stand before the Son of Man."

When we realize that Jesus is coming back to get us, that gives us the hope we need.

Read John 14:3. "And if I go and prepare a place for you, I will come again and receive you to Myself, that where I am, you may be also."

When Jesus ascended to heaven after the resurrection, angels appeared to his followers and assured their hearts:

Acts 1:7-11 "He said to them, 'It is not for you to know the times or the dates, which the Father has fixed by His own authority. [8]But you shall receive power when the Holy Spirit comes upon you. And you shall be My witnesses in Jerusalem, and in all Judea and Samaria, and to the ends of the earth.' [9]When He had spoken these things, while they looked, He was taken up. And a cloud removed Him from their sight. 10 While they looked intently toward heaven as He ascended, suddenly two men stood by them in white garments. [11]They said, 'Men of Galilee, why stand looking toward heaven? This same Jesus, who was taken up from you to heaven, will come in like manner as you saw Him go into heaven.'"

1. How does this verse encourage our hearts?

2. What did you learn from this passage?

First Thessalonians 4:16-18 also explains what the rapture will be like:

"For the Lord Himself will descend from heaven with a shout, with the voice of the archangel, and with the trumpet call of God. And the dead in Christ will rise first. [17]Then we who are alive and remain shall be caught up together with them in the clouds to meet the Lord in the air. And so we shall be forever with the Lord. [18]Therefore comfort one another with these words."

3. What are three sounds we will hear when Christ returns for us?

4. Who will rise first?

Now look up and read 1 Corinthians 15:51-53.

5. How will we be changed during the rapture?

6. Will our bodies be different?

7. How quickly will this take place?

There is the parable of the wise and foolish virgins in Matthew 25:1-12 which discusses those who were ready when the Lord came back and those who were not ready and missed the rapture.

Matthew 25:13 "Watch therefore, for you know neither the day nor the hour in which the Son of Man is coming."

8. Why does Jesus give us many warnings about the rapture?

9. What does this make you want to do?

So far we have talked about the rapture of the Church, but we need to also discuss the signs of the Last Days so we can be prepared for what is going to happen. No one knows the day or the hour He will return except the Heavenly Father, but the Lord has given us signs to watch for so we will be ready for what is coming. And while we wait, we should pray and keep ourselves unspotted from the world. He is coming back for a Bride living a holy life.

Read all of Luke chapter 21 because it has many details about the end times.

10. Will there be many false Christs saying they are the real Christ?

11. What does it say about wars and rumors of wars?

Luke 21:10-11 "Then He said to them, 'Nation will rise against nation, and kingdom against kingdom. 11 Great earthquakes will occur in various places, and there will be famines and pestilence. And there will be terrors and great signs from heaven.'"

Look up and read Luke 21:12-24.

12. List at least four things that we will see as a sign of the end of the age

13. In verses 16-19, what does it say about family relationships?

Look up and read Luke 21:25-28.

14. Describe what it says about signs in the heavens.

15. Describe how people will feel during these times.

16. What do you think the signs in the sun and the moon and the stars will be like?

Then Jesus finishes this talk with another warning to the disciples as they listen to this. Let's read and discuss this final instruction that He gave so that His disciples would not be caught unaware.

Luke 21:34-36 "Take heed to yourselves, lest your hearts become burdened by excessiveness and drunkenness and anxieties of life, and that Day comes on you unexpectedly. [35]For as a snare it will come on all those who dwell on the face of the whole earth. [36]Therefore watch always and pray that you may be counted worthy to escape all these things that will happen and to stand before the Son of Man."

17. Explain in your own words what Jesus is saying in these last few verses.

18. What should we do so that we are ready when the Lord returns?

The Bible mentions drunkenness causing the day to come upon some unexpectedly. The Bible seems to foretell and warn that alcohol would be a problem in the last days.

Memory Verse: Luke 21:36 "But keep on the alert at all times, praying that you may have strength to escape all these things that are about to take place, and to stand before the Son of Man."

LIVING AN OVERCOMING, VICTORIOUS CHRISTIAN LIFE

As you have studied these lessons, you need to make sure everything is right between you and the Lord. Take out a piece of paper and write down everyone you need to forgive. Get another piece of paper and write down every sin you have ever committed. Out loud pray to the Lord and choose to forgive everyone on your list, and confess every sin to Him on your other list. Believe you are forgiven. You understand the importance of taking communion on a regular basis, putting on the armor of God, reading your Bible, going to church, and praying every day. But, now what? How do you really live a victorious life in spite of trials that come your way? Some people have a very difficult time with this. So, let's study some more scriptures and reflect on some things so that you can really be free and live a joyful life.

I have met people who are living a "roller coaster" life in Christ. They are really happy one day and depressed the next. This cycle continues to happen all the time. It's important to really look at this and ask yourself if that describes you and why. Any time there is a negative cycle in your life, ask the Lord to show you what is wrong. And be willing to let Him show you. He may be showing you an area of your life that you have never let Him touch.

That only describes one type of person. So, let's look at something else. Let's say a person seems to be pretty happy and steadfast in their walk with God, but they seem to not be able to hang on to money no matter what they do. They are even faithfully paying their tithes. So, what could be wrong? Think of other examples now of things that may show negative cycles. Well, it could be a generational curse in your life. Your ancestors may have passed down a generational curse that has come upon you, and you can break it off of you and off of your children and grandchildren. So, let's say it's a curse of poverty. Talk to the Lord and remind Him that you are faithfully paying your tithes and obeying Him in all things, and then just break the curse of poverty off of your life. And ask the Lord if there is anything else that you were not aware of that had to do with money. Refer back to the lesson that discusses deliverance. Then **LISTEN** to what the Lord is telling you about that area of your life. We as Christians have the authority to break curses off of ourselves. You may also want to go to a pastor and have him break things off of you as well. Other generational curses might be a type of generational sickness or disease, poverty, divorce, strong struggles with a specific sin, strife in the home, early death, etc.

The need for personal deliverance and inner healing is very real. Many times people are very unstable because of the need for inner healing or personal deliverance. You may need to go through this process to be able to become stable and healthy mentally and emotionally.

Let's look at Philippians 1:6. "I am confident of this very thing, that He who began a good work in you will complete it until the day of Jesus Christ."

1. What does this tell you about the Lord's ability to complete what He is doing in your life?

Let's look at Jeremiah 29:11 together.

"For I know the plans that I have for you, says the Lord, plans for peace and not for evil, to give you a future and a hope."

2. Write down what this verse is saying to you about God and your future.

Read John 3:16-17 and then let's discuss it:

"For God so loved the world that He gave His only begotten Son, that whoever believes in Him should not perish, but have eternal life. [17]For God did not send His Son into the world to condemn the world, but that the world through Him might be saved."

3. What does this say about God's love for you?

4. Do you really, really believe that He loves you that much?

It's very important that you truly believe that God loves YOU so much that He sent His Son to die for YOU. Once that is settled in your heart, you can really love and trust Him. He wants what is best for you even when you don't understand the path He is taking you down.

Okay, let's talk about some really important things now. In a previous lesson we talked about the importance of forgiving people and having mercy on them. This is so important. Along with this comes the fact that we should not "judge" people. Let's read Matthew 7:1-5 together and then discuss it:

"Judge not, that you be not judged. [2]For with what judgment you judge, you will be judged. And with the measure you use, it will be measured again for you. [3]And why do you see the speck that is in your brother's eye, but do not consider the plank that is in your own eye? [4]Or how will you say to your brother, 'Let me pull the speck out of your eye,' when a log is in your own eye? [5]You hypocrite! First take the plank out of your own eye, and then you will see clearly to take the speck out of your brother's eye."

5. Do we have a right to judge other people?

6. What happens if we judge other people?

Did you know that when you judge another person for something, you will find yourself doing the same thing?

Let's go back to the negative cycles. Do you wonder why you keep going around in circles, especially in one or two areas of your life, and you don't know why? Maybe everything is going well for you except you are not successful in your vocation. Maybe you seem to have relationship problems but everything else is going well. Don't you want everything to go well for you? I do! When you think about judging others, if you are a typical person, I am sure you have judged many people. The Bible says there are consequences to judging others. The Bible says you will "reap what you sow" in Galatians 6:7.

We have talked about forgiving people, judging people, and reaping what you sow. There is a lot of unrighteous judgment that goes on. This can be especially true toward parents. The Bible commands us to honor parents, and our unrighteous judgment of them is dishonoring them. This can actually cause you to struggle in your life with the very things you are judging them for. This is God's justice in that you are reaping exactly what you have sown. With the measure you have judged others, you will end up being judged in the same way in your personal life.

I want to give you a few more examples here so that you will see what I mean. Let's say that you are normally happy but there is one person or a situation that just irritates you. Well, ask the Lord why that is so. Let Him talk to you about that. If you are irritated, that is a form of anger, and that's not from the Lord. Sometimes you are in a very difficult work environment and have an overbearing boss. That's where God will help you to pray for that person and to work hard for them and still live an overcoming life. Sometimes you have hidden anger in your heart that you need to let the Lord take out of you. Everyone has his/her story of difficult situations, but many times there is a root of bitterness that is coming from your heart from a wound that may have happened in your past. These wounds commonly happened when someone was a young child. Allow God to reveal things to you and heal even the most hidden hurts. Remember, the Lord wants things to go well for you, and YOU want things to go well for you! You can put this down and sincerely ask forgiveness for any unrighteous judgment of others you have done, and then ask the Lord to put the blood of Jesus and the cross in between you and any sowing and reaping. This can give you a fresh start.

Are there people in your life you have been judgmental of?

Another area that can cause a lot of problems in one's personal life is our mouth. Do you tend to speak negatively? Did you know that words have power of life and death in them?

Proverbs 18:21 "Death and life are in the power of the tongue, and those who love it will eat its fruit."

I will talk about renewing the mind at the end of this chapter, but what you continually think about and speak will be what your life will become. People who speak negatively over themselves or others will reap the very words they are speaking. Spiritually, words have great power. You have great authority over your own life, so if you keep cursing yourself by saying things like: "Things never work out for me. I hate my legs. I am such a loser. I am so stupid. Others are successful, but I have never amounted to anything." You will continue to have problems in those areas. Start changing the way you speak. Start deliberately speaking life and blessings over these areas and quote scriptures over these areas.

James 4:2-12 "You lust and do not have, so you kill. You desire to have and cannot obtain. You fight and war. Yet you do not have, because you do not ask. [3]You ask, and do not receive, because you ask amiss, that you may spend it on your passions. [4]You adulterers and adulteresses, do you not know that the friendship with the world is enmity with God? Whoever therefore will be a friend of the world is the enemy of God. [5]Do you think that the Scripture says in vain, 'He yearns jealously for the spirit that lives in us?' [6]But He gives more grace. For this reason it says: 'God resists the proud, but gives grace to the humble.' [7]Therefore submit yourselves to God. Resist the devil, and he will flee from you. [8]Draw near to God, and He will draw near to you. Cleanse your hands, you sinners, and purify your hearts, you double-minded. [9]Grieve and mourn and weep. Let your laughter be turned to mourning, and your joy to dejection. [10]Humble yourselves in the sight of the Lord, and He will lift you up. [11]Do not speak evil of one another, brothers. He who speaks evil of his brother and judges his brother speaks evil of the law and judges the law. If you judge the law, you are not a doer of the law, but a judge. [12]There is one Lawgiver who is able to save and to destroy. Who are you to judge another?"

Like the rudder of a ship, the tongue will set the course of someone's life. What a powerful revelation. Take a few minutes to ask God's forgiveness for anything you have spoken over your life or others that has negatively affected things. Ask for the blood of Jesus to wash away those words and render them null and void. Now begin to speak life and blessings.

What areas of your life could you start speaking life and blessings over?

EVIL SPEECH

Jewish scholars believe since Miriam the sister of Moses spoke evil of Moses, then got leprosy, that evil speech is connected to *metzora*. So what does the word *metzora* in Scripture mean? It translates as *leprosy* in English, but the symptoms were different from the actual physical disease. It could grow on walls of homes, and it could get into garments. This was obviously a spiritual disease that carried a lot of natural consequences. In fact, metzora would cause someone to be excommunicated and moved outside the camp to live in isolation until they repented of their sins and were consequently healed. Then the priests could restore them back into the camp. One of the great sins that opens the door to spiritual metzora, causes people to lose relationships, get hurt and hurt others, and end up leaving a church on bad terms, is gossip and slander. If you have a problem with someone, Matthew 18:15-17 teaches us to go to the person and talk it out with them. This will solve ninety percent of church problems right there. Also we need to take the matter to prayer. The Bible teaches us to absolutely never gossip or slander people. A gossip is a talebearer who shares personal information with others that is none of their business. A slanderer is someone who tears others down behind their back, destroying their good name. The Bible so strongly condemns this activity that Romans 16:17 tells us to mark divisive people and not associate with them. This means to avoid contact and conversations with them. The word the Bible uses for a gossip and slanderer is a reviler. God so hates this activity that He states that we should not even eat a meal with someone who calls himself a Christian brother but who is a reviler.

1 Corinthians 5:11-13 "But I have written to you not to keep company with any man who is called a brother, who is sexually immoral, or covetous, or an idolater, or a reviler, or a drunkard, or an extortioner. Do not even eat with such a person. [12]For what have I to do with judging those also who are outside? Do you not judge those who are inside? [13]But God judges those who are outside. Therefore 'put away from among yourselves that wicked person.'"

The Bible goes on to say that God hates the one who sows discord among the brethren. I know this is strong language in the Bible, but the reason God has such strong feelings about this subject is because of the incredible damage and destruction it does to so many individuals, families, and ministries.

Proverbs 6:16-19 "These six things the Lord hates, indeed, seven are an abomination to Him: [17]A proud look [the spirit that makes one overestimate himself and underestimate others], a lying tongue, and hands that shed innocent blood, [18]A heart that manufactures wicked thoughts and plans, feet that are swift in running to evil, [19]A false witness who breathes out lies [even under oath], and **he who sows discord among his brethren**" (AMPC, emphasis mine).

Let's take a moment here to sincerely ask God's forgiveness for any gossip and slander you have ever done. If you feel there is someone you owe an apology to because you really hurt their life with gossip, you need to apologize to them. Now is the time to stop this evil activity and stop associating with people who do these evil things.

Are there people you need to quit associating with?

PRACTICAL

If someone comes to you with gossip or slander, be a peacemaker and immediately take them to the person they are attempting to talk about so they can work it out. This person will either quit coming to you with their gossip, or they will work it out with their fellow Christian. You may have to rebuke some people to their face about this evil activity. If someone comes to you running down the pastor or leader, you need to stop them, and you need to let the leadership know of their evil activity. Take them to the pastor. You can be used of God to help stop this great evil in the body of Christ by doing these things. Whatever you do, do not participate in their evil deeds because it can bring spiritual metzora into your life, cause you to go through judgment from God, and end up destroying relationships in your life. Stay away from this evil activity. This is one of Satan's greatest tactics in the church.

THE RENEWING OF THE MIND

The final area to look at is renewing your mind. The Bible says, as a man thinks, so he is. One of the greatest battles you will win in your Christian walk is being crucified with Christ and renewing your mind. As you get up and spend time with the Lord every morning, putting your flesh under submission to Him, you will move into this crucified life. You will have to continually die to the flesh daily. In your death to the flesh, you will have to learn to renew your mind. Just like changing a baby, you don't put a clean diaper over a dirty one. Rather, you change out the old dirty diaper. Every thought that enters your mind that is evil, violent, lustful, hateful, bitter etc., needs to be thrown out and replaced with something good and wholesome. At first this can be like working out after being out of shape. It may be hard at first, but the more you do this, the more disciplined and stronger your mind will become. What you think has a lot to do with what comes out of your mouth and your behavior. The Bible states that we are transformed by the renewing of our minds.

Romans 12:1-2 "I urge you therefore, brothers, by the mercies of God, that you present your bodies as a living sacrifice, holy, and acceptable to God, which is your reasonable service of worship. 2 Do not be conformed to this world, but be transformed by the renewing of your mind, that you may prove what is the good and acceptable and perfect will of God."

Presenting your bodies as a living sacrifice is laying our lives on the altar and letting God burn out everything that needs to go. There are many times in life that you will have to make decisions your flesh does not want to make. You will have to die to that flesh. Also the word transformed is *metamorpho* in the Greek where we get the word metamorphosis from. Metamorphosis is when a caterpillar enters a cocoon, is transformed, and comes out a butterfly. When you begin to change the way you think and speak, and the company you keep, you will truly begin being transformed. You will move from a caterpillar life that moves slowly along the ground constantly running into obstacles, into a butterfly life in Christ that soars above the things of the world.

I wanted to complete this lesson and this study guide by sharing with you the "Fruit of the Spirit" that we are supposed to exhibit as we go through this life. Examine your heart, and allow the Lord to reveal things to you so that you can truly live an overcoming life for Christ.

Galatians 5:16-25 "I say then, walk in the Spirit, and you shall not fulfill the lust of the flesh. [17]For the flesh lusts against the Spirit, and the Spirit against the flesh. These are in opposition to one another, so that you may not do the things that you please. [18]But if you are led by the Spirit, you are not under the law. [19]Now the works of the flesh are revealed, which are these: adultery, sexual immorality, impurity, lewdness, [20]idolatry, sorcery, hatred, strife, jealousy, rage, selfishness, dissensions, heresies, [21]envy, murders, drunkenness, carousing, and the like. I warn you, as I previously warned you, that those who do such things shall not inherit the kingdom of God. [22]But the fruit of the Spirit is love, joy, peace, patience, gentleness, goodness, faith, [23]meekness, and self-control; against such there is no law. [24]Those who are Christ's have crucified the flesh with its passions and lusts. [25]If we live in the Spirit, let us also walk in the Spirit."

Continue to seek Him with all your heart. He is your very life.

Write in your journal what areas you feel you could change in your life concerning the company you keep and the conversations you have been involved in.

Write in your journal what you have learned about the way you think and speak.

Godly character is to keep your word, be loving/kind, humble, obedient, patient with people, not seeking recognition, not being judgmental, not being lustful, and not being fearful or controlling. These are things to meditate on. Have you struggled in some of these areas?

Some people have a tendency to try to control the lives of others. This is not love. To be honest it moves from just the sinful flesh into what the Bible calls witchcraft. Any ungodly manipulation, intimidation, or domination is witchcraft. Make sure that you pray God's will over people, and let them make their own decisions. When we raise kids, we have to balance our authority and giving direction with making sure it doesn't move into oppressive control. Control is almost always rooted in fear and sometimes in pride. Moving in true authority takes faith and humility. We have all learned valuable lessons from making poor decisions. You will have to trust God to see your kids through when they have made poor decisions. They will learn from them just as we have.

How can you bring about practical changes in regard to godly character in your life?

FINAL WORDS

Keep yourself pure, live for eternity, and be ready for Christ's return! What will matter when you stand before Christ? Live every day as though it was your last on earth. Learn to have a mindset that lives for eternity, not just for this temporary life we have on the earth. If you died today and stood before the judgment seat of Christ, what would He say about your life? If we think that way, we will live every day as though it is our last. This is living with eternity in mind.

James 1:27 "Keep oneself unstained by the world."

Ephesians 5:27 "That He might present to Himself a glorious church, not having spot, or wrinkle, or any such thing, but that it should be holy and without blemish."

Revelation 19:6-9 "Alleluia! For the Lord God Almighty reigns!
[7]Let us be glad and rejoice and give Him glory, for the marriage of the
Lamb has come, and His wife has made herself ready. [8]It was granted her to be arrayed in fine linen, clean and white. Fine linen is the
righteous deeds of the saints. [9]Then he said to me, 'Write: Blessed are
those who are invited to the marriage supper of the Lamb.' And he
said to me, 'These are the true sayings of God.'"

Section Two: Through the Bible in 56 Weeks

Now it is time to go through the second phase of Bible study. This study will take you through the entire Bible in 56 weeks. Most weeks, Pastor Scott has a free online teaching that walks you through the first five books of the Bible called the Torah. Properly understanding the first five books of the Bible lays a foundation for fully understanding the entire Word of God. Read the Torah portion in the Bible, then watch the corresponding teaching Pastor Scott offers that goes with it. You can find these teachings on our website media player under the playlist entitled "Bible Study with Pastor Scott." The rest of the week you can read the other chapters designed to take you through the entire Bible in 56 weeks. The Amplified Classic Bible (1987 version) can help bring additional depth and clarity as you read through the Bible.

There will also be weekly Bible scriptures to memorize. I recommend that you write the scripture memory for the week on something that you look at every day. Recite it over and over each day until it is truly committed to memory by the end of the week. By following this pattern, you will gain a rich understanding of Scripture. If this is too much reading for you to do in 56 weeks, just slow down and take longer to complete it. It is not about how fast you can get through the Bible, but rather, it is about truly getting a deep, rich understanding of God's Holy Word. The Modern English Version of the Bible is used in this section.

The weekly readings are labeled by the Hebrew name first to familiarize you with them. The Ketuvim are the narrative sections of the Bible. The Nevi'im are the prophets, and the Brit Chadashah is the New Testament. There will be four sections of reading weekly. When starting a new book of the Bible, you can refer to sections 5-6 to help you understand what you are reading.

WEEK ONE: WEEKLY READING

Bereshit "In the Beginning"

Torah: Genesis 1:1-6:8 (watch part 1 video after reading)

Ketuvim: Writings-Narrative: Joshua 1-6

Nevi'im: Prophets/Poetic: Psalm 1-6

Brit Chadashah: New Testament: Matthew 1-6

Scripture Memory: Genesis 1:1 "In the beginning God created the heavens and the earth." Leviticus 19:11 "You shall not steal, nor deal falsely, nor lie to one another."

WEEK TWO: WEEKLY READING

Noach "Noah"

Torah: Genesis 6:9-11:32 (watch part 2 video after reading)

Ketuvim: Writings-Narrative: Joshua 7-12

Nevi'im: Prophets/Poetic: Psalms 7-12

Brit Chadashah: New Testament: Matthew 7-12

Scripture Memory: Numbers 23:19 "God is not a man, that He should lie, nor a son of man, that He should repent. Has He spoken, and will He not do it? Or has He spoken, and will He not make it good?"

WEEK THREE: WEEKLY READING

Lech Lecha "Go forth, yourself"

Torah: Genesis 12:1–17:27 (watch part 3 "Abraham" video after reading)

Ketuvim: Writings-Narrative: Joshua 13-18

Nevi'im: Prophets/Poetic: Psalm 13-18

Brit Chadashah: New Testament: Matthew 13-18

Scripture Memory: Joshua 1:8 "This Book of the Law must not depart from your mouth. Meditate on it day and night so that you may act carefully according to all that is written in it. For then you will make your way successful, and you will be wise."

WEEK FOUR: WEEKLY READING

Vayera "And He appeared"

Torah: Genesis 18:1-22:24 (watch part 4 "God Appears to Abraham" video after reading)

Ketuvim: Writings-Narrative: Joshua 19-24

Nevi'im: Prophets/Poetic: Psalm 19-24

Brit Chadashah: New Testament: Matthew 19-24

Scripture Memory: Psalm 23:1-6 "The Lord is my shepherd; I shall not want. [2]He makes me lie down in green pastures; He leads me beside still waters .[3]He restores my soul; He leads me in paths of righteousness for His name's sake. [4]Even though I walk through the valley of the shadow of death, I will fear no evil; for You are with me; Your rod and Your staff, they comfort me. [5]You prepare a table before me in the presence of my enemies; you anoint my head with oil; my cup runs over. [6]Surely goodness and mercy shall follow me all the days of my life, and I will dwell in the house of the Lord forever."

WEEK FIVE: WEEKLY READING

Chayei Sarah "The life of Sarah"

Torah: Genesis 23:1-25:18 (watch part 5 video after reading)

Ketuvim: Writings-Narrative: Judges 1-8

Nevi'im: Prophets/Poetic: Psalm 25-31

Brit Chadashah: New Testament: Matthew 25-28; Mark 1-2

Scripture Memory: Psalm 119:9, 11 "How shall a young man keep his way pure? By keeping it according to Your word... 11Your word I have hidden in my heart, that I might not sin against You."

WEEK SIX: WEEKLY READING

Toldot "Generations"

Torah: Genesis 25:19-28:9 (watch part 6 "Jacob and Esau" video after reading)

Ketuvim: Writings-Narrative: Judges 9-15

Nevi'im: Prophets/Poetic: Psalm 32-38

Brit Chadashah: New Testament: Mark 3-9

Scripture Memory: Proverbs 3:5-6 "Trust in the Lord with all your heart, and lean not on your own understanding; 6 in all your ways acknowledge Him, and He will direct your paths." Isaiah 26:3 "You will keep him in perfect peace, whose mind is stayed on You, because he trusts in You."

WEEK SEVEN: WEEKLY READING

Vayetze "And he went out"

Torah: Genesis 28:10-32:3 (watch part 7 "Jacob Flees" video after reading)

Ketuvim: Writings-Narrative: Judges 16-21

Nevi'im: Prophets/Poetic: Psalm 39-44

Brit Chadashah: New Testament: Mark 10-15

Scripture Memory: Proverbs 3:9-10 "Honor the Lord with your substance, and with the firstfruits of all your increase; then will your barns be filled with plenty, and your vats will overflow with new wine." Malachi 3:10-12 "Bring all the tithes into the storehouse, that there may be food in My house, and test Me now in this, says the Lord of Hosts, if I will not open for you the windows of heaven and pour out for you a blessing, that there will not be room enough to receive it. [11]I will rebuke the devourer for your sakes, so that it will not destroy the fruit of your ground, and the vines in your field will not fail to bear fruit, says the Lord of Hosts. [12]Then all the nations will call you blessed, for you will be a delightful land, says the Lord of Hosts."

WEEK EIGHT: WEEKLY READING

Vayishlach "and he sent"

Torah: Genesis 32:4-36:43 (watch part 8 "Jacob faces Esau" video after reading)

Ketuvim: Writings-Narrative: Ruth 1-4

Nevi'im: Prophets/Poetic: Psalm 45-51

Brit Chadashah: New Testament: Mark16 - Luke 1-6

Scripture Memory: Isaiah 40:31 "But those who wait upon the Lord shall renew their strength; they shall mount up with wings as eagles, they shall run and not be weary, and they shall walk and not faint." Isaiah 41:10 "Do not fear, for I am with you; do not be dismayed, for I am your God. I will strengthen you, I will help you, yes, I will uphold you with My righteous right hand."

WEEK NINE: WEEKLY READING

Vayeshev "and he dwelt"

Torah: Genesis 37:1–40:23 (watch part 9 "Joseph in Slavery" video after reading)

Ketuvim: Writings-Narrative: 1 Samuel 1-6

Nevi'im: Prophets/Poetic: Psalm 52-57

Brit Chadashah: New Testament: Luke 7-12

Scripture Memory: Isaiah 53:3-6 "He was despised and rejected of men, a man of sorrows and acquainted with grief. And we hid, as it were, our faces from him; he was despised, and we did not esteem
him. 4Surely he has borne our grief and carried our sorrows; Yet we
esteemed him stricken, smitten of God, and afflicted. 5But he was
wounded for our transgressions, he was bruised for our iniquities; the chastisement of our peace was upon him, and by his stripes we
are healed. 6All of us like sheep have gone astray; each of us has
turned to his own way, but the Lord has laid on him the iniquity of us all."

WEEK TEN: WEEKLY READING

Miketz "at the end of"

Torah: Genesis 41:1-44:17 (watch part 10 "Joseph Leaves Slavery" video after reading)

Ketuvim: Writings-Narrative: 1 Samuel 7-12

Nevi'im: Prophets/Poetic: Psalm 58-63

Brit Chadashah: New Testament: Luke 13-18

Scripture Memory: Lamentation 3:22-24 "It is of the Lord's mercies that we are not consumed; His compassions do not fail. [23]They are new every morning; great is Your faithfulness. [24]'The Lord is my portion,' says my soul, 'therefore I will hope in Him.'"

WEEK ELEVEN: WEEKLY READING

Vayigash "and he drew near"

Torah: Genesis 44:18-47:27 (watch part 11 "Joseph Reveals Himself" video after reading)

Ketuvim: Writings-Narrative: 1 Samuel 13-18

Nevi'im: Prophets/Poetic: Psalm 64-69

Brit Chadashah: New Testament: Luke 19-24

Scripture Memory: Matthew 1:21 "She will bear a Son, and you shall call His name JESUS, for He will save His people from their sins (emphasis mine)." Matthew 4:19 "And He said to them, 'Follow Me, and I will make you fishers of men.'" Matthew 5:16 "Let your light so shine before men that they may see your good works and glorify your Father who is in heaven."

WEEK TWELVE: WEEKLY READING

Vayechi "and he lived"

Torah: Genesis 47:28-50:26 (watch part 12 "Jacob's Death" video after reading)

Ketuvim: Writings-Narrative: 1 Samuel 19-24

Nevi'im: Prophets/Poetic: Psalm 70-75

Brit Chadashah: New Testament: John 1-6

Scripture Memory: Matthew 5:11-12 "Blessed are you when men revile you, and persecute you, and say all kinds of evil against you falsely for My sake. [12]Rejoice and be very glad, because great is your reward in heaven, for in this manner they persecuted the prophets who were before you."

WEEK THIRTEEN: WEEKLY READING

Shemot "Names"

Torah: Exodus 1:1 - 6:1 (watch part 13 "The Call of Moses" video after reading)

Ketuvim: Writings-Narrative: 1 Samuel 25-31

Nevi'im: Prophets/Poetic: Psalm 76-80

Brit Chadashah: New Testament: John 7-12

Scripture Memory: Matthew 6:9-15 "Therefore pray in this manner: Our Father who is in heaven, hallowed be Your name. [10]Your kingdom come; Your will be done on earth, as it is in heaven. [11]Give us this day our daily bread. [12]And forgive us our debts, as we forgive our debtors. [13]And lead us not into temptation, but deliver us from evil. For Yours is the kingdom and the power and the glory forever. Amen. [14]For if you forgive men for their sins, your heavenly Father will also forgive you. [15]But if you do not forgive men for their sins, neither will your Father forgive your sins."

WEEK FOURTEEN: WEEKLY READING

Va'era "and I appeared"

Torah: Exodus 6:2-9:35 (watch part 14 "The Plagues Begin" video after reading)

Ketuvim: Writings-Narrative: 2 Samuel 1-6

Nevi'im: Prophets/Poetic: Psalm 81-86

Brit Chadashah: New Testament: John 13-18

Scripture Memory: Matthew 6:33-34 "But seek first the kingdom of God and His righteousness, and all these things shall be given to you. [34]Therefore, take no thought about tomorrow, for tomorrow will take thought about the things of itself. Sufficient to the day is the trouble thereof."

WEEK FIFTEEN: WEEKLY READING

Bo "enter"

Torah: Exodus 10:1-13:16 (watch part 15 "Passover and the Communion Table" video after reading)

Ketuvim: Writings-Narrative: 2 Samuel 7-12

Nevi'im: Prophets/Poetic: Psalm 87-92

Brit Chadashah: New Testament: John 19-21; Acts 1-3

Scripture Memory: Matthew 7:13-14 "Enter at the narrow gate, for wide is the gate and broad is the way that leads to destruction, and there are many who are going through it, 14 because small is the gate and narrow is the way which leads to life, and there are few who find it." Acts 10:38 "God anointed Jesus of Nazareth with the Holy Spirit and with power, who went about doing good and healing all who were oppressed by the devil, for God was with Him."

WEEK SIXTEEN: WEEKLY READING

Beshalach "When he sent away"

Torah: Exodus 13:17-17:16 (watch part 16 "Red Sea Crossing" video after reading)

Ketuvim: Writings-Narrative: 2 Samuel 13-18

Nevi'im: Prophets/Poetic: Psalm 93-98

Brit Chadashah: New Testament: Acts 4-9

Scripture Memory: Matthew 7:21-23 "Not everyone who says to Me, 'Lord, Lord,' shall enter the kingdom of heaven, but he who does the will of My Father who is in heaven. [22]Many will say to Me on that day, 'Lord, Lord, have we not prophesied in Your name, cast out demons in Your name, and done many wonderful works in Your name?' [23]But then I will declare to them, 'I never knew you. Depart from Me, you who practice evil.'"

WEEK SEVENTEEN: WEEKLY READING

Yitro "Jethro"

Torah: Exodus 18:1-20:23 (watch part 17 "Jethro" video after reading)

Ketuvim: Writings-Narrative: 2 Samuel 19-21

Nevi'im: Prophets/Poetic: Psalm 99-101

Brit Chadashah: New Testament: Acts 10-12

Scripture Memory: Isaiah 54:17 "No weapon that is formed against you shall prosper, and every tongue that shall rise against you in judgment, you shall condemn. This is the heritage of the servants of the LORD, and their vindication is from Me, says the LORD." Psalm 96:2 "Sing unto the Lord, bless His name; declare His salvation from day to day."

WEEK EIGHTEEN: WEEKLY READING

Mishpatim "Judgments"

Torah: Exodus 21:1-27:19 (watch part 18 "Sinai Covenant" video after reading)

Ketuvim: Writings-Narrative: 2 Samuel 22-24

Nevi'im: Prophets/Poetic: Psalm 102-104

Brit Chadashah: New Testament: Acts 13-15

Scripture Memory: Psalm 91 "He who dwells in the shelter of the Most High shall abide under the shadow of the Almighty. [2]I will say of the Lord, 'He is my refuge and my fortress, my God in whom I trust.' [3]Surely He shall deliver you from the snare of the hunter and from the deadly pestilence. [4]He shall cover you with His feathers, and under His wings you shall find protection; His faithfulness shall be your shield and wall. [5]You shall not be afraid of the terror by night, nor of the arrow that flies by day; [6]nor of the pestilence that pursues in darkness, nor of the destruction that strikes at noonday. [7]A thousand may fall at your side and ten thousand at your right hand, but it shall not come near you. [8]Only with your eyes shall you behold and see the reward of the wicked. [9]Because you have made the Lord, who is my refuge, even the Most High, your dwelling, [10]there shall be no evil befall you, neither shall any plague come near your tent; [11]for He shall give His angels charge over you to guard you in all your ways. [12]They shall bear you up in their hands, lest you strike your foot against a stone. [13]You shall tread upon the lion and adder; the young lion and the serpent you shall trample underfoot. [14]Because he has set his love upon Me, therefore I will deliver him; I will set him on high, because he has known My name. [15]He shall call upon Me, and I will answer him; I will be with him in trouble, and I will deliver him and honor him. [16]With long life I will satisfy him and show him My salvation."

WEEK NINETEEN: WEEKLY READING

Terumah "Contributions"

Torah: (watch part 19 "Priestly Garments and Tabernacle" video after reading)

Ketuvim: Writings-Narrative: 1 Kings 1-6

Nevi'im: Prophets/Poetic: Psalm 105-110

Brit Chadashah: New Testament: Acts 16-21

Scripture Memory: Deuteronomy 33:25-28 "Your sandals will be iron and brass; according to your days, so shall be your strength. [26]There is none like the God of Jeshurun, who rides through the heavens to help you, and in His majesty through the skies. [27]The eternal God is your refuge, and underneath you are the everlasting arms; He will drive out the enemy before you, and will say, 'Destroy them.' [28]Israel dwells in safety; the fountain of Jacob will be secluded."

WEEK TWENTY: WEEKLY READING

Tetzaveh "You shall command"

Torah: Exodus 27:20-30:10 (no corresponding video this week)

Ketuvim: Writings-Narrative: 1 Kings 7-12

Nevi'im: Prophets/Poetic: Psalm 111-115

Brit Chadashah: New Testament: Acts 22-28

Scripture Memory: Matthew 16:24-27 "Then Jesus said to His disciples, 'If anyone will come after Me, let him deny himself, and take up his cross, and follow Me. [25]For whoever would save his life will lose it, and whoever loses his life for My sake will find it. [26]For what will it profit a man if he gains the whole world and loses his own soul? Or what shall a man give in exchange for his soul? [27]For the Son of Man shall come with His angels in the glory of His Father, and then He will repay every man according to his works.'"

WEEK TWENTY-ONE: WEEKLY READING

Ki Tisa "When you take"

Torah: Exodus 30:11-34:35 (watch part 20 "Golden Calf" video after reading)

Ketuvim: Writings-Narrative: 1 Kings 13-18

Nevi'im: Prophets/Poetic: Psalm 116-121

Brit Chadashah: New Testament: Romans 1-6

Scripture Memory: Matthew 18:18-20 "Truly I say to you, whatever you bind on earth will be bound in heaven, and whatever you loose on earth will be loosed in heaven. 19 Again I say to you, that if two of you agree on earth about anything they ask, it will be done for them by My Father who is in heaven. 20 For where two or three are assembled in My name, there I am in their midst."

WEEK TWENTY-TWO: WEEKLY READING

Vayakhel "and he assembled"

Torah: Exodus 35:1-38:20 (watch part 21 "Tabernacle Construction" video after reading)

Ketuvim: Writings-Narrative: 1 Kings 19 – 2 Kings 3

Nevi'im: Prophets/Poetic: Psalm 122-128

Brit Chadashah: New Testament: Romans 7-13

Scripture Memory: Matthew 12:30-32 "He who is not with Me is against Me, and he who does not gather with Me scatters abroad. [31]Therefore I say to you, all kinds of sin and blasphemy will be forgiven men, but the blasphemy against the Holy Spirit will not be forgiven men. [32]Whoever speaks a word against the Son of Man will be forgiven. But whoever speaks against the Holy Spirit will not be forgiven, neither in this world, nor in the world to come."

WEEK TWENTY-THREE: WEEKLY READING

Pekudei "accounting of"

Torah: Exodus 38:21-40:38 (watch part 22 "Anointing Oil" video after reading)

Ketuvim: Writings-Narrative: 2 Kings 4-10

Nevi'im: Prophets/Poetic: Psalm 129-135

Brit Chadashah: New Testament: Romans 14-16 – 1 Corinthians 1-4

Scripture Memory: 1 John 5:4-5 "For whoever is born of God overcomes the world, and the victory that overcomes the world is our faith. [5]Who is it that overcomes the world, but the one who believes that Jesus is the Son of God?" 1 John 5:11-12 "And this is the testimony: that God has given us eternal life, and this life is in His Son. [12]Whoever has the Son has life, and whoever does not have the Son of God does not have life."

WEEK TWENTY-FOUR: WEEKLY READING

Vayikra "and he called"

Torah: Leviticus 1:1-6:7 (watch part 23 "Symbolism" video after reading)

Ketuvim: Writings-Narrative: 2 Kings 11-17

Nevi'im: Prophets/Poetic: Psalm 136-142

Brit Chadashah: New Testament: 1 Corinthians 5-10

Scripture Memory: James 4:4-5 "You adulterers and adulteresses, do you not know that the friendship with the world is enmity with God? Whoever therefore will be a friend of the world is the enemy of God. [5]Do you think that the Scripture says in vain, 'He yearns jealously for the spirit that lives in us.'" James 1:12 "Blessed is the man who endures temptation, for when he is tried, he will receive the crown of life, which the Lord has promised to those who love Him."

WEEK TWENTY-FIVE: WEEKLY READING

Tzav "Command"

Torah: Leviticus 6:8-8:36 (no corresponding video this week)

Ketuvim: Writings-Narrative: 2 Kings 18-25

Nevi'im: Prophets/Poetic: Psalm 143-150

Brit Chadashah: New Testament: 1 Corinthians 11-16

Scripture Memory: Hebrews 13:17 "Obey your leaders and submit to them, for they watch over your souls as those who must give an account. Let them do this with joy and not complaining, for that would not be profitable to you." Luke 10:18-20 "He said to them, 'I saw Satan as lightning fall from heaven. [19]Look, I give you authority to trample on serpents and scorpions, and over all the power of the enemy. And nothing shall by any means hurt you. [20]Nevertheless do not rejoice that the spirits are subject to you, but rather rejoice that your names are written in heaven.'"

WEEK TWENTY-SIX: WEEKLY READING

Shemini "eighth"

Torah: Leviticus 9:1–11:47 (watch part 24 "Fire of God" video this week)

Ketuvim: Writings-Narrative: 1 Chronicles 1-7

Nevi'im: Prophets/Poetic: Proverbs 1-7

Brit Chadashah: New Testament: 2 Corinthians 1-7

Scripture Memory: Matthew 28:18-20 "Then Jesus came and spoke to them, saying, 'All authority has been given to Me in heaven and on earth. [19]Go therefore and make disciples of all nations, baptizing them in the name of the Father and of the Son and of the Holy Spirit, [20]teaching them to observe all things I have commanded you. And remember, I am with you always, even to the end of the age.' Amen."

WEEK TWENTY-SEVEN: WEEKLY READING

Tazria "she conceives"

Torah: Leviticus 12:1-13:59 (watch part 25 "Leprosy" video this week)

Ketuvim: Writings-Narrative: 1 Chronicles 8-14

Nevi'im: Prophets/Poetic: Proverbs 8-16

Brit Chadashah: New Testament: 2 Corinthians 8-13

Scripture Memory: James 4:7-8 "Therefore submit yourselves to God. Resist the devil, and he will flee from you. [8]Draw near to God, and He will draw near to you." Galatians 5:1 "For freedom Christ freed us. Stand fast therefore and do not be entangled again with the yoke of bondage." 1 John 4:4 "You are of God, little children, and have overcome them, because He who is in you is greater than he who is in the world."

WEEK TWENTY-EIGHT: WEEKLY READING

Metzora "leper"

Torah: Leviticus 14:1–15:33 (watch part 26 "Leprosy in the Home" video this week)

Ketuvim: Writings-Narrative: 1 Chronicles 15-22

Nevi'im: Prophets/Poetic: Proverbs 17-24

Brit Chadashah: New Testament: Galatians 1-6

Scripture Memory: 1 John 3:7-10 "Little children, let no one deceive you. The one who does righteousness is righteous, just as Christ is righteous. [8]Whoever practices sin is of the devil, for the devil has been sinning from the beginning. For this purpose the Son of God was revealed, that He might destroy the works of the devil. [9]Whoever has been born of God does not practice sin, for His seed remains in him. And he cannot keep on sinning, because he has been born of God. [10]In this the children of God and the children of the devil are revealed: Whoever does not live in righteousness is not of God, nor is the one who does not love his brother."

WEEK TWENTY-NINE: WEEKLY READING

Acharei Mot "after the death"

Torah: Leviticus 16:1–18:30 (watch part 27 "After Death" video this week)

Ketuvim: Writings-Narrative: 1 Chronicles 23-29

Nevi'im: Prophets/Poetic: Proverbs 25-31; Ecclesiastes 1

Brit Chadashah: New Testament: Ephesians 1-6

Scripture Memory: Philippians 2:9-11 "Therefore God highly exalted Him and gave Him the name which is above every name, [10]that at the name of Jesus every knee should bow, of those in heaven and on earth and under the earth, [11]and every tongue should confess that Jesus Christ is Lord, to the glory of God the Father."

WEEK THIRTY: WEEKLY READING

Kedoshim "holy ones"

Torah: Leviticus 19:1–20:27 (no corresponding video this week)

Ketuvim: Writings-Narrative: 2 Chronicles 1-3

Nevi'im: Prophets/Poetic: Ecclesiastes 2-5

Brit Chadashah: New Testament: Philippians 1-2; Colossians 1-2

Scripture Memory: Ephesians 1:16-23 "Mentioning you in my prayers, [17]so that the God of our Lord Jesus Christ, the Father of glory, may give you the Spirit of wisdom and revelation in the knowledge of Him, [18]that the eyes of your understanding may be enlightened, that you may know what is the hope of His calling and what are the riches of the glory of His inheritance among the saints, [19]and what is the surpassing greatness of His power toward us who believe, according to the working of His mighty power, [20]which He performed in Christ when He raised Him from the dead and seated Him at His own right hand in the heavenly places, [21]far above all principalities, and power, and might, and dominion, and every name that is named, not only in this age but also in that which is to come. [22]And He put all things in subjection under His feet and made Him the head over all things for the church, [23]which is His body, the fullness of Him who fills all things in all ways."

WEEK THIRTY-ONE: WEEKLY READING

Emor "say, speak!"

Torah: Leviticus 21:1–24:23 (watch part 28 "Called to Be Different" video)

Ketuvim: Writings-Narrative: 2 Chronicles 4-6

Nevi'im: Prophets/Poetic: Ecclesiastes 6-9

Brit Chadashah: New Testament: Philippians 3-4; Colossians 3-4

Scripture Memory: Colossians 2:13-15 "And you, being dead in your sins and the uncircumcision of your flesh, He has resurrected together with Him, having forgiven you all sins. [14]He blotted out the handwriting of ordinances that was against us and contrary to us, and He took it out of the way, nailing it to the cross. [15]And having disarmed authorities and powers, He made a show of them openly, triumphing over them by the cross."

WEEK THIRTY-TWO: WEEKLY READING

Behar "one the mountain"

Torah: Leviticus 25:1-26:2 (watch part 29 "Restoration" video)

Ketuvim: Writings-Narrative: 2 Chronicles 7-13

Nevi'im: Prophets/Poetic: Ecclesiastes 10-12; Song of Solomon 1-8

Brit Chadashah: New Testament: 1 Thessalonians 1-5

Scripture Memory: Ephesians 2:4-10 "But God, being rich in mercy, because of His great love with which He loved us, [5]even when we were dead in sins, made us alive together with Christ (by grace you have been saved), [6]and He raised us up and seated us together in the heavenly places in Christ Jesus, [7]so that in the coming ages He might show the surpassing riches of His grace in kindness toward us in Christ Jesus. [8]For by grace you have been saved through faith, and this is not of yourselves. It is the gift of God, [9]not of works, so that no one should boast. [10]For we are His workmanship, created in Christ Jesus for good works, which God prepared beforehand, so that we should walk in them."

WEEK THIRTY-THREE: WEEKLY READING

Bechukotai "in my statutes"

Torah: Leviticus 26:3-27:34 (watch part 30 "Obedience" video this week)

Ketuvim: Writings-Narrative: 2 Chronicles 14-20

Nevi'im: Prophets/Poetic: Isaiah 1-7

Brit Chadashah: New Testament: 2 Thessalonians 1-3; 1 Timothy 1-6

Scripture Memory: Romans 5:17-18 "For if by one man's trespass death reigned through him, then how much more will those who receive abundance of grace and the gift of righteousness reign in life through the One, Jesus Christ. [18]Therefore just as through the trespass of one man came condemnation for all men, so through the righteous act of One came justification of life for all men."

WEEK THIRTY-FOUR: WEEKLY READING

Bamidbar "in the desert"

Torah: Numbers 1:1–4:20 (no video this week)

Ketuvim: Writings-Narrative: 2 Chronicles 21-26

Nevi'im: Prophets/Poetic: Isaiah 8-14

Brit Chadashah: New Testament: 2 Timothy 1-4; Titus 1-3

Scripture Memory: John 16:33 "I have told you these things so that in Me you may have peace. In the world you will have distress. But be of good cheer. I have overcome the world." Revelation 21:6-7 "He said to me, 'It is done. I am the Alpha and the Omega, the Beginning and the End. I will give of the spring of the water of life to him who thirsts. [7]He who overcomes shall inherit all things, and I will be his God and he shall be My son.'"

WEEK THIRTY-FIVE: WEEKLY READING

Naso "lift up"

Torah: Numbers 4:21–7:89 (watch part 31 "Fear of the Lord" video)

Ketuvim: Writings-Narrative: 2 Chronicles 27-36

Nevi'im: Prophets/Poetic: Isaiah 15-21

Brit Chadashah: New Testament: Philemon 1; Hebrews 1-2

Scripture Memory: 2 Corinthians 2:14 "Now thanks be to God who always causes us to triumph in Christ and through us reveals the fragrance of His knowledge in every place." Revelation 1:5-6 "Jesus Christ, who is the faithful witness, the firstborn from the dead, and the ruler of the kings of the earth. To Him who loved us and washed us from our sins in His own blood, [6]and has made us kings and priests to His God and Father, to Him be glory and dominion forever and ever. Amen."

WEEK THIRTY-SIX: WEEKLY READING

Beha'alotecha "when you set up"

Torah: Numbers 8:1–12:16 (watch part 32 "Following the Cloud" video)

Ketuvim: Writings-Narrative: Ezra 1-10

Nevi'im: Prophets/Poetic: Isaiah 22-26

Brit Chadashah: New Testament: Hebrews 3-7

Scripture Memory: 1 Corinthians 15:54-57 "When this corruptible will have put on incorruption, and this mortal will have put on immortality, then the saying that is written shall come to pass: 'Death is swallowed up in victory. [55]O death, where is your sting? O grave, where is your victory?' [56]The sting of death is sin, and the strength of sin is the law. [57]But thanks be to God, who gives us the victory through our Lord Jesus Christ!"

WEEK THIRTY-SEVEN: WEEKLY READING

Shelach Lekha "send for yourself"

Torah: Numbers 13:1–15:41 (watch part 33 "Faith" video)

Ketuvim: Writings-Narrative: Nehemiah 1-13

Nevi'im: Prophets/Poetic: Isaiah 27-30

Brit Chadashah: New Testament: Hebrews 8-11

Scripture Memory: Romans 8:14-17 "For as many as are led by the Spirit of God, these are the sons of God. [15]For you have not received the spirit of slavery again to fear. But you have received the Spirit of adoption, by whom we cry, 'Abba, Father.' [16]The Spirit Himself bears witness with our spirits that we are the children of God, [17]and if children, then heirs: heirs of God and joint-heirs with Christ, if indeed we suffer with Him, that we may also be glorified with Him."

WEEK THIRTY-EIGHT: WEEKLY READING

Korach "Korah"

Torah: Numbers 16:1–18:32 (watch part 34 "Rebellion" video)

Ketuvim: Writings-Narrative: Esther 1-10

Nevi'im: Prophets/Poetic: Isaiah 31-34

Brit Chadashah: New Testament: Hebrews 12-13; James 1-5

Scripture Memory: Hebrews 2:14-16 "So then, as the children share in flesh and blood, He likewise took part in these, so that through death He might destroy him who has the power of death, that is, the devil, [15]and deliver those who through fear of death were throughout their lives subject to bondage. [16]For surely He does not help the angels, but He helps the seed of Abraham."

WEEK THIRTY-NINE: WEEKLY READING

Chukat "decree of"

Torah: Numbers 19:1–22:1 (watch part 35 "Red Heifer and the Cross" video)

Ketuvim: Writings-Narrative: Job 1-8

Nevi'im: Prophets/Poetic: Isaiah 35-43

Brit Chadashah: New Testament: 1 Peter 1-4

Scripture Memory: Mark 16:15-18 "He said to them, 'Go into all the world, and preach the gospel to every creature. [16]He who believes and is baptized will be saved. But he who does not believe will be condemned. [17]These signs will accompany those who believe: In My name they will cast out demons; they will speak with new tongues; [18]they will take up serpents; if they drink any deadly thing, it will not hurt them; they will lay hands on the sick, and they will recover.'"

WEEK FORTY: WEEKLY READING

Balak "Devastator"

Torah: Numbers 22:2–25:9 (watch part 36 "Witchcraft" video)

Ketuvim: Writings-Narrative: Job 9-17

Nevi'im: Prophets/Poetic: Isaiah 44-51

Brit Chadashah: New Testament: 1 Peter 5 – 2 Peter 1-3

Scripture Memory: Mark 6:4-6 "Jesus said to them, 'A prophet is not without honor, except in his own country, and among his own relatives, and in his own house.' 5He could not do any miracles there, except that He laid His hands on a few sick people and healed them. 6And He was amazed because of their unbelief."

WEEK FORTY-ONE: WEEKLY READING

Pinchas "Phinehas"

Torah: Numbers 25:10–30:1 (watch part 37 "Spirit of Elijah" video)

Ketuvim: Writings-Narrative: Job 18-28

Nevi'im: Prophets/Poetic: Isaiah 52-58

Brit Chadashah: New Testament: 1 John 1-5

Scripture Memory: Luke 9:1-2 "Then He called His twelve disciples together and gave them power and authority over all demons and to cure diseases. 2And He sent them to preach the kingdom of God and to heal the sick."

WEEK FORTY-TWO: WEEKLY READING

Matot "Tribes"

Torah: Numbers 30:2–32:42 (watch part 38 "Tribes" video)

Ketuvim: Writings-Narrative: Job 29-38

Nevi'im: Prophets/Poetic: Isaiah 59-62

Brit Chadashah: New Testament: 2 John

Scripture Memory: 2 Timothy 1:6-7 "Therefore I remind you to stir up the gift of God, which is in you by the laying on of my hands. [7]For God has not given us the spirit of fear, but of power, and love, and self-control." Luke 11:28 "But He said, 'Indeed, blessed are those who hear the word of God and keep it.'"

WEEK FORTY-THREE: WEEKLY READING

Masei "journeys of"

Torah: Numbers 33:1–36:13 (watch part 39 "Journey" video)

Ketuvim: Writings-Narrative: Job 39-42

Nevi'im: Prophets/Poetic: Isaiah 63-66

Brit Chadashah: New Testament: 3 John - Jude

Scripture Memory: Mark 12:29-31 Jesus answered him, "The first of all the commandments is, 'Hear, O Israel, the Lord our God is one Lord. [30]You shall love the Lord your God with all your heart, and with all your soul, and with all your mind, and with all your strength.' This is the first commandment. [31]The second is this: 'You shall love your neighbor as yourself.' There is no other commandment greater than these."

WEEK FORTY-FOUR: WEEKLY READING

Devarim "words"

Torah: Deuteronomy 1:1–3:22 (watch part 40 "Deuteronomy" video)

Nevi'im: Prophets/Poetic: Jeremiah 1-12

Brit Chadashah: New Testament: Revelation 1-2

Scripture Memory: Luke 9:23-24 "Then He said to them all, 'If anyone will come after Me, let him deny himself, and take up his cross daily, and follow Me. [24]For whoever will save his life will lose it, but whoever loses his life for My sake will save it.'" 1 John 3:13 "Do not marvel, my brothers, if the world hates you."

WEEK FORTY-FIVE: WEEKLY READING

Va'etchanan "and I pleaded"

Torah: Deuteronomy 3:23–7:11 (watch part 41 "Pleading" video)

Nevi'im: Prophets/Poetic: Jeremiah 13-21; Ezekiel 1-9

Brit Chadashah: New Testament: Revelation 3-4

Scripture Memory: 1 John 2:15-17 "Do not love the world or the things in the world. If anyone loves the world, the love of the Father is not in him. [16]For all that is in the world—the lust of the flesh, the lust of the eyes, and the pride of life—is not of the Father, but is of the world. [17]The world and its desires are passing away, but the one who does the will of God lives forever."

WEEK FORTY-SIX: WEEKLY READING

Eikev "on the heel of, because"

Torah: Deuteronomy 7:12–11:25 (no corresponding video this week)

Nevi'im: Prophets/Poetic: Jeremiah 22-30; Ezekiel 10-18

Brit Chadashah: New Testament: Revelation 5-6

Scripture Memory: 1 John 1:6-10 "If we say that we have fellowship with Him, yet walk in darkness, we lie and do not practice the truth. [7]But if we walk in the light as He is in the light, we have fellowship one with another, and the blood of Jesus Christ His Son cleanses us from all sin. [8]If we say that we have no sin, we deceive ourselves, and the truth is not in us. [9]If we confess our sins, He is faithful and just to forgive us our sins and cleanse us from all unrighteousness. [10]If we say that we have not sinned, we make Him a liar and His word is not in us."

WEEK FORTY-SEVEN: WEEKLY READING

Re'eh "see"

Torah: Deuteronomy 11:26–16:17 (no corresponding video)

Nevi'im: Prophets/Poetic: Jeremiah 31-39; Ezekiel 19-27

Brit Chadashah: New Testament: Revelation 7-8

Scripture Memory: 1 Peter 5:5-7 "Likewise you younger ones, submit yourselves to the elders. Yes, all of you be submissive one to another and clothe yourselves with humility, because 'God resists the proud, but gives grace to the humble.' [6]Humble yourselves under the mighty hand of God, that He may exalt you in due time. [7]Cast all your care upon Him, because He cares for you."

WEEK FORTY-EIGHT: WEEKLY READING

Shoftim "Judges"

Torah: Deuteronomy 16:18–21:9 (watch part 42 "Judges" video)

Nevi'im: Prophets/Poetic: Jeremiah 40-48; Ezekiel 28-36

Brit Chadashah: New Testament: Revelation 9-10

Scripture Memory: Galatians 6:7-9 "Be not deceived. God is not mocked. For whatever a man sows, that will he also reap. [8]For the one who sows to his own flesh will from the flesh reap corruption, but the one who sows to the Spirit will from the Spirit reap eternal life. [9]And let us not grow weary in doing good, for in due season we shall reap, if we do not give up."

WEEK FORTY-NINE: WEEKLY READING

Ki Teitzei "when you go out"

Torah: Deuteronomy 21:10–25:19 (watch part 43 "When You Go to War" video)

Nevi'im: Prophets/Poetic: Jeremiah 49-52; Lamentations 1-5; Ezekiel 37-45

Brit Chadashah: New Testament: Revelation 11

Scripture Memory: Galatians 2:20 "I have been crucified with Christ. It is no longer I who live, but Christ who lives in me. And the life I now live in the flesh, I live by faith in the Son of God, who loved me and gave Himself for me." Ephesians 4:29-30 "Let no unwholesome word proceed out of your mouth, but only that which is good for building up, that it may give grace to the listeners. [30]And do not grieve the Holy Spirit of God, in whom you are sealed for the day of redemption."

WEEK FIFTY: WEEKLY READING

Ki Tavo "when you go in"

Torah: Deuteronomy 26:1-29:8 (watch part 44 "When You Go In" video)

Nevi'im: Prophets/Poetic: Ezekiel 46-48; Daniel 1-6; Hosea 1-9

Brit Chadashah: New Testament: Revelation 12

Scripture Memory: Ephesians 4:32 "And be kind one to another, tenderhearted, forgiving one another, just as God in Christ also forgave you." Ephesians 5:1-3 "Therefore be imitators of God as beloved children. [2]Walk in love, as Christ loved us and gave Himself for us as a fragrant offering and a sacrifice to God. [3]And do not let sexual immorality, or any impurity, or greed be named among you, as these are not proper among saints."

WEEK FIFTY-ONE: WEEKLY READING

Nitzavim "standing"

Torah: Deuteronomy 29:9-30:20 (watch part 45 "Standing" video)

Nevi'im: Prophets/Poetic: Daniel 7-12; Hosea 10-14; Joel 1-3; Amos 1-2

Brit Chadashah: New Testament: Revelation 13-14

Scripture Memory: 2 Corinthians 13:5 "Examine yourselves, seeing whether you are in the faith; test yourselves. Do you not know that Jesus Christ is in you?—unless indeed you are disqualified." 2 Corinthians 5:17 "Therefore, if any man is in Christ, he is a new creature. Old things have passed away. Behold, all things have become new."

WEEK FIFTY-TWO: WEEKLY READING

Vayeilech "and he went"

Torah: Deuteronomy 31:1-30 (watch part 46 "Moses' Final Appeal" video)

Nevi'im: Prophets/Poetic: Amos 3-9; Zechariah 1-14

Brit Chadashah: New Testament: Revelation 15-16

Scripture Memory: John 15:18-21 "If the world hates you, you know that it hated Me before it hated you. [19]If you were of the world, the world would love you as its own. But because you are not of the world, since I chose you out of the world, the world therefore hates you. [20]Remember the word that I said to you: 'A servant is not greater than his master.' If they persecuted Me, they will also persecute you. If they kept My words, they will keep yours also. [21]But all these things they will do to you for My name's sake, because they do not know Him who sent Me."

WEEK FIFTY-THREE: WEEKLY READING

Ha'azinu "give ear"

Torah: Deuteronomy 32:1-52 (watch part 47 "Give Ear" video)

Nevi'im: Prophets/Poetic: Obadiah; Jonah 1-4; Micah 1-7; Malachi 1-4

Brit Chadashah: New Testament: Revelation 17-19

Scripture Memory: Luke 24:49 "And behold, I am sending the promise of My Father upon you. But wait in the city of Jerusalem until you are clothed with power from on high." Acts 1:8 "you shall receive power when the Holy Spirit comes upon you. And you shall be My witnesses in Jerusalem, and in all Judea and Samaria, and to the ends of the earth."

WEEK FIFTY-FOUR: WEEKLY READING

V'Zot HaBerachah "and this blessing"

Torah: Deuteronomy 33:1-34:12 (watch part 48 "Final Blessing" video)

Nevi'im: Prophets/Poetic: Nahum 1-3; Habakkuk 1-3; Zephaniah 1-2

Brit Chadashah: New Testament: Revelation 19-22

Scripture Memory: Philippians 4:4-7 "Rejoice in the Lord always. Again I will say, rejoice! [5]Let everyone come to know your gentleness. The Lord is near. [6]Be anxious for nothing, but in everything, by prayer and supplication with gratitude, make your requests known to God. [7]And the peace of God, which surpasses all understanding, will protect your hearts and minds through Christ Jesus."

WEEK FIFTY-FIVE: FOLLOW-UP: UNDERSTANDING THE HEBREW ROOTS

Follow-up: watch part 49 "Seven Benefits of the Feasts" video

Read: Romans 9-11 and 1 Corinthians 10:1-22

Scripture Memory: Matthew 5:17-18 "Do not think that I have come to abolish the Law or the Prophets. I have not come to abolish, but to fulfill. [18]For truly I say to you, until heaven and earth pass away, not one dot or one mark will pass from the law until all be fulfilled."≠

WEEK FIFTY-SIX: WATCH FINAL VIDEOS TO BETTER UNDERSTAND THE OLD TESTAMENT

Watch Video Part 50 "Joshua and Judges"

Watch Video Part 51 "1st and 2nd Samuel"

Watch Video Part 52 "1st Kings through Malachi"

Scripture Memory: 2 Timothy 2:15 "Study to show yourself approved by God, a workman who need not be ashamed, rightly dividing the word of truth."

Section Three: Understanding Hebrew Roots and Biblical Symbolism

The reason understanding symbolism in the Bible is so important is that God speaks so much through symbolism. Many read the book of Revelation and do not understand anything they have read. This is because they do not understand Biblical symbolism. The symbolism for the entire Bible has its roots in the symbolism of the Tabernacle. This is the "law of first mention" that Biblical scholars understand. I hope this list of symbolism helps open up the scriptures to you in a new way.

THE PRIESTLY GARMENTS

Exodus 19:6 "And you will be to me a kingdom of priests and a holy nation." 1 Peter 2:5, 9 "You also, as living stones, are being built up into a spiritual house as a holy priesthood to offer up spiritual sacrifices that are acceptable to God through Jesus Christ… [9]But you are a chosen race, a royal priesthood, a holy nation, a people for God's own possession."

We are priests unto God as Christians. We are living stones that come together to form a temple for God's presence to dwell in corporately. Individually we are clothed in righteousness and power, and we carry God's glorious presence. As you read below you will see how the five major offerings are fulfilled in the New Covenant and it shows how New Testament priests offer these spiritual sacrifices unto God. What Israel had in the natural, we now have fulfilled in the spiritual.

THE PRIESTLY GARMENTS OF AARON

1. **White**: Garments of Salvation (Isaiah 61:10-11; Revelation 3:5; Ephesians 5:26-27; Revelation 7:13; Revelation 19:6-9)
    a. White turban of salvation with a gold plate on the forehead which reads "holy unto God."
    b. White robe of righteousness that covers down to the wrist and ankles.
    c. White undergarments of salvation that cover shameful nakedness.
2. **Blue**: Baptism in the Holy Spirit
    a. The infilling and baptism into the Holy Spirit (Matthew 3:11)
    b. The clothing of power from on high (Acts 1:8; Luke 24:49)
    c. Bells on the bottom speak of gifts of the Spirit
    d. Pomegranates on the bottom speak of fruit of the Holy Spirit
3. **Gold**: Carriers of the glory (Numbers 4:15; Deuteronomy 31:9; Joshua 3:3)
    a. Clothed in God's presence; the sash speaks of humble service.

b. Shoulder pieces speak of our responsibility to carry God's presence. The ark was always supposed to be carried on the shoulders of the priests.

c. Breastplate with twelve tribes on the chest is our responsibility as priests to intercede for the people of God.

SCRIPTURAL SYMBOLISM: WHAT DO COLORS REPRESENT?

1. White: righteousness and purity
2. Scarlet or red: blood of Jesus, sacrifice, suffering
3. Blue: power coming down from above (ex. blue sky)
4. Purple: royalty (blue mixed with red)
5. There will be no green or brown in the Tabernacle. They are earth colors and the Tabernacle is a heavenly dwelling.

WHAT DO DIFFERENT METALS SPEAK OF IN THE BIBLE?

1. Gold: divinity (from heaven, ex. heavenly streets of gold)
2. Silver: redemption, Christ purchasing us at the cross
3. Bronze: judgment and suffering
4. Iron: warfare (iron will not be in the Tabernacle because it speaks of weapons of war)

WHAT DO DIFFERENT MATERIALS FOR THE TABERNACLE REPRESENT?

1. White linen: righteousness
2. Goat's hair: prophetic ministry (Jesus as a prophet)
3. Ram's skins dyed red: The blood of Jesus as a sin offering
4. Black goat's hair: sin

5. Badger skins: plain skins that covered the tent area (this shows how on the outside Christianity looks boring like a set of rules, but when you come in, it is beautiful and wonderful). As Christians we have the treasure of the Holy Spirit inside us as earthen vessels (2 Corinthians 4:7).
6. Lamb: Jesus as the Lamb of God
7. Goat: Evil counterpart of the Lamb (usually represents Satan)
8. Oil: Anointing of the Holy Spirit
9. Incense: praise, worship, prayer, and intercession going up to God

THE CHERUBIM AND COLORS: EZEKIEL 1:10; 10:21; REVELATIONS 4:7

1. **The Ox:** symbolic of Mark's Gospel as Christ represented as a servant. The color that speaks of Mark's Gospel is red, as Jesus is seen also as the suffering savior.
2. **The Lion:** symbolic of Matthew's Gospel representing Christ as the king of the Jews. The color that corresponds with Matthew's Gospel is purple which speaks of royalty.
3. **The Eagle:** symbolic of John's Gospel representing Jesus as the Son of God. The color that corresponds is blue, speaking of Jesus' coming from heaven.
4. **The Man:** symbolic of Luke's Gospel. This speaks of Jesus as the righteous man. The color that would correspond with this Gospel is white which speaks of righteousness.
    - Purple speaks of Jesus as our king.
    - Blue speaks of Jesus as the Son of God.
    - Red speaks of the suffering savior.
    - Goat's hair speaks of Jesus as a prophet.
    - Linen speaks of Jesus as our Great High Priest.

WHAT SYMBOLISM IS SEEN IN THE NUMBERS OF THE BIBLE?

1. God is one (meaning perfect unity among the Godhead) Deuteronomy 6:4, John 17:11
2. Fellowship, unity, agreement
3. Resurrection (Trinity, God's number)
4. Earth
    a. Eden's four streams Genesis 2:10
    b. Four winds Ezekiel 37:9
    c. Four corners Isaiah 11:12
    d. Four Gospels to be preached in all the earth
5. God's grace
    a. The five major offerings in the Old Covenant
    b. The offerings under Aaron would be cut into five pieces
    c. Christ was pierced in five places
6. Sinful man
    a. Man was created on the sixth day
    b. 666 seen in revelation is sinful man trying to be like God
7. Complete Perfection
    a. Four plus three (God's creation of the earth was originally perfect)
    b. God's rest in perfection
    c. 7 Spirits of God speak of the complete perfect Holy Spirit, not seven different spirits
8. New beginnings
    a. New birth
    b. Noah had eight members of his family on the ark
9. Judgment
10. Completion like the closure of something
11. Government under man

a. Falling short—not twelve
b. Six (sinful man) plus five (grace) is sinful man trying to obtain God's grace without repentance

12. God's government

13. Rebellion
    a. 6 (sinful man) plus 7 (perfection) speaks of sinful man trying to be perfect in their own eyes
    b. 13 is a satanic number associated many times with witchcraft

14. Deliverance (double perfection and double portion); it is interesting that David's name numerically is 14 in Hebrew.

15. Bride of Christ

20. 2x10

24. Divine worship (kingly messianic rule 12 plus 12)

30. Immaturity (child stage), 60 speaks of youth stage, 100 speaks of full maturity

40. Testing
    a. Christ in the wilderness
    b. Israel in the wilderness
    c. Noah in the ark

50. Jubilee (restoring all that has been lost)
    a. Liberty
    b. Pentecost

70. Gentile number (Daniel's seventy weeks; fullness of the time of the gentiles)

100.10x10 or 2x50 or 5x20

1000. Perfect fruitfulness and full maturity

WHAT DO THE FIVE MAJOR OFFERINGS OF THE OLD TESTAMENT MEAN TO US TODAY?

The Hebrew word *mishkan* that is used for the Tabernacle comes from a root word which means to *dwell.* This word implies a place where God's presence continually dwells. That was evident with the initial shekinah glory seen in the cloud by day and fire by night. The other word commonly used for the Tabernacle was *mikdash* and is translated *sanctuary.* A sanctuary implies holy ground. The Hebrew word *korban* is translated in English as offerings or sacrifices. It comes from a root word which means to draw near. Putting this together we see that God gives prescribed ways (offerings) to come onto His holy ground where His presence dwells. As New Testament priests, God has given us a pattern to offer up "spiritual sacrifices (offerings) which are acceptable to God" (see 1 Peter 2:5-9). I believe below will help explain how this scripture is to be truly understood from a New Covenant perspective based on the pattern given us in Scripture.

1. **Burnt offering: Living Sacrifice**
    a. References: Leviticus 1:1-17; 6:8-13; Ephesians 5:1-2; Hebrews 10:7; Romans 12:1-2

    b. Offering includes bullocks, goats, sheep, rams, lambs, young pigeons, turtle doves, all male only

    c. God's part: all that was burned

    d. Priest's part: skin

    e. New Testament Fulfillment: Offerer consecrates his/her life to the Lord as a living sacrifice; the fully burning of this animal is us being fully consumed and crucified with Christ. We lay our lives on the altar and let the fire of the Holy Spirit burn up all that is not of Christ. (Rom 12:1-2)

2. **Grain offering: Service for God**
    a. References: Leviticus 6:14-23; 7:1-16; Hebrews 7:26; 13:15

b. Offering included fine flour, frankincense, oil, salt, green ears of grain

c. God's part: handful of frankincense, part of oil, all priest's offering

d. Priest's part: all remainder

e. New Testament Fulfillment: Offerer gives his life for service for the Lord; the flour (works for the harvest), frankincense (worship), oil (anointing), salt (purity), green ears of corn (firstfruits). All of this speaks of the type of service we have. The service we offer is for the harvest, in worship (thankful attitude), led and anointed by the Holy Spirit, in purity (clean hands before God), and putting the Lord before our own needs. We need to do the work God has called each of us to do.

3. Fellowship offering: Personal and Corporate Prayer Lives

a. References: Leviticus 3:1-17; 7:11-34; Romans 5:1; Colossians 1:20

b. Offering included male or female of herd or flock, bullocks, lambs, or goats

c. God's part: all the fat

d. Priest's part: heave shoulder (heave offering) and wave breast (wave offering)

e. The offerer was given the rest as those who brought the offering would eat it with the priest in the presence of the Lord.

f. New Testament Fulfillment: The offerer is in fellowship with the Lord. The heaving of the shoulder and waving the breast speak of our responsibility (calling, service) and our hearts (breast) for the Lord. In all our work for the Lord we must make time to stay intimate (with our hearts) with the Lord.

Many fall into the trap of doing things for the Lord and losing their fellowship with the Lord. Fellowship must come first before service. We must have strong personal prayer lives.

4. Sin offering: Confessing and Repenting of our Sins

a. References: Leviticus 4:1-5, 13; 6:24-30; 2 Corinthians 5:21

b. Offering included male and female from the herd or flock, turtle doves, young pigeons, 1/10th deal of fine flour. The reason for doves, pigeons, and flour was so that even the poorest of people could make this sacrifice. On the Day of Atonement, the blood was applied even to the altar of incense (altar of worship) to enter the Holy of Holies (Leviticus 16).

c. God's part: all the fat on the bronze altar, and the blood poured at the bottom of the altar.

d. Priest's part: The blood applied to horns of bronze altar, and the bullock burned outside camp.

e. New Testament Fulfillment: The offerer is forgiven as a sinner. We can see the emphasis of blood in this offering as Christ shed His blood for the sin of the world once and for all. "If we confess our sins, He is faithful and just to forgive us our sins and cleanse us from all unrighteousness" (see 1 John 1:9). The sin offering has to do with our salvation, and being made the righteousness of God in Christ Jesus.

5. Guilt offering: Removing Blockages

a. References: Leviticus 5:13-6:7; 7:1-10; Colossians 3:13-14; 1 Peter 2:24

b. Offering included male and female from the herd or flock, turtle doves, young pigeons, 1/10th deal of fine flour. The reason for doves, pigeons, and flour was so that even the poorest of people could make this sacrifice.

c. Certain sins seem to bring guilt even if we are a Christian. Where the sin offering deals with our sin nature, the guilt offering deals with our sinful actions that are a result of our sin nature. We can see examples:

    1. Withholding the truth (Leviticus 5:1)
    2. Defiling the body (or spirit) through touching the unclean (Leviticus 5:2-3; 2 Corinthians 6:14-18)
    3. Making rash vows or promises that are not kept (Leviticus 5:4)
    4. Sinning due to ignorance of God's Word, or failure to learn and obey His will (Leviticus 5:17)
    5. Being irresponsible with someone's possessions (Leviticus 6:2)
    6. Theft of another's belongings or extorting someone (Leviticus 6:2)
    7. Taking someone's belonging through deception (Leviticus 6:2)
    8. Failure to return someone's lost belongings (Leviticus 6:2)

d. In studying the guilt offering, we see that restitution was required, or a fine paid, to the person that was wronged. In other words, it was not just a matter of asking God's forgiveness, but the guilty party had to make things right with the person they wronged (Job 42:7-10). Jesus taught along these lines when stating "leave your gift at the altar (approaching God), and first be reconciled to your brother, then bring your gift to God" (see Matthew 5:23-24). Trying to approach God after wronging someone else can greatly hinder your prayers. The scriptures teach that a husband's prayers can be hindered if they have been hurtful to their wives (1 Peter 3:7). The Lord would first require the husband to apologize and reconcile with his wife before attempting to pray to Him. True repentance is not just confession, but it is a changed life. We must be careful how we treat others, and remember the words of the Lord that taught us "what you do to the least of these, you have done to me" (see Matthew 25:40). And again when the Lord said, "Do to others the way you would have them do to you (see Luke 6:31)." One of the greatest ways a Christian can be defiled is through unforgiveness. The King James Version reads "forgive us our trespasses (another word for guilt offering is a trespass offering) as we forgive those that have trespassed against us (Matthew 6:12-14)." The sin offering deals with our right standing before God, but the guilt offering deals with our lifestyle being right before a holy God.

Before Abraham, Noah was the righteous leader of the world. Many scholars understood that Noah was a priest and that priesthood was passed onto Shem through whom Abraham would be a descendent. Many scholars believe that Shem spent time with Abraham, teaching him the ways of God, and that Shem was actually Melchizedek. When Abraham went out to meet Melchizedek after defeating four kings, he was seeing an old friend and spiritual father. It is also believed that Noah taught the world of that time seven basic laws called the Noahide Laws. These laws were: **Idolatry** was forbidden, to hold **God's holy name** with reverence, the prohibition of **murder, sexual immorality, and theft**. The last two of the seven laws were: establish a **court system** to judge in righteousness and not to eat blood (i.e., limb torn from a live animal). Notice the similarity to the Ten Commandments given later to Moses.

WHAT DO THE SEVEN MAJOR FEAST DAYS MEAN TO US TODAY?

This speaks of God's prophetic timeline before Christ returns to reign on the earth for a thousand years. It begins at Christ's death at the cross.

1. **Passover**- (in Hebrew *Pesach*)
   a. References: Leviticus 23:5; Exodus 12:2-14; 21-24

   b. Date: Nisan (Abib) 14 at twilight

   c. Event that occurs: Lamb sacrificed—its blood applied to the doorpost of the home, eat all the meat of the lamb after roasted (Exodus 12:7), and remain in the house under the blood of the lamb throughout the night.

   d. Special offerings the priesthood performed included: 2 bulls, 1 ram, 7 lambs, and 1 goat. Also, every male in Israel would bring a lamb to the temple to be sacrificed as an offering from his family.

   e. Significance: We are redeemed from judgment by the blood of the lamb and protected from God's wrath. We are God's blood covenant people. The communion table was taken directly out of Passover. Jesus was crucified and died as our Passover Lamb on the day of Passover.

2. **Unleavened Bread** (Chag Ha Matzot)
   a. References: Leviticus 23:6-8; Exodus 12:15-20

   b. Date: Nisan 15 through 21st day (totaling 7 days)

   c. Event that occurs: Partake of unleavened bread instead of leavened (Exodus 12:15; 18-20). Leaven or yeast always speaks of sin. Jesus' body is symbolized as bread without yeast (without sin). Israel left Egypt on the Sabbath: Numbers 33:3, Exodus 12:17; 13:3-4; Deuteronomy 5:15

d. Significance: Christ's death has removed the leaven from our lives and prepared us for the baptism in the Holy Spirit. Jesus' sinless body laid in the tomb for three full days and nights during the feast of unleavened bread.

3. **Firstfruits** (Chag Ha Bikkurim)
   a. References: Leviticus 23:10-14
   b. Date: Nisan 16
   c. Event that occurs: The day after the Sabbath (after Passover), wave the sheaf of barley firstfruits as an act of praise and thanksgiving for the harvest. This is to be done in the temple and the counting to 50 days (till Pentecost) begins. This is the first day of the counting of the omer.
   d. Significance: This occurred the Sunday (day after Sabbath) when Christ rose from the dead as the firstfruits of the resurrection. Jesus died on Wednesday, lay in the tomb Thursday through Saturday, and raised from the dead on Sunday. It represents the first of the harvest. It speaks of Christ's resurrection from the dead. After this resurrection, there are 50 days (Jubilee) until Pentecost.

The first three feasts are in the first month (Nisan) of the Jewish year. This is springtime (falls in either March or April). This is the harvest of barley, and these were all fulfilled in Christ's death, burial, and resurrection.

4. **Pentecost** (also called the "feast of weeks" which in Hebrew is "Shavuot")
   a. References: Leviticus 23:15-22
   b. Date: Sivan 6
   c. Special offerings the priesthood performed included: 2 bulls, 1 ram, 7 lambs, and 1 goat.

d. Event that occurs: In the third month after Israel left Egypt, the law given on Mount Sinai Exodus 19:1. Israel was made a kingdom of priests and a holy nation (Exodus 19:6). Two wave loaves, a new offering. This is the time of the harvest of wheat (Gentile harvest) and speaks of the gentile age of the people of God. The gentiles are symbolically becoming a part of God's people. We see this in that Egyptians and Jews left Egypt together (prophetically shows both Jew and gentile leaving bondage). The two wave loaves speak of both Jew and gentile. The "stranger" of Leviticus 23:22 is a gentile.

e. Significance: This obviously speaks of Acts 1:8 when Jesus said wait until you are clothed with power from on high. This symbolizes being baptized in the Holy Spirit (clothed in power) to bring in the harvest of both Jew and gentile. This is the birth of the "church age" in God's prophetic calendar. We are living in this age awaiting Christ's return to the earth to reign for 1,000 years. This is the time gentiles and Jews become God's true people circumcised in the hearts, and natural Israel is scattered.

f. It is also connected to the bringing of the firstfruits offering unto God at the temple.

g. In the first Shavuot God gave His people His Word, and 1,500 years later on the same feast day God gave His people His Spirit. As God's blood covenant people, He has given us His Word and Spirit for our spiritual growth.

There is a long interval of the third to the sixth month until the feast of trumpets. There are four months from Pentecost to the feast of trumpets. This speaks of the summer working the fields to prepare for the coming final harvest (John 4:35). We seem to be moving into this final harvest and end-time revival now. The first four feasts have been fulfilled, but the next feast on God's calendar is the rapture of the remnant bride as we see symbolized in the feast of trumpets.

1. **Feast of Trumpets** (Yom Teruah "shofarot")
    a. References: Leviticus 23:23-25

    b. Date: Tishra 1

    c. Special offerings the priesthood performed included: 1 bull, 1 ram, 7 lambs, and 1 goat.

    d. Event that occurs: Memorial of the blowing of the trumpets (shofars). Remembering all events announced by the trumpets. There are four distinct blasts of the shofar sounded at least one hundred times. Then the last trump is when all the shofars let out the loudest and longest shofar blast called tekiah ha gadol. Scholars believe this is symbolic of Christ's return as we read in 1 Thessalonians 4:16.

    e. Significance: This speaks of Christ's coming at the blast of the shofar! This season is the harvest of the corn (grain), nuts, oil, and wine. The time frame of the last three feasts is in the seventh month, which falls in autumn (September or October). The Feast of Trumpets is the rapture of the true bride of Christ—for those that have made themselves ready.

2. **Day of Atonement** (Yom Kippur)
    a. References: Leviticus 23:26; Leviticus 16

    b. Date: Tishra 10

    c. Special offerings the priesthood performed included: 1 bull for the sin of the priest's family, 1 ram, 7 lambs, 1 goat for the sin of Israel, and the azazel scapegoat was released.

    d. Event that occurs: The soul is afflicted through fasting, repentance, sorrow over sin, and mourning. No work is to be done except for that of the high priest as he makes atonement for Israel's sin. Blood is shed for this atonement and sprinkled on the mercy seat (Leviticus 17:11).

e. Significance: Aaron the high priest came out of the Holy of Holies twice before the goat was sent away taking the sin of Israel with it. First, it was regarding the Priestly family. Then it had to do with all of Israel. So the Lord Jesus will come twice from the heavenlies. First, he will come to meet His bride (Priestly family) in the air; then He will come again to the earth in relationship to Israel. During this time, the church will be seven years at the marriage supper of the Lamb while the earth endures the seven-year tribulation. This is also a time referred to as Jacob's trouble because Israel will suffer a great deal during this time. So Yom Kippur refers to the tribulation time also known as the days of Jacob's trouble.

3. **Tabernacles** (Succoth)

a. References: Leviticus 23:33-44; Deuteronomy 16:13-15

b. Date: Tishri 15

c. Special offerings the priesthood performed included: over the course of seven days 70 bulls, 14 rams, 98 lambs, and 7 goats.

d. Event that occurs: A very joyful season of ingathering in the corn, oil, nuts, and wine harvests of the year. Israel would dwell in booths or tabernacles to remind them of God's dwelling with them in their journey to the Promised Land (Exodus 23:16).

e. Significance: This speaks of Christ's second coming to earth to set up His kingdom in Jerusalem for a thousand years. We see both Jew and gentile gathered unto Christ in this great ingathering (Revelation 7:9-10). John 1 shows us that the word (Christ) became flesh to tabernacle among us. It is believed by many that Jesus was actually conceived at Hanukkah/Christmastime, but He was actually born during the feast of Tabernacles. Jesus will ultimately come again to Tabernacle on the earth, from the millennial temple, and sit on the throne of his father David to reign for 1,000 years.

GOD'S EARTHLY PEOPLE (ISRAEL) AND HEAVENLY PEOPLE (CHURCH)

"Scripture bears out the fact that God will have an earthly and a heavenly people forever. He will keep his covenant with the House of Israel, His earthly people (Jeremiah 31:31-34). Israel will be forever (Jeremiah 31:35-37). God will keep His promise to Israel that their Messiah will be Ruler-King over them as we read in Micah 5:2. In Messiah's first coming He was not actually their King. God will keep His promise to Abraham that his seed will be as the stars and sand for multitudes: Stars = heavenly people. Sands = earthly people. He will keep His promise that once Israel was not a people during their rejection but in the latter days would once more be His people = Hosea 1:9,10; 2:23; 3:4-5. All those of Israel and the gentiles who were redeemed up until the fulfilling of the Feast of Trumpets are God's heavenly people. All those of Israel who will be dealt with by God during "Jacob's trouble" and who will repent when they accept Jesus as their Messiah during that time, are God's earthly people. Jesus will be King of the Jews, a holy nation (Exodus 19:6). He is never called King of the church. He will be King of Kings and Lord of Lords over the Kingdom of Priests, the heavenly people." (written by: Ruth Specter Lascelle 1980)

OTHER BIBLE SYMBOLISM:

1. Mountains and hills speak of governments.

2. Night, venomous, violent, or wild creatures usually speak of demons [(ex. owls, jackals, snakes, scorpions, lions (sometimes speak of Jesus), wolves, wild dogs, etc.]
3. Light speaks of truth and revelation from God while darkness speaks of deception and lies.
4. Flies speak of lies.
5. Stars represent angels, fallen angels, God's servants depending on the scripture.
6. Beasts (animals like bear, lion, or leopard) speak of different things. The bear and lion often refer to the strength of something. The leopard will speak of speed. Eagles will speak of vision. In the books of Daniel and Revelation the bear represents the kingdom of the Medes and Persians because of their great numbers and resulting strength. The lion speaks of Babylon because of its rulership and strength. The leopard with wings speaks of Greece and Alexander the Great because the great swiftness he had in conquering the world of his day. Rome was seen connected with iron because of its incredible strength.
7. Heads and crowns speak of authority (ex. a gold *God's* crown *authority*).
8. Horns of an animal or altar speak of power.
9. Robes, mantles, and color of purple all speak of royalty.
10. Rivers, fire, dove, rain, wind can speak of the Holy Spirit.
11. Fire can also speak of judgment and/or cleansing.
12. Height speaks of levels of authority, which is why God's throne is in the third (highest) heaven.
13. Large bodies of water, like oceans or seas, usually speak of large masses of people like nations or humanity in general.
14. Yeast speaks of sin.

Section Four: Personal Growth

HOW TO PRAY EFFECTIVELY AN HOUR A DAY
Based on the Lord's Prayer in Matthew 6:5-15

1. **<u>Our Father, who is in heaven</u>** (approaching God)

Hebrews 10:19-22 "Therefore, brothers, we have confidence to enter the Most Holy Place by the blood of Jesus, [20]by a new and living way that He has opened for us through the veil, that is to say, His flesh, [21]and since we have a High Priest over the house of God, [22]let us draw near with a true heart in full assurance of faith, having our hearts sprinkled to cleanse them from an evil conscience, and our bodies washed with pure water."

a. Picture the cross and thank God we are His children by the blood of Jesus.

b. Acknowledge you are coming through Jesus' name and blood to approach the Father.

c. Understand you are of the seed of Abraham, a child of blood covenant.

Faith confession: By the blood of Jesus I am justified, sanctified as holy, and the righteousness of God in Christ Jesus. Therefore, Satan has nothing in me, over me, no claim to my life, no access to me, no power over me, and no accusation can stand against me. I am a son/

daughter of Abraham, a child of blood covenant, and the oath and blessings given to Abraham are my inheritance and are at work in my life.

2. **<u>hallowed be Your name</u>** (the incense of worship)

Psalm 141:1-2 "O Lord, I cry unto You; make haste to me; give ear to my voice, when I cry unto You. [2]Let my prayer be set forth before You as incense, and the lifting up of my hands as the evening sacrifice."

a. Hallowing God's name is the opposite of using it in vain.

b. This is a time to worship in spirit and truth.

c. Understanding God's nature and promises revealed in His names.

- **Sin**: Jehovah Tzidkenu "our righteousness;" Jehovah M'kaddesh "our sanctification"
- **Presence**: Jehovah Shalom "our peace;" Jehovah Shammah "His Presence with us"
- **Health**: Jehovah Rophe "our healer"
- Prosperity: Jehovah Jireh "the one who sees the need and provides"
- **Protection**: Jehovah Nissi "our banner;" Jehovah Rohi "our shepherd;" Jehovah Tzevaot "God of angel armies"

3. **<u>Your kingdom come; Your will be done on earth, as it is in heaven</u>** (intercession: praying in tongues)

1 Samuel 12:23 "Moreover as for me, God forbid that I should sin against the Lord in ceasing to pray for you. But I will teach you the good and the right way."

a. Yourself

b. Your family (spouse, children, extended family)

c. Your church (pastor, leaders, faithfulness in people, and harvest)

d. Nation (city, state, nation, spiritual leaders, harvest)

e. Israel

4. **Give us each day our daily bread**

Philippians 4:19 "But my God shall supply your every need according to His riches in glory by Christ Jesus."

a. Be in the will of God in all things including church attendance, giving, and being a witness.

b. Believe it is God's will to prosper you.

c. Be specific in presenting your needs.

d. Be tenacious, calling in from the north, south, east, and west.

e. Take authority over the enemy trying to hinder your provision.

5. **And forgive us our sins, for we also forgive everyone who is indebted to us**

Mark 11:25-26 "And when you stand praying, forgive if you have anything against anyone, so that your Father who is in heaven may also forgive you your sins. [26]But if you do not forgive, neither will your Father who is in heaven forgive your sins."

a. Choose to forgive everyone who has wronged you.

b. Use the Ten Commandments as a guide and ask God's forgiveness in your personal life.

c. Ask God for the grace to walk in forgiveness, love, and humility.

d. Ask God for grace, wisdom, and discernment.

6. **And lead us not into temptation, but deliver us from evil**

a. Ask for God's grace to live a holy, righteous life before Him.

b. Put on the full armor of God: Ephesians 6:10-19
   i. Helmet of salvation over the mind
   ii. Breastplate of righteousness over the heart
   iii. The belt of truth
   iv. Shoes of peace
   v. Shield of faith
   vi. Sword of the Spirit (God's Word)
   vii. Praying in the Spirit always
   viii. The armor of light (glory) Romans 13:12

c. Pray for a hedge of protection around you and your family and all you own. God will be around us as a wall of fire and a glory in our midst Zechariah 2:5.

d. Memorize and say out loud Psalm 91 over your family.

7. For Yours is the kingdom and the power and the glory forever. Amen.
   a. Make faith declarations and thank God for hearing and answering prayers.
   b. Finish with praise and thanksgiving.
   c. Soaking in His presence.
   d. Bible reading and study.

Inspired by the teachings of Dr. David Yonggi Cho and Dr. Larry Lea

EFFECTIVE PRAYERS

HOW TO PRAY EFFECTIVELY FOR ISRAEL

Heavenly Father, rock of Israel and its redeemer, bless the state of Israel. Strengthen the hands of those that defend the Holy Land, and give them swift decisive victories in all battles. Let there be accuracy in their intelligence gathered, precision in the weaponry, and grant wisdom and good counsel to all the leaders of Israel. Pour out the Spirit of grace and supplication on Israel and upon the Jewish people around the world. Gather in a great harvest of souls, and send them laborers they will receive. Establish your shalom in the land of Israel, everlasting joy for its inhabitants. May all who to try to touch Israel and Jerusalem find themselves reeling backwards. Let there be peace and prosperity for Jerusalem.

PRAYER POINTS:

1. The outpouring of "a spirit of grace and supplication" (Zechariah 12: 10), leading to the salvation of Jews, Arabs, others in Israel, and among the Jewish people (Isaiah 30:19; Romans 10:1; 1 Timothy 2:3– 4).
2. Strengthen and mature the Body of Messiah in Israel and among the messianic communities (John 17; Acts 4:29– 31; Romans 15:26–27), and raise up laborers for the harvest (Luke 10:2).
3. Righteousness and wisdom for all spiritual, governmental, social, military, and all other authorities (1 Timothy 2:1– 2; Proverbs 21:1).
4. Internal unity and peace within Israel (Psalm 122:3, 8).
5. Physical restoration through God's regathering of the Jewish people (aliyah) and material prosperity and provision (Psalm 147:2; Jeremiah 30:17; Psalm 122:9).
6. Security, protection and defense from attack (Psalm 91; Psalm 125), including salvation for Israel's enemies who seek to overtake her (Psalm 83:18).
7. The outworking of end-time prophetic events according to the ideal timing of God (Ecclesiastes 3:1– 8; Matthew 24:22).

8. Pray that your family, your church, and your nation will stand with and bless Israel (Genesis 12:3; Obadiah), the Lord will prosper those who love Jerusalem.
9. Pray the Lord will raise up true end-time intercessors who give God "no rest till He establishes Jerusalem and makes her the praise of the earth" (Isaiah 62:6– 7).
10. Fulfillment of Jerusalem's destiny as the City of the Great King (Matthew 5:35) that blesses all nations (Psalm 48; Isaiah 2:2– 3; 62:1– 2).

Thank you to Kerry and Sandra Teplinsky for compiling these biblical prayer requests.

HOW TO PRAY EFFECTIVELY FOR AMERICA

NATIONAL LEADERSHIP

Heavenly Father, we ask you to raise up godly leaders into places of influence in our government, judicial system, education, media, and other spheres of influence. We also pray for city and state government leaders. Raise up those that will bring you glory, align with your purposes, honor your Son, and honor your Word. Turn their hearts the way you would have them go, give them grace and wisdom to lead, and give us peace and harmony in our nation. Pull down those that oppose your purposes, and set your hand against them so they are unable to succeed, and make it impossible for them to rise to influence. I thank you for your mighty angels walking through America making sure every plan of Satan is cancelled and destroyed, but the plans and purposes of God will take place and be established.

Lord, we lift up our local and national law enforcement, and we pray that you would expose and purify them from all corruption. We pray that you would raise up godly law enforcement that will establish true righteousness, justice, and compassion. We pray they will execute your perfect will in protecting and serving our communities.

We ask that you will cause a sincere love and appreciation among the people for the good protection that serves their community. We ask that you will surround law enforcement with your angels that keep them safe from all acts of violence. Lord, give them wisdom and grace in their duties, and cause them to be able to understand and solve even the most difficult cases.

We pray for our judicial systems. We ask you to raise up godly judges that will honor you, your Son, your Word, and our constitution. Also, pull down the wicked that pervert justice or promote an ungodly agenda. We ask that these judges will have great wisdom in their duties to execute your true will and truth, justice, and righteousness. We pray for our judicial systems, that all corruption be exposed and purged out. Raise up those who will promote true justice in our land.

We pray for our military here in America and the IDF in Israel. As both our militaries are trying to do what is right in your eyes to defend our respective nations and keep peace among other nations, we ask you to bless and protect them. Surround our troops and their vehicles with your angels to prevent them from being harmed. We pray great wisdom with our military leaders in executing various operations. Give our militaries precision in their weaponry, accurate intelligence to confuse and paralyze our enemies, and swift victory in all battles. Let the presence of angels around our troops cause a heavenly atmosphere that will result in a huge harvest of souls. Raise up chaplains that will help minister to them, and make them disciples of Christ. Gives these chaplains great wisdom and grace in their ministries.

SCHOOL SYSTEMS

We ask you, Lord, to raise up those who will work in the education system of this nation to honor you, your Son, and your Word. Place them in positions of influence and use them to lead people to you and unto repentance. Purify the educational systems, and remove those that promote any ungodly agenda. Let revival sweep through the educational systems that will yield a great harvest. Grant repentance and eternal life.

PRAYER POINTS FOR AMERICA:

1. PRAY FOR THE LOST TO BE SAVED AND FOR SPIRITUAL AWAKENING. Pray that people's hearts will be opened to repent of their sins and receive the gospel. Romans 10:1; 2 Peter 3:9; Matthew 9:37-38; Acts 26:18
2. PRAY FOR UNITY AMONG PASTORS AND CHURCHES. Pray that denominational, theological, and ethnic walls will come down so that pastors will love each other, pray together, and serve each other. John 17:20-23; Psalm 133:1; Ephesians 4:3-6
3. PRAY FOR RACIAL RECONCILIATION. Pray that God will heal our nation of racism and that God will use the church to stand against racial conflict, violence, and prejudice. The church must lead the way in racial reconciliation by modeling love and respect for every person regardless of the color of their skin or their ethnic background. Romans 10:12-13; Galatians 3:28; Acts 10:28; Acts 10:34-35; John 7:24; 1 John 2:9; James 2:9; Revelation 7:9
4. PRAY FOR LIFE TO BE VALUED AND PROTECTED THROUGH ALL STAGES OF LIFE BEGINNING AT CONCEPTION. God will oppose and cancel abortion throughout this nation. Psalm 139:13-16; Jeremiah 1:5; Proverbs 24:11; Deuteronomy 21:8-9
5. PRAY FOR SEXUAL PURITY, REPENTANCE FROM THE OCCULT, AND ALL FORMS OF IDOLATRY AND WORSHIP OF OTHER GODS. Exodus 20

HOW TO PRAY EFFECTIVELY FOR THE NATIONS

THE PERSECUTED CHURCH

We pray for those that are suffering for your name's sake among the nations. Give them great boldness in the midst of persecution like you did Peter and John as they stood before the Sanhedrin. We ask that you stretch out your hand and release signs, wonders, a harvest, and revival around them. Let them be enveloped in your glory in an awesome way, for the Word says if we share in your suffering we share in your glory. Let your manifest presence so saturate them, it takes the sting out of what they are going through. I pray you will deliver them out of the hands of evil men, and restore them to their loved ones. Send your angels to deliver them as you did Peter when he was in prison. If it is your will that they die a martyr's death, I pray they will die well like Stephen did. Let their face shine and a song be on their lips, so it will bring great glory to you among those present. We ask that you would remember the blood of the martyrs, and send great revival and a harvest of souls.

THE GLOBAL CHURCH

Lord, we ask you to send a great shaking among your people, for it is written that all that can be shaken will be shaken. We know that judgment begins in the household of God, therefore we ask you to bring down that which is high and lofty in pride. All that is man, the world, and what is satanic, let it come down. That which is humble, pure, and of you, let that be thrust upward. Place your true fivefold ministry in their true place of authority, and purify your people, getting a bride ready for the coming of the Lord. Let your people be brought to full maturity, perfect unity of the faith, and every part of the body of Christ doing it's part. Let the high places be brought down, the low places brought up, the crooked places made straight, and every stumbling block removed. Send your mighty angels to remove all hindrances to your purposes, and clear out all the Jezebels, Judases, and those that sow discord and rebellion among your people.

INTERNATIONAL

Raise up right leaders in the nations of the earth in realms of influence that will bring you glory and will work in tandem with your purposes. Pull down those that oppose you. Set your hand against those that have evil agendas or oppose the gospel. Move the nations into end-time purposes of the Lord! Send your mighty angels to ride the heavens and descend into the nations to break open harvest fields and revivals. We ask you to lay your sickle across the nations and bring in the fullness of this last-day harvest. Pour out your Spirit on all flesh and get a bride pure and ready for the coming bridegroom. Lord, we ask that you continue to reveal yourself to the Muslims, Hindus, and those of other religions, and draw them unto you.

Raise up your end-time laborers, anoint them mightily, and thrust them into the harvest fields. Raise up mighty intercessors all over the world that will give you no peace until your purposes are fulfilled in the earth. Let the gospel of the kingdom be preached to all. Let your remnant bride be without spot or blemish, and be wise virgins with extra oil.

SPIRITUAL WARFARE PRAYERS FOR YOUR CHURCH AND FAMILY

As the seed of Abraham, sons and daughters of blood covenant, the oath and blessing given to Abraham are our inheritance. You bless those who bless us and curse those who curse us. I thank you that anyone trying to strike us in word or deed will find themselves hitting a thorn from the Lord and reeling backwards. Anyone seeking to hinder God's plans or purposes for our lives in any way:

- I thank you, Lord, for pursuing them with your tempest and terrifying them with your great storm as you fill their faces with shame. They are ashamed, dismayed, humiliated, and defeated before you, that they may know that you, whose name is the Lord, are the most high over the earth (Psalm 83).

- I thank you for overshadowing them with your fear and let them tremble with your terror, drying up the finances they would use against us, and paralyzing their agenda as you did Pharoah, Abimelek, and on behalf of Jacob. Like the grass upon the housetops withering before coming to maturity, they cannot get roots down or bear fruit for Satan's kingdom against us (Psalm 129:6).
- As in the days of Hezekiah and Gideon, may they drown in confusion and may division break out in their camp as you confuse the wicked and divide their tongues (Psalm 55:9). I thank you that you are confusing their counsel against us into foolishness as you did for David regarding Ahithophel (2 Samuel 15:31).
- As they pursue our harm in any way, or try to hinder our destiny in God, I thank you for their ways becoming dark and slippery and the angels of the Lord sent to persecute and block them as you dealt with Balaam in his wickedness (Psalm 35:6). I thank you for your angels going before us to plow the road and clear out all people or circumstances that desire our destruction in any way, for angels are sent to minister unto those that are heirs of salvation, accompany us in all our ways to bear us up in their hands lest we dash our foot against a stone, and encamp around us to deliver us because we fear the Lord.
- I thank you that you are a wall of fire around us and a glory in our midst (Zechariah 2:5). You are hiding us from the secret counsel of the wicked who use their tongue like a sword. I thank you for shooting your arrow at them, Lord, that hits its mark; they are made to stumble, as their own tongues turn against them. All who look at them will shake their head and flee away from them (Psalm 64). For every weapon formed against us shall not pros-

per, and every tongue that rises up against us, we will condemn (Isaiah 54:17). Because our ways please the Lord, we have peace with our enemies, and the Lord is confusing the tokens of liars against us. Those that lay a snare for us, will be ensnared in their own devices as we walk safely around their traps. The Lord is with us as a mighty, terrible one; our persecutors will stumble, not prevail, and be greatly ashamed. They will not prosper and their shame will not be forgotten (Jeremiah 20:11-12).

- Through this great resistance from the Lord, may these truly find Jesus as their Savior and repent of their evil ways. Let this result in a great harvest of souls that you may be glorified in the earth.

I thank you, Lord, that we are being delivered from all demonic forces, works of Satan, or the attacks of Satan's servants in anyway. We are seeing a sevenfold restoration in our lives and ministry as you restore the years the locust have eaten. We are among those that are rebuilding ancient ruins, raising up age-old foundations, repairing the breach and streets to dwell in as you heal our land (Isaiah 58; Joel 1-2; 2 Chronicles 7:14).

A curse without cause cannot light upon us, but it returns from where it was sent (Proverbs 26:2).

I thank you that the harvest is being gathered in from the north, south, east, and west, as your angels are sent to those that shall inherit salvation to gather in the sheaves. You are removing the crookedness out of their thinking, and the blindness out of their minds. You are drying up the pleasures of sin in their lives, and removing the numbness to the conviction of the Holy Spirit. I thank you for softening their hearts to the gospel, and opening them up to salvation as the Holy Spirit is drawing them unto Jesus.

At night, the Lord grants sleep to those He loves as we have sweet rest in the glory. We will lie down and awake, for the Lord sustains us. We abide under the shadow of the almighty, and no plague, calamity, nor disaster will come near us nor our dwelling. We fear no evil, for angels with flaming swords encamp around us and our dwelling.

By Christ's stripes we are being healed and restored from the top of our heads to the souls of our feet. We are being healed in our spirit and soul, for the Lord has come to bind up and heal the brokenhearted. Our youth is renewed as the eagle, and we are in divine health and prosperity and have prospering souls. As Abraham was blessed in all things, we are also blessed in every area and detail of our lives. The Lord is with us as a mighty, terrible one, and He is an enemy to our enemies.

PRAYER POINTS FOR WARFARE IN AMERICA:

1. Removal of the wicked. "Take away the wicked from before the king, and his throne will be established in righteousness" (Proverbs 25:5).
2. Psalm 129:5-6 "May all who hate Zion (Israel/Church) be put to shame and turned backward. Let them be like grass upon the housetops that withers before it grows up." Make Jerusalem a cup of trembling and all that try to touch it find themselves reeling backwards (Zechariah 12:2).
3. Cause a great shaking in Satan's kingdom, and a great shaking and collapse of the satanic strongholds that have been set up against your people (Hebrews 12:27).
4. To those that serve the enemy, "**let their way be dark and slippery**: and let the angel of the Lord pursue and persecute them" (Psalm 35:6).
5. **Confuse** the wicked and divide their tongues (Psalm 55:9).
6. According to Psalm 83:15-18: To those that make war against your people, we ask you to "pursue them with your tempest and terrify them with your storm. [16]Fill their faces with dishonor, that they may seek your name, O Lord. [17]Let them be ashamed

and dismayed, and let them be humiliated and be defeated, 18 that they may know that you alone, whose name is the Lord, are the Most High over all the earth."

7. Confuse the tokens of liars and cause a love for truth. May those who dig a pit for your people fall into their own trap, while the righteous escape.
8. Confuse the satanic counselors turning their counsel into foolishness (2 Samuel 15).
9. Invade their satanic meeting places with the terror of the Almighty. Let them either fall on their faces before Christ, and accept Him as Savior, or flee in abject terror from that place... never wanting to return there again.
10. Disband their groups: bring division in their satanic relationships that Satan depends on (Matthew 12:25).
11. Dry up their finances that serve Satan and paralyze their agendas. For the wealth of the wicked is laid up for the righteous (Proverbs 13:22).
12. Disrupt and cancel their plans made in secret: disorganize those that serve Satan's purposes in the earth.
13. Divine delays for the enemy and no more delays for God's people (Revelation 10:6).
14. Reveal what is hidden (Luke 8:17). Things the devil desperately wanted to be hidden will be exposed.
15. Dismantle their structures set in place like Jericho's walls.
16. From among God's people remove all dividers, stumbling blocks, and those who sow confusion (1 Corinthians 8:9).
17. Deal with witchcraft in the church. Send your angels to remove all agents Satan would try to use to hinder or abort people's destinies in God. Clear out all manipulation, intimidation, ungodly control, and counterfeit revelation.

HUSBANDS, WIVES, AND CHILDREN

1. Bring your family under the blood of Jesus.
2. Bind the enemy and command him to leave your family.

PRAYING FOR HUSBANDS IN YOUR CHURCH:

- Psalm 1:1-3 "Blessed is the man who walks not in the counsel of the ungodly, nor stands in the path of sinners, nor sits in the seat of scoffers; [2]but his delight is in the law of the Lord, and in His law he meditates day and night. [3]He will be like a tree planted by the rivers of water, that brings forth its fruit in its season; its leaf will not wither, and whatever he does will prosper."
- Proverbs 24:3-4 "Through wisdom is a house built, and by understanding it is established; [4]and by knowledge the rooms will be filled with all precious and pleasant riches."
- Psalm 142:7 "The righteous shall surround me, for you shall deal bountifully with me."
- Isaiah 11:2-4 "The Spirit of the Lord shall rest upon him, the Spirit of wisdom and understanding, the Spirit of counsel and might, the Spirit of knowledge and of the fear of the Lord. [3]He shall delight in the fear of the Lord, and he shall not judge by what his eyes see, nor reprove by what his ears hear; [4]but with righteousness he shall judge."
- Proverbs 21:1 "The king's heart is in the hand of the Lord, as the rivers of water; He turns it to any place He will."
- Malachi 4:6 "He will turn the hearts of the fathers to their children, and the hearts of the children to their fathers."
- 2 Timothy 1:7 "God has not given us the spirit of fear, but of power, and love, and self-control."
- Proverbs 28:1 "The righteous are bold as a lion."

- Psalms 90:17 "Let the favor of the Lord our God be upon us, and establish the work of our hands among us; yes, establish the work of our hands."
- 1 Timothy 6:6 "Godliness with contentment is great gain."

PRAYING FOR WIVES IN YOUR CHURCH ALSO:

- Proverbs 14:1 "Every wise woman builds her house."
- Proverbs 31:11-31 "The heart of her husband safely trusts in her, so that he will have no lack of gain. [12]She will do him good and not evil all the days of her life. [13]She seeks wool and flax, and works willingly with her hands. [14]She is like the merchant ships, she brings her food from afar. [15]She also rises while it is yet night, and gives food to her household, and a portion to her maidens. [16]She considers a field and buys it; with the fruit of her hands she plants a vineyard. [17]She clothes herself with strength, and strengthens her arms. [18]She perceives that her merchandise is good; her candle does not go out by night. [19]She lays her hands to the spindle, and her hands hold the distaff. [20]She stretches out her hand to the poor; yes, she reaches forth her hands to the needy. [21]She is not afraid of the snow for her household, for all her household are clothed with scarlet. [22]She makes herself coverings of tapestry; her clothing is silk and purple. [23]Her husband is known in the gates, when he sits among the elders of the land. [24]She makes fine linen and sells it, and delivers sashes to the merchant. [25]Strength and honor are her clothing, and she will rejoice in time to come. [26]She opens her mouth with wisdom, and in her tongue is the teaching of kindness. [27]She looks well to the ways of her household, and does not eat the bread of idleness. [28]Her children rise up and call her blessed; her husband also, and he praises her: [29]"Many daughters have done virtuously, but you excel them all a woman who fears the Lord, she shall be praised. [30]Charm is deceitful, and beauty is vain, but a woman who fears the Lord,

she shall be praised. [31]Give her of the fruit of her hands, and let her own works praise her in the gates."

- Proverbs 12:4 "A virtuous woman is a crown to her husband."

PRAYING FOR CHILDREN AND GRANDCHILDREN IN YOUR CHURCH:

- Isaiah 54:13 "All your sons shall be taught of the Lord, and great shall be the peace of your sons."
- Proverbs 23:12 "Apply your heart to instruction, and your ears to the words of knowledge."
- Proverbs 9:9-10 "Give instruction to a wise man, and he will be yet wiser; teach a just man, and he will increase in learning. [10]The fear of the Lord is the beginning of wisdom, and the knowledge of the Holy One is understanding."
- Proverbs 20:12 "The hearing ear and the seeing eye, the Lord has made both of them."
- Ephesians 6:1-3 "Children, obey your parents in the Lord, for this is right. [2]'Honor your father and mother,' which is the first commandment with a promise, [3]'so that it may be well with you and you may live long on the earth.'"
- Luke 2:52 "Jesus increased in wisdom and in stature and in favor with God and men."
- Psalm 138:8 "The Lord will fulfill His purpose for me; Your mercy, O Lord, endures forever; do not forsake the works of Your hands."

PRAYING FOR OUR DESCENDANTS IN THE CHURCH:

- Isaiah 8:18 "See, I and the children whom the Lord has given me are for signs and for wonders in Israel from the Lord of Hosts who dwells in Mount Zion."

- Psalms 112:1-4 "Blessed is the man who fears the Lord, who delights greatly in His commandments. [2]His offspring shall be mighty in the land; the generation of the upright shall be blessed. [3]Wealth and riches shall be in his house, and his righteousness endures forever. [4]To the upright there arises light in the darkness; he is gracious, and full of compassion, and righteous."
- Psalms 127:3-5 "Look, children are a gift of the Lord, and the fruit of the womb is a reward. [4]As arrows in the hand of a mighty warrior, so are the children of one's youth. [5]Happy is the man who has his quiver full of them; he shall not be ashamed when he speaks with the enemies at the gate."
- Isaiah 59:21 "As for Me, this is My covenant with them, says the Lord: My Spirit who is upon you, and My words which I have put in your mouth shall not depart out of your mouth, nor out of the mouth of your descendants, nor out of the mouth of your descendants' descendants, says the Lord, from this time forth and forever."
- Exodus 20:6 "Showing lovingkindness to thousands of them (blessing them) who love Me and keep My commandments."

PRAYING FOR PASTORS AND LEADERS

- Open doors of ministry God has for them (Colossians 4:2-3)
- Boldness to speak God's word fearlessly (Ephesians 6:18-19)
- Wisdom to respond well in all situations (Ephesians 6:19-20)
- The Word to spread rapidly and be honored as it should (2 Thessalonians 3:1)
- Protection and deliverance (2 Thessalonians 3:2)
- Their ministry accepted and honored by the greater body of Christ (Romans 15:31)
- Guidance and safety in travels (Romans 15:31)

- Angels around them to deliver them (Psalm 34:7-9), keep their steps and prosper their ways (Psalm 91:11-12), and minister unto them (Matthew 4:11)
- Fresh anointing, fruitfulness, and refreshment (Romans 15:32)
- Their harvest to come in (Matthew 9:38)
- Peace and harmony in all relationships in their lives (Romans 12:18)
- Divine health and financial prosperity (3 John 2)

EFFECTIVE PRAYERS IN THE COURTROOM OF HEAVEN: DESTROYING SATANIC ALTARS

If you haven't already, make sure and listen to the sermon The Courtroom of Heaven in the sermon series entitled Keys to an Effective Prayer Life. Getting a breakthrough in the courts of heaven will create huge results in answered prayers.

1. ENTER HIS GATES WITH THANKSGIVING AND PRAISE

Psalm 100:4-5 "Enter into his gates with thanksgiving, and into his courts with praise: be thankful unto him, and bless his name. [5]For the Lord is good; his mercy is everlasting; and his truth endures to all generations (emphasis added)."

2. ENTER THROUGH YESHUA'S NAME AND HIS BLOOD

Our Father (by blood covenant) Hallowed be thy name (Matt 6:9-11)

Hebrews 10:19-23 "Since therefore, brethren, we have confidence to enter the holy place by the blood of Jesus, 20. by a new and living way which He inaugurated for us through the veil, that is, His flesh, 21. and since we have a great priest over the house of God, 22. let us draw near with a sincere heart in full assurance of faith, having our hearts sprinkled clean from an evil conscience and our bodies washed with pure water. 23. Let us hold fast the confession of our hope without wavering, for He who promised is faithful."

3. ASSERT WE ARE A PEOPLE OF BLOOD COVENANT—SONS AND DAUGHTERS OF GOD—AND SONS AND DAUGHTERS OF ABRAHAM (GALATIANS 3:13-14).

Names of God

- Yahweh (covenant) Jireh (provider): one who saw and provided a ram in the thicket. Christ's sacrifice is the complete provision for humanity
- Yahweh Mishpat: our righteous judge and vindication
- Yahweh Tzevaot (Lord of hosts-angels armies), Yahweh Nissi (banner) "arise oh Lord let your enemies be scattered and those who hate you flee before you
- Yahweh Roi (shepherd), Yahweh Rapha (healer)
- Yahweh Shalom (peace), Yahweh Shammah (divine presence with us)
- Yahweh Makadesh (sanctification), Yahweh Tzikeinu (righteousness)

The Lord has justified us, sanctified us as holy unto Him, and made us the righteousness of God in Christ Jesus. We are a people of blood covenant. The enemy has no power over our lives in any way. God is an enemy to our enemies, and drives out our enemies, saying destroy them.

4. ASK THE COURTS TO BE SEATED (DAN 7:9-10)

We ask that the hosts of heaven would bear witness to God's righteous judgments, and the angels carry them out so that every earthly institution, human being, and satanic being will have to obey them and come into alignment with the will of God.

5. SURRENDER SELF-REPRESENTATION (1 JOHN 2:1-2) AND AGREE WITH ADVERSARY (MATTHEW 5:25)

We humbly ask that Jesus be our advocate, who is our Great High Priest and intercessor. He is the one who ever lives to make intercession, and He is touched with the feelings of our infirmities. We agree with our adversary, and ask that the blood of Jesus speak on our behalf in the courts of heaven, as we confess and repent of our sins.

6. ASK THAT THE EVIL ALTAR WITH THE IDOL UPON IT APPEAR IN THE COURTROOM FOR JUDGMENT (INIQUITY: WITCHCRAFT, PRIDE, REBELLION, ETC.)

1 Corinthians 6:3 "Do you not know that we will judge angels? How much more matters of this life?" (NASB).

7. DEEP REPENTANCE, THE BLOOD WASH AWAY ALL SIN, AND DISMISS ALL SATAN'S LEGAL CLAIMS (ACCUSATIONS AND CHARGES)

- Deep repentance of sins, transgressions, and iniquity you have committed and that of your ancestors (blood wash away)
- All things you or others have spoken that is not the will of God be washed away by the blood of Jesus and stricken from the record
- All covenants with demon powers or dedications to other gods and idols be revoked and washed away by the blood of Jesus
- We give back anything the enemy would say is his, as we only want what the blood of Jesus has secured for us

8. ASK FOR THE ENEMY BOUND AND RESTRAINING ORDERS AGAINST HIM

The Lord would see that Satan has come to steal, kill, and destroy, but Christ has come to give abundant life. The enemy seeks great injury to our lives, great destruction of our families, severe hindrance to our destiny (cause some to go to hell), and very significant damage to God's kingdom purposes on the earth. Therefore we ask that the enemy is bound and restraining orders against him from this day forward.

9. ASK FOR SEVENFOLD RESTORATION

Proverbs 6:30 "Men do not despise a thief if he steals, to satisfy himself when he is hungry; 31. But when he is found, **he must repay sevenfold**; he must give all the substance of his house."

10. SEALING THE VERDICT

We know that, God, you are Yahweh Mishpat, our righteous judge. Righteousness and justice are the foundations of your throne. If the persistent widow of Luke 18 got justice from an evil judge, how much more so will we receive justice as your blood covenant people.

Thank you for hearing and answering our prayers. We have confidence that if we pray according to your will, you hear us, and if we know you hear us, we have what we ask. You are faithful and just to forgive our sins, and the prayers of the righteous make tremendous power available, dynamic in its working.

Let all these proceedings be sealed by the blood of Jesus, and the angels dispatched to carry them out. Thank you for hearing and answering every prayer. We believe we have received it now in Jesus' name.

CLEANSING, BLESSING, DEDICATING HOMES AND LAND

God is interested in your home being a place of health, protection, and blessing! This section on cleansing, blessing, and dedicating property is intensely powerful. I have been so blessed to see such a revival and presence of God in my home. This will be an added level of protection to your dwelling place, and help make it a dwelling place for God.

PREPARATION: AN OUNCE OF PREVENTION IS WORTH A POUND OF CURE

First, it is important to remove anything that would displease God. In regard to entertainment, there are filters that keep out unwanted language or scenes in television shows or movies. With that said, go through your home and remove anything that has to do with the occult, connected to a false god, pornographic (or has nudity or sex), has ungodly violence in it, or if it has foul language (filthy language or using God's name in vain). This will require going room by room, through boxes, drawers, attics, basements, garages, and every area of the home. This may take some time.

Then you can proceed. **Walk completely around your property line** praying and applying the blood of Jesus by faith. You can pour something out representing the blood of Jesus, or you can just simply use your faith to apply it. The blood of Jesus is applied by faith. Stop at corners and bury communion at each corner, consecrating the land as God's property. This is a deep consecration and dedication of that land. There is nothing more powerful than the body and blood of the Lord applied to that land. You can also drive a stake of some kind (can write scriptures on it) at each corner of your property. Now use your faith that the body and blood of our Lord is in that land, it is set apart as holy unto God, and there are distinct lines of demarcation that you are laying down regarding your property and what the enemy is NOT ALLOWED to trespass on. Last, pour out some anointing oil on the land, separating it and consecrating it to be used for God's service. Try to end up in the backyard last so there won't be distractions. Now you can speak this over your property.

CONFESSION OF THE SINS OF THE LAND AND HOME

Lord I ask forgiveness on behalf of this land and home for any:

- Idolatry, witchcraft, occult activity, sorcery, worship of other gods, satanic objects, or dark arts of any kind. I break all curses and works of Satan associated with these things off this property and home, bind all satanic spirits associated with these things, and command everything associated with this in any way to leave my property right now in the name of Jesus and never return.
- I renounce any dedications to false gods, idols, or curses placed on this home or property. I destroy that now in the name of Jesus.
- Lord, I ask your forgiveness for any sexual sins or perversions that have taken place on this property or in this home.
- I confess as sin and repent of any shedding of innocent blood, violence, murder, or criminal activity that has taken place on this land or in this home. I ask you to cleanse this property by the blood of Jesus right now. We must remit the stain of innocent blood on any land.
- Forgive us for any substance abuse or addictions that have been here on this land or in this home. I command any spirits of bondage, addictions, or drug use to leave this property right now in Jesus' name.
- Lord, forgive us for the strife, fighting, divorce, family alienation, or bickering that has taken place here. We repent of any disorder

and division that has been on this property. I command these spirits to leave this property now!

- We confess as sin and repent of any racism or anti-Semitism that has been associated with this land or home.
- Forgive us if there has been any persecution of the righteous here.
- I ask your forgiveness for any ungodly entertainment of any kind that has polluted this property. I command all that filth to leave this property now in Jesus' name.
- Forgive us for words that have been spoken here that have grieved you and are not the will of God. We break those words off this property and home and command them to be removed from here.
- Forgive us, Lord, for any broken vows or covenants that have taken place on this land or in this home.
- So in the name of Jesus I command every satanic spirit to leave this property and home right now! I destroy every curse and work of Satan associated with this land or home. By the blood of Jesus I cancel any legal rights Satan has had to this home or land right now. I bring this property under the blood of Jesus right now. I ask you to release your angels to purge and cleanse this property from anything unclean before you in the name of Jesus.

OPENING PRAYER OF DEDICATION: PRAY THIS OUT LOUD

Lord, I now dedicate this land and home to you, Almighty God, creator of heaven and earth; The God of Abraham, Isaac, and Jacob, the holy one of Israel. May it be for the glory of God, our Father, from whom comes every good and perfect gift. We dedicate this land and home to the honor of Jesus, His Son, our Lord and Savior. May it be the praise of the Holy Spirit, the comforter, whose presence is welcome to tabernacle here. To you, Holy Spirit, we also dedicate this property. Let your presence, glory, and power dwell here.

BLESSING TO SPEAK: LIFT A HAND AND SPEAK THIS OVER YOUR HOME AND PROPERTY

May the Lord bless you—home, land, and vehicles—to be a sanctuary of rest, renewal, and refreshing. May you be a haven of God's perfect peace and the manifest atmosphere of heaven. The Lord grant you to be a place of unity, harmony, and submission to authority. May the sounds of joy and laughter be heard in you as people continually love and enjoy each other in you. The Lord bless you to be a place of unconditional love and acceptance of one another and warm loving affection, as people love and appreciate what they have in each other in you. The Lord bless you that there is a continual open heaven over you and continual showers of God's blessings and the outpouring of the Holy Spirit that takes place in you. As you are dedicated for God's service, may you be fruitful for the kingdom of God, a place where many are born again and discipled in Christ. May you be a place where many are healed, delivered, the works of Satan destroyed and replaced with the works of Christ. May many be baptized in the Holy Spirit and receive impartation from Jesus in you. May you be a place where the things of God and the Word of God are honored and cherished. May you be holy ground of praise, worship, prayer, and intercession that is in Spirit and truth, and may that which is evil be hated in you and kept from you. May you be a place of sweet rest and pleasant dreams. In this place shall the direction of God's will be learned and revealed, and the Bible be read and lived out. May dreams and visions from God and the gifts of the Spirit be in you, bringing direction, revelation, and truth. Here may the inhabitants of this home, and their relatives, and friends enjoy supernatural peace and safety from all acts of violence, including break-ins, theft, fire, and storm. May they find sweet rest and sense the Lord's nearness.

CLOSING PRAYER FOR OUTDOORS

So Lord, we have dedicated this dwelling to you and blessed it. We ask you to arise and enter into this house. Put your Holy Name in this place. Let your eyes be open toward it. Hear the supplication of this family. Establish the works of this family's hands. Let your angels envelope this dwelling with protection, peace, and bring the presence of God. Let this be a place that brings you glory. Let people's prayer lives and times in the Word be rich and powerful in this place, filled with the atmosphere of heaven, and sweet fellowship of the Holy Spirit. We thank you for hearing and answering us now, in Jesus' name. Amen.

ANOINTING AND BLESSING HOME INTERIOR

Entrance of the Home: Place the blood of Jesus (fruit of the vine) on the front door posts and top of door posts, symbolizing the Blood of the Passover Lamb, Jesus. Then speak this: I pronounce that the __________ family are overcomers by the Blood of the Lamb of God and the word of their testimony. I speak that this home will have a hedge of protection around it, no curse can rest on it, and that satanic forces will have to pass over it, not bringing any harm to it or those in it, in Jesus' name.

ANOINT DOOR POSTS OF ROOMS:

MEV version of the Bible used here in this section

1. **In bedrooms:** I speak blessings of restful sleep and pleasant dreams according to Psalm 3:5: "I lay down and slept; I awoke, for the Lord sustained me." Psalm 4:8 "I will both lie down in peace and sleep; for You, Lord, make me dwell safely and securely."
2. **In bathrooms:** May the Lord bless you with health according to Exodus 15:26: "If you diligently listen to the voice of

the Lord your God, and do what is right in His sight, and give ear to His commandments, and keep all His statutes, I will not afflict you with any of the diseases with which I have afflicted the Egyptians. For I am the Lord who heals you."

3. **In Kitchen:** I bless you with pleasant conversation and God's presence. May God give you provision and strength for the word of God says, Exodus 23:25-26: "You shall serve the Lord your God, and He shall bless your bread and your water, and I will remove sickness from your midst. [26]No one shall be miscarrying or be barren in your land. I will fulfill the number of your days."
4. **In the living room and den:** Joshua 24:15 "As for me and my house, we will serve the Lord." May the Lord bless these rooms that singing and praise, and talking of God's goodness and faithfulness be often heard in them.
5. **In the entry and hall:** God said, He will bless your going out and your coming in and that if we acknowledge him in all our ways, he will direct our paths. May the going from you and coming in be in peace and safety.
6. **Anoint vehicles:** Psalm 91:9-10 "Because you have made the Lord, who is my refuge, even the Most High, your dwelling, [10]there shall be no evil befall you, neither shall any plague come near your dwelling." May the Lord keep you from any wrecks, vandalism, theft, or any harm from ever coming near you. May you be a place of pleasant conversations, anointed prayer times, learning the Word of God, and spiritual growth. May the angels of the Lord always be with you to take you safely from destination to destination. I bless you in Jesus' name.
7. **Anoint checkbook representing your finances:** Proverbs 10:22 "It is the blessing of the Lord that makes rich, And He adds no sorrow with it." May the Lord rebuke the devourer from you,

open the heavens above you, and give you great prosperity and abundance for we are tithers and givers. May raises and bonuses and increase come to you and satanic forces never be able to steal from you. I bless you in Jesus' name.

8. **Anoint animals:** Psalms 24:1 "The earth belongs to the Lord, and its fullness, the world, and those who dwell in it." May the Lord bless you with long healthy lives and all go well with you. May you have favor and be a joy to us. The Lord set you apart unto Him as holy so nothing evil can touch you. I bless you in Jesus' name.
9. **Gateways:** Matthew 16:18 "And I tell you that you are Peter, and on this rock I will build My church, and the gates of Hades shall not prevail against it." Take communion juice and go to points of entry like your Wi-Fi connection, DVR, garage/back door and apply the blood and ask the Lord to seal these entry ways. Witches commonly use mirrors to enter places. You may want to apply the blood to mirrors. Nowadays Muslims have allowed halal meat in markets which has been sacrificed to Allah. I would simply pray over all groceries and things you buy and bring into your home and bring it all under the blood of Jesus.

CLOSING PRAYER

Blessed are you, Lord our God, king of the universe who has kept us and sustained us. You are the Lord of Hosts and the guardian of the gates of Israel. So, Lord, we dedicate all we have unto you and ask you to set it apart as holy unto you and release your angels to watch over it and protect it. Position mighty warring angels around our property and around our beds at night. Let no evil come near us. Seal off our families and all we own in the protection of your blood. Be about us as a wall of fire and a glory in our midst. Thank you for hearing us today. In Jesus' name we pray. Amen.

FINAL THOUGHTS

Fill your home with anointed worship and powerful revival church services. With most homes having a computer in it now this should not be difficult. I play anointed worship and powerful revival services in my home especially at night while sleeping. The glory of the Lord will fill your home as you do this. May God's anointing and glory fill your home, soak into the soil of your land, and reside in the walls of your dwelling. May your home become a dwelling place for God where no evil dwells.

FATHER'S BLESSING

Speak over children or grandchildren

The Lord bless you men to be as Ephraim and Manasseh, and women to be as Sarah, Rebecca, Rachael, and Leah.

I bless you with a long and healthy life. No sickness or disease will come near you, and you will live in perfect health. I bless you with financial prosperity and abundance.

May the works of your hands be blessed and prosperous, and you be successful in all things. As the Bible says, may you be the head and not the tail, the top and not the bottom. May you have the ability to gain wealth, and have durable riches on all you own.

May every place the soles of your feet tread, God give you victory. I bless you that the angels of the Lord continually be with you to minister to you and protect you, and God always give you victory over Satan's kingdom in all things. May you have peace and favor with all people and complete victory over all your enemies.

I bless your marriage, family, and all relationships to be filled with peace. May they be wonderful, satisfying, and fulfilling for you. May your home be a place of God's peace, and His presence, and sounds of joy and laughter be heard in them and unconditional love be consistent in them. May you and your spouse be godly and virtuous in all ways. May all your children grow up godly and bring honor to your family name. May you enjoy your children, and they honor, obey, and respect you.

May you have mental and emotional health and well-being as you live a righteous life before the Lord, and God give you the grace to forgive everyone from your heart. I bless your night's rest to be sweet in God's presence. May you continually walk in the fullness of the freedom, victory, and dominion that Jesus paid for you to have at the cross.

May you have: clear direction and leading of the Holy Spirit, wisdom from the Lord, spiritual discernment, a controlled and disciplined life, courage, faithfulness, boldness, peace, happiness, fulfillment, contentment, hope, a good outlook on life, a listening ear to God, knowledge of God's Word, an obedient heart to God's Word, a pleasant personality, pleasant speech, protection, provision, safety, an assurance of God's love and grace, strength, the grace to live a righteous life, and success in all things.

May the Lord make you and keep you healthy and strong physically, mentally, emotionally, and spiritually. May any weakness in your life become a strength in Christ.

As the Bible declares for you, may the blessings of Abraham, every spiritual blessing in Christ, and the promises of God be yours. May goodness and mercy follow you all the days of your life, and you dwell in the house of the Lord forever.

The Lord bless you and keep you. May His face shine upon you. May He be gracious unto you and lift up His countenance upon you and establish your life in His peace and manifest presence.

So now, may these blessings come on you, your family, and descendants. I bless you now in the name of Jesus.

A special thank you to John Kilpatrick for his powerful teachings entitled The Mystery and Power of a Blessing *that have influenced this father's blessing.*

Section Five: Understanding the Old Testament Synopsis

GENESIS

In the Hebrew Bible the name for this book of the Bible is Bereshit which means "in the beginning." The Greek word used for this book of the Bible is Genesis which means "origin" or "beginning."

This is the first of the five books Moses wrote while on Mt. Sinai. These five books (Genesis, Exodus, Leviticus, Numbers, and Deuteronomy) are always seen together and comprise what we call the Torah today. The Bible indicates this was given to Moses directly from God through angels so he could write it down with precision (Acts 7:53). The Torah was written fifteen hundred years before Jesus came to the earth. From Adam's fall to Abraham's time was around two thousand years. From Abraham's time to the time of Jesus was also around two thousand years. From Jesus' resurrection until the present time we live is around two thousand years. So we see from Adam's fall until the end times will be a total of six thousand years. When Jesus comes, he will reign on the earth for the seventh thousandth year which is a Sabbath rest for the world after six thousand years of torment under Satan's oppression.

Genesis answers the question of where we came from and how the world came into being. At the beginning, God tells His story of creation and the focus is broad on all humanity. As Genesis continues we see the story focusing more on the righteous of the earth, namely Noah, his son Shem, to Abraham, Isaac, Jacob, and finally Joseph.

Genesis shows the fall of man and the results of the fall. In regard to the fall of man, the entire Bible is God's revelation of redemption and restoration through Jesus Christ.

Here are some interesting facts in Genesis. The light appeared before the sun, moon, and stars. This is because it was God's glory as seen in Psalm 104:2-3. Adam and Eve were naked (Hebrew word *arom* which means partially nude) and they did not know it. After the fall, they were naked (Hebrew word *erom* which means completely nude) and were ashamed. What happened was that God created them in His image. They were also wrapped in the light of God's glory, which they saw and felt. When they sinned, the glory left. For all have sinned and fall short of the glory. God gave them the gospel when saying the seed of the woman (Christ) would come and crush the head of the serpent. Then God killed an animal and clothed them in that skin, showing Adam and Eve that there had to be shedding of blood for the forgiveness of sins.

The Bible speaks of a weird race of beings that were in the earth during Noah's days. They were the hybrid offspring of fallen angels and human women. No doubt Satan was trying to pollute the human race and stop the coming of the Messiah. These beings were on the earth for over a thousand years, corrupting mankind and the earth. It seems almost the entire human race's DNA became polluted with this corruption except for Noah and his sons who were blameless in their generation. Scholars believe the Nephilim giants are responsible for the ancient stone megalithic structures that still exist around the world today. This Hebrew phrase "blameless in their generation" implies blameless in their bloodline (generations). Extrabiblical writings indicate that these fallen angels and their offspring taught the entire world the occult and forbidden knowledge. They promoted sexual immorality and extreme violence which included cannibalism. God saw this evil and had Noah build an ark. Through the flood, God removed all this corruption from the earth and started over with Noah. Bible scholars believe Shem was the righteous spiritual leader after the death of Noah. Scholars believe he was known as Melchizedek which is translated "king of righteousness." Some Hebrew writings state that Shem took Abram into his home when Abram fled for his life from Nimrod. Shem taught Abram about the one true God. Later, Melchizedek became the king/priest of Salem which would become known as Jerusalem. After Abram's great victory over four kings, Melchizedek took the bread and wine (communion) with Abram and blessed him. It appears that Melchizedek could have been Abram's spiritual father and mentor. This would make sense as to why he came to bless Abram.

God is revealed as the Elohim (creator) and Yahweh (covenant) God in Genesis. Abraham followed the leading of God throughout his journeys in Canaan, building altars and inscribing the names of God that were revealed to him. The best known account of this was in the binding of Isaac known as the *akedah*, which was one of the clearest pictures of the crucifixion we see in the Old Testament. God revealed Himself to Abraham as Yahweh Yireh (Jehovah Jireh) "the one who sees (the need and provides a sacrifice)." Abraham also dug wells (of revival) that his children could benefit from.

Finally, I would add that the triune God is seen even at creation. We see God the Father as the great mastermind, the Holy Spirit (ruach) brooding over the waters, and the word being spoken is Christ.

John 1:1-5 "In the beginning was the Word, and the Word was with God, and the Word was God. [2]He was in the beginning with God. [3]All things were created through Him, and without Him nothing was created that was created. [4]In Him was life, and the life was the light of mankind. [5]The light shines in darkness, but the darkness has not overcome it."

A BASIC OUTLINE FOR GENESIS CAN BE SEEN THIS WAY:

1. Creation of the universe, the earth, and mankind as we know it. Chapters 1:1-2:25
2. The activity of Satan, the fall of man, and consequences of sin entering the world. Chapters 3-5
3. The flood, Nephilim, and Noah's family spared. Chapters 6-9
4. The tower of Babel and the scattering of mankind out of the middle east. Chapters 10-11
5. The call and life of Abraham. Chapters 12-25
6. Isaac, Jacob, and Esau. Chapters 25:19-26:35
7. Jacob and his children. Chapters 27-37
8. The life of Joseph and Israel entering Egypt. Chapters 37-50

Finally, there could be a gap of millions of years between Genesis 1:1 and Genesis 1:2. In the beginning, God created the heavens (plural) and the earth. The Hebrew implies in verse 2, "and the earth became void." It could be that the earth was millions of years old when Satan and one-third of the angels were cast down to it. God destroyed the earth of that time, making it like a dark, deserted penal colony for Satan and his rebellious angels. This is a possible explanation for dinosaurs. Some scholars believe this was the first flood and Noah experienced the second flood of destruction. After Noah's flood, God promised to never destroy the earth by a flood again.

It is interesting to note that God chose the earth to turn into a beautiful place once again. He did not choose another planet. God has a special place in His heart for the earth, His covenant people, and the city of Jerusalem.

MEMORABLE SCRIPTURES IN GENESIS:

Genesis 1:3 "God said, 'Let there be light,' and there was light."

Genesis 6:8 "But Noah found grace in the eyes of the Lord."

Genesis 12:1-3 "Now the Lord said to Abram, 'Go from your country, your family, and your father's house to the land that I will show you. [2]I will make of you a great nation; I will bless you and make your name great, so that you will be a blessing. [3]I will bless them who bless you and curse him who curses you, and in you all families of the earth will be blessed.'"

Genesis 15:6 "Abram believed the Lord, and He credited it to him as righteousness."

EXODUS

The book of Exodus records Israel's escape from the bondage of Egypt, the institution of Passover, and finally the construction of the Tabernacle. Jacob took his family of 70 into the land of Goshen, and a few hundred years later Israel grew to around six hundred thousand men (Exodus 12:37). The new Pharaoh, believed to be Ramses II, rose to power and did not know or care about Joseph or what he had previously done for the nation. He saw how powerful Israel had become, and wanted to subdue them and make sure they never rose up against Egypt.

The word Exodus means "departure" or "exit." This is the second of the five books written by Moses called the Torah or Pentateuch. Jesus quotes from Exodus in Mark 12:26, calling it "the book of Moses." The Hebrew name given to this book of the Bible is Shemot which means "names" and comes from the first sentence of the book which reads, "These are the names of the sons of Israel who came into Egypt with Jacob."

Exodus is an amazing story of Abraham's grandson, Jacob, taking his family into a foreign land in which God mightily blessed and prospered them to the point that Pharaoh was afraid of their strength. Exodus takes us on a journey of deliverance. Pharaoh is a picture and type of Satan; Egypt is like the sinful world, and the task-masters are like demonic oppressors. God's people were sent a deliverer named

Moses who is a picture and type of Christ. The people of God were delivered by the blood of the lamb (salvation), through the waters of baptism of the red sea, the baptism in the Holy Spirit as symbolized by the cloud, and ended up at Sinai which is a foreshadowing of the day of Pentecost to come (see 1 Corinthians 10).

A BASIC OUTLINE OF EXODUS IS:

1. Moses' call to be a deliverer to Israel. Chapters 1-4
2. The confrontation with Pharaoh and the release of the plagues. Chapters 5-13
3. Israel leaving Egypt and coming to Sinai (picture and type of salvation found in Christ). Chapters 13-19
4. God entering a covenant with Israel. Chapters 19-24
5. God using Moses to build a Tabernacle for His presence to dwell among His people. Chapters 24-40

God has always had a blood-covenant people in the earth. The book of Exodus shows Israel entering a blood covenant as a nation with the God of Abraham. Passover is a beautiful picture of what Jesus has accomplished on the cross. The plagues of Egypt show God's power over Satan's and cause the utter humiliation of the false gods of Egypt. God openly displayed His power over these false gods, declaring He would execute judgments on the gods of Egypt (Exodus 12:12). This is probably why some Egyptians left Egypt with Israel as a "mixed multitude." The realization came to many Egyptians that the God of Abraham was the true God to follow as they saw God's power openly displayed over the gods of Egypt.

HERE IS A LIST OF THE PLAGUES AND THE EGYPTIAN GODS THAT WERE JUDGED:

1. Water to blood – Hapi, the god of death and the Nile
2. Frogs – Heket, the god of fertility and water

3. Gnats – Geb, the god of the earth
4. Flies – Shu, the god that supposedly held the sky off the earth and god of the flies and beetles
5. Death of the livestock – Apis, the bull god which symbolized the strength of the king
6. Boils – Heka, the god of medicine and magic
7. Hail – Nut, the god of the firmament that was supposed to protect man from the heavens
8. Locusts – Min, the god of vegetation
9. Darkness – Ra, the sun god
10. Death of first born - Ammon Ra, the god of creation

Paul mentions the names Jannes and Jambres in 2 Timothy 3:8 as the magicians that stood in Pharaoh's court and could mimic through occult powers the first few plagues. Jewish writings indicate these were the sons of wicked Balaam who was one of the most powerful sorcerers of that day.

MEMORABLE SCRIPTURES IN EXODUS:

Exodus 3:14 "And God said to Moses, 'I AM WHO I AM,' and He said, 'You will say this to the children of Israel, 'I AM has sent me to you.'"

Exodus 8:1 Then the Lord said to Moses, "Go to Pharaoh and say to him, 'Thus says the Lord: Let My people go, so that they may serve Me.'"

Exodus 12:13 "The blood shall be to you for a sign on the houses where you are. And when I see the blood, I will pass over you, and the plague shall not be upon you to destroy you when I smite the land of Egypt."

Exodus 20:3 "You shall have no other gods before Me."

Exodus 25:8 "Let them make Me a sanctuary that I may dwell among them."

LEVITICUS

The book of Leviticus is the third book of the Torah written by Moses. It was an instructional guide to the priests and Levites on holy living and performing the duties of the Tabernacle. It is important to understand Leviticus from a New Testament perspective. The book of Hebrews would be the New Testament counterpart to the book of Leviticus. The first chapter of John shows Jesus dwelling or "Tabernacling" among us. Jesus is clearly seen in every aspect of the Tabernacle of Moses. The apostle Paul spoke of us as being the temple (or tabernacle) of the Spirit. Peter spoke of us as being a royal priesthood offering spiritual sacrifices that are pleasing to God. In Exodus God spoke from Sinai and Moses was given the Torah through angels. Moses wrote it word for word like a scribe. In Leviticus God spoke out of the Holy of Holies from the Tabernacle and called out to Moses fifty-six times.

Refer to the Hebrew Roots and Symbolism at the beginning of the Bible to understand the priestly garments, offerings, feast days, etc.

A BASIC OUTLINE FOR LEVITICUS IS:

1. The laws for the five major offerings. Chapters 1-7
2. Aaron's priesthood. Chapters 8-10
3. Regulations for holy living. Chapters 11-15
4. Law concerning Yom Kippur (Day of Atonement). Chapter 16
5. Living a holy life. Chapters 17-22
6. Teachings on the feasts of the Lord. Chapters 23-25
7. Blessings for obedience and curses for disobedience. Chapters 26-27

MEMORABLE SCRIPTURES IN LEVITICUS:

Leviticus 11:44 "For I am the Lord your God. You shall therefore sanctify yourselves, and you shall be holy, for I am holy." (notice 2 Corinthians 6:14-18)

Leviticus 17:10 "Whoever from the house of Israel, or from the strangers who sojourn among you, who eats any manner of blood, I will set My face against that person who eats blood, and will cut him off from among his people." (notice Acts15:29)

Leviticus 17:11 "For the life of the flesh is in the blood, and I have given it to you on the altar to make atonement for your lives; for it is the blood that makes atonement for the soul." (notice Hebrews 9:22)

Leviticus 18:29 "For whoever shall commit any of these abominations, those persons who commit them shall be cut off from among their people." (notice 1 Corinthians 5:1-12)

Leviticus 23:1 "And the Lord spoke to Moses, saying: [2]Speak to the children of Israel, and say to them: Concerning the feasts of the Lord that you shall proclaim to be holy convocations, these are My appointed feasts." (notice Zechariah 14:16-19)

NUMBERS

The book of Numbers is the fourth book of the Torah written by Moses at Sinai. The Hebrew name given to this book is BaMidbar which means "in the wilderness." This book starts with a census, but is mainly the story of unfaithful Israel wandering forty years in the wilderness because of testing God ten times. The census shows that God cares for and counts each individual of great value regardless of socioeconomic status. The Israelites continually tested God by complaining about food and water, and rebelling against Moses and Aaron. Finally, as they stand before the Promised Land, they shrink back in fear about entering the rest God had for them (see Hebrews 4). The book of Numbers shows God's ability to provide manna, quail, and water for well over 600,000 men, not counting Levites, women, and children. The book of Numbers also shows God's presence as seen in the cloud by day and fire by night that dwelled in the midst of Israel and led the nation.

The book of Numbers shows the twelve tribes were required to leave their encampment at the sound of the silver trumpets in an orderly manner. The first group of three to depart were Judah, Issachar, and Zebulun which were encamped at the east side of the Tabernacle. They were followed by the Levites carrying the supplies. The second group was Rueben, Gad, and Simeon encamped on the south side of the Tabernacle. They were followed by the Kohathites carrying the sacred furnishings like the Ark Menorah, Altar of Incense, etc. This placed the sacred items right in the middle of the caravan. The third camp to leave was the western side made up of Manasseh, Ephraim, and Benjamin (sons of Rachel). The final camp to leave, making up the rear guard, were Dan, Asher, and Naphtali. They had to be a rear guard. The rear guard was significant because we read the Amalekites were attacking Israel from the rear picking off the weak, poor, and defenseless that fell behind (see Deuteronomy 25:17-18).

The Levites had three families: the Kohathites (Moses was a close relative) carried the most holy articles; the Gershonites would carry the curtains and skins; and the Merarites would carry the framework. The priests would follow the cloud and fire of God's presence which led them. When it was time to move, the silver trumpets would blast a distinct sound to let the people know what to do. There are four distinct sounds to this day used by Israel when the shofar blasts. The tekiah is a long unbroken blast; shevarim are three distinct blasts; teruah is at least nine staccato blasts; and the tekiah ha gadol is a loud held-out blast.

Signaled events: gathering all Israel—tekiah, both silver trumpets; gathering just the leaders—tekiah, one silver trumpet; departure from camp—teruah/tekiah both silver trumpets (see Numbers 10).

It is important to mention the articles that made up the Tabernacle here and what they mean for us today as believers.

The Tabernacle in every way speaks of Christ as He has come to dwell or tabernacle among us according to John 1:14. There is a heavenly Tabernacle where God dwells in the third heaven. What God gave Moses is only a replica of this heavenly reality (see Hebrews 8:5).

The outer court (represents the human body, age of the law), the holy place (represents the human soul, church age), and the holy of holies (represents the human spirit, millennial reign of Christ).

The outer court has hangings of white linen (righteousness) in silver (redemption) sockets. The fact there is only one way into the outer court speaks of hearing the gospel, as Christ is the only way to the Father. The four colors of the entrance speak of the four Gospels.

The first thing we see entering the outer court is the bronze (judgment) altar where animals were cut into five pieces and burned. This speaks of the cross, and the sufferings Christ endured, and how he was pierced in five places as the true Lamb of God that takes away the sins of the world. This speaks of the sprinkling of the blood to cleanse us (see Revelation 6:11).

Next is the laver where the hands and feet of the priests were washed before entering the tent. This speaks of water baptism and the washing of the water of the Word (see Revelation 4:6).

We then look at the tent which had the first covering with interwoven cherubim that could be seen as walls and the ceiling from the inside. The cherubim were always seen as guardians of the glory of God. The next layer is the black goat skin which speaks of our sin nature. Over the goat skin was ram's skin died red. The red ram's skin speaks of the blood of Jesus to cleanse our sin. Finally, the outer covering seen by all was badger's skin which was very plain. The badger skins speak of how the things of God look mundane to the outsider, but when someone comes into Christ and enters the tent, one can see the true beauty of the things of God (see 2 Corinthians 4:4).

Entering the holy place, we see the table of the bread of presence on the right. In Hebrew the bread is lechem panim, literally "bread of faces." This speaks of us being intimate with the Lord. He stands at the door and knocks; if anyone opens, He will come in and eat with him. This speaks of the communion and/or Passover table. Passover was the time of the barley harvest (Jewish harvest) (see Revelation 3:20; Luke 24:13-35).

On the left, one would see the seven branch golden menorah with oil in it. The wicks were made of the soiled Levitical white garments. The menorah is seen as a mix of the olive and almond tree. The almond tree buds first in Israel and has beautiful white blossoms, while the olive tree is God's anointed family tree. The root system of this tree is the faith of the patriarchs, the center branch is Christ, and we are the Jew and gentile branches that make up this family tree. God has given His family His Word, which is a lamp to our feet. The totaling 66 knobs, buds and bowls speak of the 66 books of the Bible we have today. The oil and fire speak of the Holy Spirit. So God has given His family His Word and His Spirit. God gave us His initial Word at Sinai on the first Pentecost, and gave us His Spirit fifteen hundred years later on Pentecost. The Table of Showbread speaks of Passover, and the menorah speaks of Pentecost. The menorah speaks of the harvest that takes place in the church age. Pentecost was the time of firstfruits and the wheat harvest (gentile harvest) (see Revelation 2:1).

The last piece of furniture in the Holy Place right up against the veil was the golden altar of incense. This speaks of the Feast of Tabernacles. The incense was made of four equal parts. This speaks of praise, worship, prayer, and intercession. The golden altar of incense speaks of the Feast of Tabernacles which took place at the final harvest of the year which involved grapes, olives, and nuts. The grape harvest speaks of the very last harvest which occurs during the Lord treading out the wine press of His wrath. Jesus will come to tabernacle among us for one thousand years as He sits on the throne of David (see Zechariah 14:16-19).

The priest twice a day (evening and morning) would offer a lamb, unleavened bread, and pour out a libation of the fruit of the vine. This obviously speaks of personal prayer, worship, and the communion table. Then he would enter the Holy Place to partake of the bread of presence (if he desired), trim the menorah, and burn incense praying for God's people. People knew the time this was happening, which was around nine in the morning and three in the afternoon. That is why you see references to around the time of the evening or morning sacrifice something significant would happen (see 1 Kings 18:36-38; Acts 10:3; Daniel 8:14; Ezra 9:4).

On the Passover when Jesus died, the evening sacrifice was moved back from three in the afternoon to twelve noon. This was to accommodate the special Passover Lamb being offered which would take place at three in the afternoon. So Jesus was nailed to the cross at the time of the morning sacrifice, darkness covered the land during the evening sacrifice at noon when Jesus cried out, "Why have you forsaken me?" and Jesus died saying, "It is finished," at the time of the Passover offering. There was an earthquake and the veil separating the Holy of Holies from the Holy Place was ripped open (see Luke 23:44-49).

The Holy of Holies was only entered into once a year when the high priest wore only white, and had deeply consecrated himself. First, he hid away for several days and water immersed to cleanse himself. Then he took incense into the Holy of Holies and allowed it to be filled with smoke. Second, he had to offer a special bull for himself and his family and bring that blood into the Holy of Holies and sprinkle it before the mercy seat to cleanse his family. Third, he came out to offer a goat for the sins of Israel. He placed his hands on the head of the second goat called the azazel. He placed the sins of the nation on that goat and it was led away out of the camp. Then he took the blood of the first goat, and entered the Holy of Holies to sprinkle it on the Mercy Seat, and ask forgiveness for the sins of the nation. That was the third time he entered the Holy of Holies. He then would enter a fourth and final time to retrieve the censer that burned the incense. It is interesting to note that after Jesus died, He took the sins of the world upon Himself, but He had a secret ascension right after He told Mary not to touch Him because He hadn't ascended to the Father. Many scholars believe He entered the Holy of Holies of heaven to make atonement for us, and to even cleanse the sin of Lucifer's rebellion who led worship in heaven before his fall. Jesus is our Great High Priest who ever lives to make intercession. The Ark of the Covenant represents God's throne of grace. Inside the Ark was a jar of manna, Aaron's rod that budded, and the Ten Commandments (see John 20:16-18).

ALTARS IN THE BIBLE

There was a total of eleven altars mentioned in the Bible. Eleven is grace (number five) for sinful man (number six). Here are the eleven altars: 1. Noah builds an altar after the flood (Genesis 8:20); Abram builds an altar near Bethel (Genesis 12:7); Abram builds an altar on Mount Moriah where God reveals Himself as Jehovah Jireh "God who sees the need and provides" (Genesis 22:9-14); Isaac builds an altar at Beer Sheba (Genesis 26:25); Jacob builds an altar at Shechem and called the place El Elohe Israel "the God of Israel" (Gen 33:20); Moses builds an altar and called it Jehovah Nissi "God my banner" (Exodus 17:15); Joshua builds an altar on Mount Ebal (Joshua 8:30); Gideon builds an altar and called it Jehovah Shalom "God of Peace" (Judges 6:24); Manoah builds an altar on a rock (Judges 13:19-20); King Saul builds an altar to the Lord (1 Samuel 14:35); and finally David builds an altar in the threshing floor of Ornan the Jebusite to stop a plague in Israel (2 Samuel 24:21-25). Christ will have the twelfth and final altar in the millennial temple where nations will bring their offerings to worship Him (Ezekiel 43:13-27).

There were three types of altars mentioned in the Scripture. The first was stone altars that we see built without an iron tool on it. This was what Isaac would have laid on. It spoke of personal sacrifice. The second altar God sanctioned was the bronze altar where animals were offered up to God. This spoke of Christ's sacrifice on the cross. The final altar was the golden altar of incense. Before Christ came, the righteous would face the temple and pray during the times of the evening and morning sacrifices. It was believed all the prayers of the righteous intermingled with the incense and prayers of the priest and would go up to God. Before Christ, this was probably true (see Revelation 8:3-5).

A BASIC OUTLINE FOR NUMBERS IS:

1. God gives instructions about encampment and departure. Chapters 1-10
2. Leaving Sinai for the plains of Moab. Chapters 10-21
3. Balaam, Balak, and Israel. Chapters 22-25
4. Teachings on conquests and occupation. Chapters 26-36

MEMORABLE SCRIPTURES IN NUMBERS:

Numbers 6:22-27 "The LORD spoke to Moses, saying: 23Speak to
Aaron and to his sons, saying, This is how you will bless the children of Israel, saying to them, 24The Lord bless you and keep you;
25the Lord make His face to shine upon you, and be gracious unto you;
26the Lord lift His countenance upon you, and give you peace. 27They
will put My name upon the children of Israel, and I will bless them."

Numbers 9:15-17 "And on the day that the tabernacle was erected, the cloud covered the tabernacle, the tent of the testimony, and at evening there was over the tabernacle the appearance of fire until the morning. 16So it was always. The cloud covered it by day, and the
appearance of fire by night. 17When the cloud was lifted up from over
the tabernacle, then after it the children of Israel journeyed, and in the place where the cloud settled, there the children of Israel camped."

Numbers 10:9-10 "If you go to war in your land against the enemy that oppresses you, then you will blow an alarm with the trumpets, and you will be remembered before the Lord your God, and you will be saved from your enemies. 10Also in the day of your gladness, and at
your appointed days, and in the beginnings of your months, you shall

blow the trumpets over your burnt offerings, and over the sacrifices of your peace offerings that they may be a memorial for you before your God. I am the Lord your God."

Numbers 14:18 "The Lord is slow to anger and abounding in mercy, forgiving iniquity and transgression; but He will by no means clear the guilty, visiting the iniquity of the fathers upon the children to the third and fourth generation."

As a picture and type of the Law, Moses himself was not able to enter the Promised Land. This shows us that the Law was simply not enough, and that is why Jesus came to fulfill the Law and bring true salvation. Moses struck the rock in his anger toward the people in Numbers 20:1-13, and it cost him dearly. We must fully obey the Lord and not allow our emotions to take control of our actions.

DEUTERONOMY

Deuteronomy is the fifth and final book of the Torah written by Moses who received it directly from God through angels as he was on Mount Sinai. We see this referenced in 31:9 "Moses wrote this law and delivered it to the priests, the sons of Levi who bore the ark of the covenant of the Lord, and to all the elders of Israel." Also we see this referenced in the rebuke Stephen gave the Sanhedrin in Acts 7:53 "who have received the law by the disposition of angels, but have not kept it."

The name Deuteronomy comes from the Greek word Deuteronomion which means "second law." Moses emphasizes covenant in this book more than law. Moses places great importance on Israel loving the Lord with all their heart and teaching their children to love and obey God (see 4:9-10; 6:7; 30:19).

We see that Jesus quoted Deuteronomy 8:3; 6:16; and 6:13 when facing Satan as we read in Matthew 4:1-11. The New Testament quotes Deuteronomy dozens of times. The Shema which is quoted by observant Jews and written on Mezuzot scrolls is found in Deuteronomy.

The Hebrew name for Deuteronomy is Devarim which literally translates "words." This is a retelling of the stories of the first four books and Moses' final words as Israel is about to enter the Promised Land. At this writing forty years has passed and Moses is telling the younger generation the stories and preparing them to enter the Promised Land their fathers did not enter because of God's judgment. God did not allow Moses to enter Canaan. He saw it from Mount Nebo, died, and God buried Moses (34:5-6). The reason God buried Moses was so that Israel would not worship his bones or tomb. Moses was 120 years old when he died and Joshua was his successor.

A BASIC OUTLINE FOR DEUTERONOMY IS:

1. The younger generation learning from the history of the last forty years. Chapters 1-4
2. The importance of observing the Law. Chapters 4-11
3. The importance of living righteously. Chapters 12-26
4. Warnings and predictions. Chapters 27-30
5. Vision for new leadership. Chapters 31-34

MEMORABLE SCRIPTURES IN DEUTERONOMY:

Deuteronomy 6:4-5 "Hear, O Israel: The Lord is our God. The Lord is one! [5]And you shall love the LORD your God with all your heart and with all your soul and with all your might."

Deuteronomy 6:13-19 "You shall fear the Lord your God and serve Him and shall swear by His name. [14]You shall not go after other gods, the gods of the people which surround you [15](for the Lord your God is a jealous God among you). Otherwise the anger of the Lord your God will be inflamed against you and destroy you from off the face of the earth. [16]You shall not tempt the Lord your God, as you tempted Him in Massah. [17]You shall diligently keep the commandments of the Lord your God, and His testimonies and His statutes which He has commanded you. [18]You shall do what is right and good in the sight of the Lord that it may be well with you and that you may go in and possess the good land which the Lord swore to your fathers, [19]to drive out all your enemies before you, just as the Lord has spoken."

Deuteronomy 8:3 "He humbled you and let you suffer hunger, and fed you with manna, which you did not know, nor did your fathers know, that He might make you know that man does not live by bread alone; but man lives by every word that proceeds out of the mouth of the Lord."

Deuteronomy 30:19 "I call heaven and earth to witnesses against you this day, that I have set before you life and death, blessing and curse. Therefore choose life, that both you and your descendants may live; [20]that you may love the Lord your God, that you may obey His voice, and that you may cling to Him, for He is your life and the length of your days; and that you may dwell in the land that the Lord swore to your fathers, to Abraham, Isaac, and Jacob, to give them."

OBEDIENCE

Deuteronomy 6:3 "Hear therefore, O Israel, and be careful to do it, so that it may be well with you and so that you may multiply greatly, as the Lord the God of your fathers has promised you in the land that flows with milk and honey."

One of the important teachings of Scripture is that of giving to the Lord. If we want to live a blessed life, we must learn to obey the Lord in our finances. There are seven realms of giving taught in the scriptures. Here they are in condensed form:

1. **Don't glean the corners of your fields**, but leave them for the poor in the land (Leviticus 23:22). In a practical sense this is simply letting your overflow be a blessing to others in need around you.
2. **The Firstfruits** as taught in Deuteronomy 26:1-2. This is the first and best of what God has given us.

Ancient Jewish writings record large processions of Jewish farmers placing special baskets on oxen adorned with garlands of flowers in a grand parade to the temple in Jerusalem at Pentecost (Shavuot). The oxen would later be sacrificed as peace offerings. As the pilgrims passed through various towns along the way they would be accompanied by others who wanted to rejoice with them. These farmers had previously marked their fields and trees that ripened first. These were their firstfruits of what ripened brought to the temple and specifically given to the priesthood (Aaron's descendants).

3. **The Tithe** (ten percent) as read in Malachi 3:6-15. After the farmers gathered in their full harvest, they would separate one-tenth unto God. This was then taken to the local Levites who lived closest to them. The Levites lived in the six walled cities of refuge located throughout the land. These tithes met the needs of the Levites who were not supposed to work secular jobs but focus on temple ministry. The Levites would also distribute the tithe to the poor who would come to them for help.
4. **The Second Tithe** as mentioned in Deuteronomy 16:16. This was separated and kept back for the three journeys to Jerusalem at Passover, Pentecost, and Tabernacles. We always associate fasting and mourning with spirituality, but God wanted Israel to put aside money to feast and celebrate before Him.
5. **The Musaf Special Offerings** we also read about in Deuteronomy 16:16. The Lord commanded Israel to not come before the Lord at Passover, Pentecost, or Tabernacles empty-handed. There were to be special offerings brought to the Lord at these special times.
6. **The Tzedakah Offering** (Deuteronomy 14:28-29) was special offerings to specifically help the poor in the land. God has always had a deep concern for the poor, widows, and orphans. We see God's heart for the poor in these scriptures below:

Psalm 41:1-3 "Blessed are those who consider the poor; the Lord will deliver them in the day of trouble. [2]The Lord will preserve them and keep them alive, and they will be blessed on the earth, and You will not deliver them to the will of their enemies. [3]The Lord will sustain them on the sickbed; You will restore all his lying down in his illness."

Proverbs 19:17 "He who has pity on the poor lends to the Lord, and He will repay what he has given."

Proverbs 11:24-26 "There is one who scatters, yet increases; and there is one who withholds more than is right, but it leads to poverty. [25]The generous soul will be made rich, and he who waters will be watered also himself. [26]The people will curse him who withholds grain, but blessing will be upon the head of him who sells it."

Exodus 22:21-27 "You must neither wrong a foreigner nor oppress him, for you were foreigners in the land of Egypt. [22]You shall not afflict any widow or orphan. [23]If you afflict them in any way and they cry at all to Me, I will surely hear their cry. [24]And My anger will burn, and I will kill you with the sword, and your wives will become widows, and your children fatherless. [25]If you lend money to any of My people who is poor among you, do not be a creditor to him, and do not charge him interest. [26]If you take your neighbor's garment as a pledge, you shall return it to him before the sun goes down, [27]for that is his only covering; it is his garment for his body. In what else will he sleep? And when he cries out to Me, I will hear, for I am gracious."

7. **The Freewill Offerings** we read about in Psalm 54:6. There are times that a church is simply needing supplies, maintenance, or some special need arises. God's blessing will be upon those who are willing to give freewill offerings that help the house of God and the people of God when there are needs. God loves a cheerful giver.

JOSHUA

Scholars agree that Joshua Son of Nun authored this book himself except for 24:29-33 which describes his death and legacy. Many times an author would dictate to a scribe, who would meticulously write down what was spoken verbatim. This might have been the case with Joshua. This book was written around 1375 BC documenting the next phase of what God was doing with His people as they entered the Promised Land, conquering the nations before them.

Joshua and Caleb were now eighty years old. They were the only two spies that had faith and brought a good report. It seems that God kept them as young, healthy, and strong at the age of eighty as they were at the age of forty (Joshua 14:11). Joshua was faithful to serve under his spiritual father, Moses, all the years Israel wandered through the wilderness. Now God has exalted him to the highest place over Israel.

This book makes it clear that the Nephilim serpent seed were on the earth again. The Lord purged them from the earth during the flood, but Genesis 6:4 states "The Nephilim were on the earth in those days, **and also after that**, when the sons of God came in to the daughters of men, and they bore children to them. These were the mighty men who were of old, men of renown (emphasis mine)." We notice verse 4 states "and also after that," indicating the giants were also in the earth after the flood. It is little wonder that this was the case in Canaan. The land of Canaan was literally filled with witchcraft and satanism. All seven tribes that inhabited the land were deeply involved in the occult (see Deuteronomy 18:9-14). The city of Jericho could have been a Nephilim stronghold, and that might be why God marked it for destruction first before other cities. God used Joshua to begin the annihilation of the Nephilim, but David and his men seem to finish the job as they killed Goliath and his brothers. Joshua did not conquer the land of the Philistines and David had to fight them and subdue them later is Israel's history. It is interesting to note that the land called Gaza in southern Israel is the ancient land of the Philistines. With that said, Israel is still fighting a battle from that land mass to this day. One could conclude that the principality of the Philistines is still trying to destroy Israel to the present day as fallen angels never die.

God prepared Joshua for ministry through leading the military against the Amalekites in Exodus 17:8-16, assisting Moses as we see in Exodus 33:11, and was one of the twelve spies sent to spy out the land in Numbers 13-14.

Joshua stayed the course and strived to do everything right in the eyes of the Lord. He was faithful all the days of his life. Joshua remembered Caleb's faithfulness and gave him the land promised him (Joshua 15:13-19). Caleb drove out the Anakites who were Nephilim. Caleb was a fierce warrior before the Lord. Joshua never fell into sin, nor did he disobey the voice of the Lord. The only recorded mistake Joshua made was the covenant with the Gibeonites (Joshua 9:14). If Joshua had asked the Lord in prayer, God would have exposed this plot. God encouraged Joshua to be strong and courageous because of the fierce, life-threatening battles he would have to engage in. One of the most notable attributes of Joshua is that after Moses would leave his prayer time, Joshua would linger in the presence of God (Exodus 33:11). Could this have something to do with why Joshua ended up being Moses' successor? Joshua knew the presence and voice of the Lord, and God made a special promise to be with Joshua everywhere he went.

Joshua (whose name means salvation) had to be strong to discipline Achan for the sin of taking the devoted things out of Jericho because of greed. The city of Jericho was to be like a firstfruit offering and a tithe to God of the conquered lands. God told Joshua that if he did not deal with the sin, He would not be with him anymore (Joshua 7:10-12). Joshua refused to compromise, and was more concerned with pleasing God than man. Joshua fulfilled his destiny, but Israel did not fully drive out the inhabitants of the land, and God told them these nations would be a snare to them (Joshua 23:13). We see this fulfilled throughout the book of Judges and on until the Babylonian exile in the days of Jeremiah the prophet.

Upon entering the land, Joshua circumcised the sons of Israel whose rebellious parents refused to do so while in the wilderness. He celebrated Passover with all Israel renewing the covenant. The angel of the Lord appeared to him, and God gave him Jericho, which was one of the greatest miracles recorded in the Bible (see Joshua 5-6). Joshua also led a military campaign to clear the idol-worshipping Hittites, Amorites, Perizzites, Hivites, and Jebusites from the land. One time in battle God heard Joshua's cry to cause the sun to stand still to give them more time to complete the battle (Joshua 10:1-15). What an incredible miracle that God caused the rotation of the earth to pause at the prayer of this mighty man of God. Hebrew sages state that Moses was like the sun and Joshua like the moon. Joshua reflected what he learned from his spiritual father. Joshua was of the tribe of Ephraim as mentioned in Numbers 13:8. Moses honored and commissioned Joshua before Israel right before his death as recorded in Deuteronomy 31.

Joshua was faithful to give the Levites 48 cities spread throughout the nation. Even though the tribes of Reuben, Gad, and the half-tribe of Manasseh stayed on the east bank of the Jordan, Joshua allocated the land to the remaining tribes before his death, thus establishing Israel in the land God promised Abraham his seed would possess.

A BASIC OUTLINE FOR JOSHUA IS:

1. The sons of Israel being prepared to take the Promised Land. Chapters 1-5
2. The conquest of the Promised Land. Chapters 6-12
3. The allocation of conquered land. Chapters 13-21
4. The farewell and death of Joshua. Chapters 22-24

MEMORABLE SCRIPTURES IN JOSHUA:

Joshua 1:9 "Have not I commanded you? Be strong and courageous. Do not be afraid or dismayed, for the Lord your God is with you wherever you go."

Joshua 23:10 "One man from among you can make a thousand flee, for it is the Lord your God who wages war for you, as He told you."

Joshua 24:15 "If it is displeasing to you to serve the Lord, then choose today whom you will serve, if it should be the gods your fathers served beyond the River or the gods of the Amorites' land where you are now living. Yet as for me and my house, we will serve the Lord."

JUDGES

Some scholars believe the prophet Samuel wrote the book of Judges, but the author is unknown. The book of Judges shows how strange and deceptive things can become when God's people are ignorant of His Word. The book reads as a continual cycle of Israel falling into sin. Because of their sin, they are ravaged and in bondage to their enemies. And finally, God raises up a deliverer. It was most likely written around 1050 BC, but the events covered go as far back as 1375 BC.

Later in their history, one of Israel's greatest mistakes was desiring a king. God was their king and leader. The phrase "ask of the Lord" is found in the book of Judges and in Samuel. This implied seeking the Lord's headship and direction found through prophets and the high priest who had the urim and thummin in his breastplate (see Exodus 28:30). After Israel told Samuel they wanted a king, this phrase was rarely found throughout the time of the kings.

After the death of Joshua, Israel lost the momentum of cleansing the land and driving out the inhabitants. When Israel did not completely drive out the nations, God told Israel these remaining nations would be thorns in their sides and a snare to them (see Judges 2:2-3). This is exactly what happened as we see Israel continually going into idolatry. The Bible goes on to say "that entire generation passed away, and after them grew up a generation who did not know the Lord or the deeds that He had done for Israel (see Judges 2:10)." There was also widespread ignorance of the Word of God. The book of Judges has some of the most bizarre stories recorded in the Bible:

- Samson's supernatural physical strength and moral failures. Judges 13-16
- Jephthah making a foolish vow and consequently sacrificing his daughter. Judges 11:29-15:20
- The story of Micah and his idols. Judges 17
- The Levite and his concubine. Judges 19
- The tribe of Benjamin committing sins similar to Sodom and Gomorrah and causing civil war in Israel because of their stubborn refusal to repent. Judges 20-21

Judges tells of the period between Joshua and Samuel. Samuel, like John the Baptist, was used in history to move Israel into a new era. John the Baptist moved Israel out of the period of the Old Covenant, and helped usher in the period of the New Covenant. Samuel moved Israel out of the period of the Judges into the era of Kings.

The Hebrew name for this book is Shoftim, literally translated "judges" or "ruling leaders." Over a period of 410 years there were fifteen leaders God raised up to deliver Israel from the oppressive nations of Midian, Canaan, Philistia, Ammon, and Moab. The message of Judges is that we get in trouble when we don't know the Bible and we do what is right in our own eyes (see 17:6; 21:25).

Some well-known figures like Samson, Deborah, and Gideon have their introduction in the book of Judges, while there are lesser known judges like Othniel, Ehud, Tola, Jair, and Jepthah. The book of Hebrews chapter 11 mentions some of these great judges operating in faith and being used mightily by God.

A BASIC OUTLINE FOR JUDGES:

1. The spiritual condition of the era. Chapters 1-3
2. Cycles of oppression and God raising up Judges. Chapter 3:7-16
3. Idolatry, immorality, and civil war. Chapters 17-21

MEMORABLE SCRIPTURES IN JUDGES:

Judges 2:12 "They forsook the Lord, the God of their ancestors, who had brought them out of Egypt. They followed and worshiped various gods of the peoples around them. They aroused the Lord's anger."

Judges 2:16 "Then the Lord raised up judges, who saved them out of the hands of these raiders."

Judges 7:2 "The Lord said to Gideon, 'You have too many men. I cannot deliver Midian into their hands, or Israel would boast against me, My own strength has saved me.'"

RUTH

Some believe that Samuel wrote the book of Ruth, but the author is officially unknown. Based on information gleaned in Ruth chapter 4, scholars believe the events of Ruth probably took place during the time of the judge Ehud (see Judges 3:12-30). Ruth probably lived around 1100 BC. She was the great-grandmother of King David who later reigned approximately from 1010 BC to 970 BC. This places Ruth in the bloodline of Jesus Christ Himself who physically descended from David's bloodline. It is interesting to note that Rahab (prostitute), Tamar (gentile who slept with her father-in-law), Ruth (Moabite), and Bathsheba (who committed adultery) were mentioned in Matthew chapter 1 specifically as being in the bloodline of Christ. The message is that God would cause a people to become cleansed and become His blood-covenant people who were once unclean and far from Him in many ways. This is a picture of the gentile church being engrafted into God's family, as we see in 1 Peter 2:9-10:

"But you are a chosen race, a royal priesthood, a holy nation, a people for God's own possession, so that you may declare the goodness of Him who has called you out of darkness into His marvelous light. [10]In times past, you were not a people, but now you are the people of God. You had not received mercy, but now you have received mercy."

In a metaphoric sense, Ruth is a picture and type of the gentile church (bride) betrothed to our kinsmen redeemer Boaz (Jesus Christ). Ruth was taught how to please Boaz by Naomi (Israel). We learn so much about what pleases God through the Hebrew heritage passed to us. We would not even have the Bible if it wasn't for Israel. Ruth then turns around and takes care of Naomi. In the same way the church is called to be a blessing to Israel. Israel has blessed us spiritually, and we are in turn called to bless Israel materially and by bringing the gospel to them.

Naomi understood the ancient Jewish culture and taught Ruth to beautify herself and lay at Boaz's feet in the night during the reaping of the barley harvest. This culture would have been strange and foreign to her as a gentile from Moab, but she learned of it from Naomi. So much can be gleaned by learning the Hebrew roots of our faith. Naomi taught Ruth to wash herself (cleanse her life), anoint herself (filled with the Holy Spirit), and change her clothes (our priestly role as believers) to get Boaz's attention. We can learn from this how to please Jesus in our walk with God today.

Ruth marries Boaz and becomes a Jew by being grafted in through marriage with a kinsman redeemer. We can see this as a beautiful picture of what the apostle Paul was teaching in Romans 9-11. The elders of ancient Bethlehem spoke a blessing over Boaz and Ruth's wedding which stated:

"We are witnesses. May the Lord make the woman who is coming to your house like Rachel and Leah, who together built up the house of Israel. May you do well in Ephrathah [ancient name for Bethlehem] and be famous in Bethlehem! [12]May your house be like the house of Perez, whom Tamar bore to Judah, through the offspring that the Lord will give you by this young woman" (Ruth 4:11-12).

Jesus was a direct descendent of this union and He is famous from Bethlehem. Even Tamar who also was in this bloodline was mentioned here. Bethlehem is the Hebrew words beit which means "house" and lechem which is translated "bread." The bread of life was born in the house of bread. Jesus is truly living bread like manna from heaven.

A Jewish legend states that Orpah, who forsook Naomi in her time of need, ended up becoming the matriarch of the evil bloodline from which Goliath and his brothers came. Ruth stayed faithful to Naomi in her difficulty and became the matriarch to King David who killed Goliath and cut off his head.

The concept of a near kinsman redeemer is certainly foreign to us in the western gentile culture of today, but this was very common during the time of Ruth. The laying at Boaz's feet was to show him that she was interested in his redemption if he was willing. In Leviticus 25:25 God provided a way for one to redeem their property. Deuteronomy 25:5 shows that a near kin would marry the widow and help carry on the family name through that union. This marriage would be recognized by the elders who sat at the gate of the city as judges. Ruth's kindness to Naomi caused her to be blessed beyond measure.

A BASIC OUTLINE FOR RUTH:

1. Naomi's departure from Moab and return to the land of Judah. Chapter 1:1-22
2. Ruth returns with Naomi and meets Boaz. Chapters 2-3
3. Boaz and Ruth. Chapter 4:1-22

MEMORABLE SCRIPTURES IN RUTH:

Ruth 1:16-18 "But Ruth said, 'Do not urge me to leave you or to turn back from following you. For wherever you go, I will go, and wherever you stay, I will stay. Your people shall be my people and your

God my God. [17]Where you die, I will die, and there I will be buried. May the Lord do thus to me, and worse, if anything but death separates you and me!' [18]When Naomi saw that she was determined to go with her, she said no more to her."

Ruth 3:3-4 "Now wash and anoint yourself, and put on your best clothes. Then go down to the threshing floor, but do not let the man know you are there until he has finished eating and drinking. [4]When he lies down, notice the place where he is lying. Go in and uncover his feet and lie down. He will tell you what you will do."

Ruth 4:11-14 "Then all the people who were at the gate, along with the elders, said, 'We are witnesses. May the Lord make the woman who is coming to your house like Rachel and Leah, who together built up the house of Israel. May you do well in Ephrathah and be famous in Bethlehem! [12]May your house be like the house of Perez, whom Tamar bore to Judah, through the offspring that the Lord will give you by this young woman.' [13]So Boaz took Ruth, and she became his wife. When they came together, the Lord enabled her to conceive, and she bore a son. [14]Then the women said to Naomi, 'Blessed be the Lord, who has not left you without a redeemer. May he become famous in Israel!'"

1 SAMUEL

The events and writing of 1 Samuel most likely took place between 1100-1000 BC. Most scholars believe Samuel had a hand in the writing of 1 Samuel, but he could not have been the sole author of 1 and 2 Samuel since his death is recorded in 1 Samuel 25. Whoever wrote 1and 2 Samuel probably drew from the book of Jasher, which is mentioned in 2 Samuel 18, and possibly the writings of Samuel, Nathan, and Gad referenced in 1 Chronicles 29:29.

First Samuel records that Elkanah was the father of Samuel, and his ancestry was from the territory known as Ephrathah. Ephrathah was an ancient name for Bethlehem. It is interesting that Elkanah's son Samuel would one day anoint David who was also from Bethlehem (see Micah 5:2; 1 Samuel 16:13). Samuel was a very influential figure as a prophet, priest, and judge. Because Samuel had authority with God, when he came into an area, the people were afraid at his coming (see 1 Samuel 16:4-5).

Judges 21:19 shows us that Shiloh was located in Ephraim. Shiloh is where the Tabernacle rested for almost four hundred years (see Joshua 18:1). The word Shiloh, which means "tranquil" in Hebrew, is derived from the same root word as Salem or Shalom which are translated as "peace." Shiloh was a place, but it is also a metaphor for the coming Messiah who will come and Tabernacle among us. It seemed that Jacob spoke of this in Genesis 49:10 when it is stated, "The scepter shall not depart from Judah, nor a lawgiver from between his feet, until Shiloh comes; and to him will be the obedience of the people." Jacob seemed to be prophetically seeing the millennial reign of Christ. Balaam saw this when he said, "I will see him, but not now; I will behold him, but not near; a star will come out of Jacob, and a scepter will rise out of Israel" (see Numbers 24:17). The thousand-year reign of Christ will truly lead to worldwide peace and prosperity.

The first chapter of 1 Samuel shows us the story of infertile Hannah earnestly praying for a son at the Tabernacle located in Shiloh. Eli blessed her, and God caused her to conceive the prophet Samuel. Eli was of the bloodline of Ithamar. God cursed Eli's bloodline to cease to be in the priesthood (see 1 Samuel 2:27-36; 3:11-14).

Later we read in 1 Kings 2:27 that Solomon removed Abiathar from priesthood so that any of the descendants of Ithamar would no longer serve before the Lord. Zadok was a faithful priest descended from the bloodline of Eliezer. Remember the zeal of Phinehas who was of the bloodline of Eliezer (Numbers 25)? It seems that the bloodline of Eliezer was the remaining faithful priests who served in the temple during the days Jesus walked the earth. John the Baptist was a direct descendant of Aaron through the bloodline of Eliezer. It is interesting that the descendants of David and Eliezer began to intermarry at some point as Jesus and John the Baptist were first cousins.

The book of 1 Samuel records one of the greatest mistakes of Israel's history. Israel rejected God as their true headship speaking to them through the prophets and priests. Rather, they wanted a king like all the other nations around them. The history of Israel from that point on shows how tragic this decision was. Almost every king of Israel led them astray into idolatry and eventually into captivity. In like manner, Jesus is called the head of the church in Ephesians 1:22-23, but there are very few churches that really consult Him and obey what He tells them to do. Most simply run the church the same way one would run a secular business. How different will things be if God is truly our headship whom we consult and obey in all things?

A BASIC OUTLINE FOR 1 SAMUEL

1. Samuel's miraculous birth and dedication to God's service. Chapters 1-2
2. Eli as the high priest and judge of Israel at the Tabernacle in Shiloh. Chapters 3-4
3. Samuel's leadership in Israel as a prophet, priest, and judge. Chapters 5-8
4. Saul becoming Israel's first king as anointed by Samuel. Chapters 9-31

MEMORABLE SCRIPTURES IN 1 SAMUEL:

1 Samuel 8:9 "And all the elders of Israel gathered together and they
came to Samuel at Ramah. [5]They said to him, 'You are old and your
sons do not walk in your ways. Now, install for us a king to govern
us like all the nations.' [6]But the thing was evil in the eyes of Samuel,
because they said, 'Give us a king to govern us.' And Samuel prayed to
the Lord. [7]The Lord said to Samuel, 'Obey the voice of the people in
relation to all that they say to you. For it is not you they have rejected,
but Me they have rejected from reigning over them. [8]Just as all the
deeds which they have done to Me, from the day I brought them up

from Egypt even to this day, in that they have forsaken Me and have served other gods, so they are doing also to you now. [9]Now then, obey their voice. Only you will testify against them and proclaim to them the judgment concerning the king who will reign over them.'"

1 Samuel 15:22-23 "Samuel said, 'Does the Lord delight in burnt offerings and sacrifices as much as in obeying the voice of the Lord? Obedience is better than sacrifice, a listening ear than the fat of rams. [23]For rebellion is as the sin of witchcraft, and stubbornness is as iniquity and idolatry. Because you have rejected the word of the Lord, He has also rejected you from being king."

1 Samuel 16:13 "Then Samuel took the horn of oil, and anointed him in the midst of his brothers. And the Spirit of the Lord came on David from that day forward. So Samuel arose and went to Ramah."

1 Samuel 17:45-46 "Then David said to the Philistine, 'You come to me with a sword, a spear, and a shield, but I come to you in the name of the Lord of Hosts, the God of the armies of Israel, whom you have reviled. [46]This day will the Lord deliver you into my hand. And I will strike you down and cut off your head. Then I will give the corpses of the Philistine camp this day to the birds of the air and to the beasts of the earth so that all the earth may know that there is a God in Israel. "

2 SAMUEL

The author could not have been Samuel since the events of 2 Samuel take place after Samuel's death. Some Bible scholars have suggested Abiathar the priest (2 Samuel 15:35), but it is impossible to say for certain. The events and writing of this book likely happened during the reign of King David approximately 1010-970 BC. It is also important to note that both 1 and 2 Samuel where one scroll written together. Second Samuel picks up as David learns of Saul and Jonathan's death at the hands of the Philistines.

This book speaks of David's kingship over Israel. God spoke through Samuel that David was to be the next king. Samuel even told Saul he would lose his kingship, but the house of Saul insisted on keeping power. God was with those who obeyed the voice of the Lord and supported David's rise to power, and God resisted those who supported the house of Saul (see 2 Samuel 3).

David began his reign after Saul's death. Saul opened himself up to premature death by being rebellious to God and also visiting a witch (see Deuteronomy 18:9-13). David is first anointed in Hebron and reigned over the southern territory of Israel. Saul's son Ishbosheth illegitimately took power after Saul's death and reigned for seven years. After his death, David became king over all Israel. David is the only Bible figure to have been anointed three separate times. The first anointing by Samuel, the second when reigning over Hebron for seven years, and the third to reign over all Israel for thirty-three years. David's entire reign was forty years. God made a covenant with David that he would have an heir on the throne forever. This is ultimately fulfilled in Christ, the son of David, who will reign eternally (see Luke 1:28-38).

We also read how David's sin with Bathsheba opened him up to judgment and his family to destruction. Sadly, David dies wasting away in sickness. This is most likely because of the sin of adultery and murder. David's family enters great turmoil as predicted by Nathan the prophet "you are the (guilty) man" (12:7). Nathan goes on to say "the sword will not depart from your house" (12:10-14).

God cannot trust someone with authority if they cannot submit to and honor authority. David was a man who honored authority. He refused to do anything against Saul, "God's anointed." Therefore God raised him up to the highest authority. We can also see that man will always want a Saul, but God will always choose a David. Saul was handsome, tall, and looked like a king, but David had a heart for God.

David truly repented of his sin, and God forgave him. Even though the consequences of his sin lived on in his health and family, God forgave David and restored him. During the dark time of repentance David wrote the beautiful Psalm 51. We see David's heart in this psalm as we read, "Have mercy on me, O God, according to Your lovingkindness; according to the abundance of Your compassion, blot out my transgressions. [2]Wash me thoroughly from my iniquity, and cleanse me from my sin. [10]Create in me a clean heart, O God, and renew a right spirit within me. [11]Do not cast me away from Your presence, and do not take Your Holy Spirit from me. [12]Restore to me the joy of Your salvation, and uphold me with Your willing spirit." David's life shows us that we must be careful in the decisions we make as it can affect many others. The more authority we have, the more disastrous our bad decisions can be for many others.

In 2 Samuel we see David capture Jerusalem and make it the capital of all Israel (5:6-16). God spoke to David that his son would build a temple and not David himself (7-8). David's sin and consequences are recorded in 2 Samuel: David's unfortunate sin with Bathsheba (11:1-27); David's son Amnon raping his sister Tamar (13:1-20); David's son Absalom's rebellion to seize the throne (13-20).

A BASIC OUTLINE FOR 2 SAMUEL

1. David as king in Hebron over the southern area of Judah. Chapters 1-4
2. David's troubled reign over all Israel. Chapters 5-24

MEMORABLE SCRIPTURES IN 2 SAMUEL:

2 Samuel 1:25 "How the mighty ones have fallen in the midst of battle! Jonathan was slain on your high places."

2 Samuel 7:18-19 "Then King David went in and sat before the Lord. He said, 'Who am I, O Lord God, and what is my house that You have brought me this far? [19]Yet this was comparatively insignificant in Your sight, Lord God, for You have also spoken about Your servant's house into the distant future. Is this Your manner with man, Lord God?'"

2 Samuel 18:33 "The king was deeply moved and went up to the upper chamber of the gate and wept. As he went he said, 'O my son Absalom, my son, my son Absalom! If only I could have given my death in your stead, Absalom, my son, my son!'"

1 KINGS

The author is unknown, but some have suggested Jeremiah the prophet as the author of 1 and 2 Kings. First and 2 Kings were probably written during the Babylonian exile after the destruction of Jerusalem and the temple in 586 BC.

First Kings begins with David placing Solomon as king of Israel and Solomon asking God for wisdom. Unfortunately, Solomon moved far from God and God's wisdom. He marries seven hundred women, many of them foreigners, that turn his heart from God. He goes on to have four hundred concubines, so that his harem totaled one thousand. The Torah specifically taught that a king should not multiply horses or wives who would lead him astray (see Deuteronomy 17:16-17). This is exactly what Solomon did.

First Kings covers the events from 970-850 BC when Israel divides into northern and southern independent nations. The ten northern tribes comprising Israel is symbolically called Ephraim by God through the prophets, and its capital became Samaria. Rehoboam, the son of Solomon and heir to the throne, foolishly taunts the leaders of Israel. Israel splits from Solomon's line and placed one of Solomon's former officials named Jeroboam as their king. From the time of Jeroboam until their exile to Assyria, northern Israel was apostate and completely unfaithful to God. King Jeroboam placed idols in the far north area of Dan and far south area of Beersheba so that Israel would never take their offerings to Jerusalem, be faithful to God, and return their loyalty to the house of David. Unfortunately the sin of Jeroboam was never really repented of by Israel. Israel also provoked the Lord's anger by having high places on which they offered sacrifices and burned incense such as on hills and mountains. Sacrifices and burning incense to God was only to be done at the tabernacle (later temple), specifically according to what was laid out in the Torah, and by the descendants of Aaron alone.

The southern nation of Judah, comprising both Judah and Benjamin, wavered in their loyalty to God depending on the king in power. David's descendants reigned until their exile to Babylon under Nebuchadnezzar. The southern kingdom of Judah does have some stand-out kings that were righteous, like Asa, Jehoshaphat, Hezekiah, and Josiah. Sadly many of their kings were wicked and lead the nation into idolatry.

First Kings introduces the mysterious prophet Elijah. It also details some of Israel's darkest days as Jezebel ruled through Ahab over the northern ten tribes, and through marriage, the spirit of Jezebel entered the royal family of Judah through Athaliah. God raised up Elijah to confront this wickedness. The showdown on Mt. Carmel, and the miracles of Elijah are detailed in 1 Kings.

Jezebel was not just an evil woman alone. There was a very strong spirit she walked in that tried to infest and destroy Israel. It took Elijah anointing Elisha, thus bringing the prophetic ministry, with a double portion anointing, to expose her. In addition to the prophetic, it took King Jehu's ruthless slaughter of her and all her descendants under God's command. God allowed Hazael's reign over Syria, bringing national judgment to Israel. Finally, it took the holy priesthood under Jehoiada to finish this spiritual cleansing in the death of Athaliah and establishing Joash, a descendent of David, back on the throne. This was a major spiritual battle over Israel in which Elijah was used to initiate the victory, but it took an anointed prophet, anointed king, and anointed priest to fully defeat this spirit. It is noteworthy that all three of Israel's first kings reigned for forty years each (Saul, David, and Solomon) totaling 120 years.

A BASIC OUTLINE FOR 1 KINGS

1. David places Solomon as king and his reign. Chapters 1-11
2. The national split of Israel. Chapters 12-14
3. The divided kingdom. Chapters 15-22

4. The notable story of Jezebel verses Elijah. Chapters 18-19

5. God's judgment on Ahab's reign. Chapters 20-22

MEMORABLE SCRIPTURES IN 1 KINGS:

1 Kings 2:2-3 "I am going the way of all the earth. Be strong, and show yourself to be a man. [3]And keep the charge of the Lord your God, walking in His ways, keeping His statutes, His commandments, His judgments, and His testimonies, as it is written in the Law of Moses, that you may prosper in all that you do and wherever you turn."

1 Kings 3:9 "Give Your servant therefore an understanding heart to judge Your people, that I may discern between good and bad, for who is able to judge among so great a people?"

1 Kings 18:21 "Elijah came to all the people and said, 'How long will you stay between two opinions? If the Lord is God, follow Him, but if Baal, then follow him.'"

1 Kings 18:37-39 "Elijah the prophet came near and said, 'The Lord, God of Abraham, Isaac, and of Israel, let it be known this day that You are God in Israel and that I am Your servant and that I have done all these things at Your word. [37]Hear me, O Lord, hear me, so that this people may know that You are the Lord God and that You have turned their hearts back again.' [38]Then the fire of the Lord fell and consumed the burnt sacrifice and the wood and the stones and the dust and licked up the water that was in the trench. [39]When all the people saw it, they fell on their faces and said, 'The Lord, He is God! The Lord, He is God!'"

2 KINGS

Traditionally some scholars believe Jeremiah the prophet wrote 1 and 2 Kings as originally one scroll. This scroll was originally written during the Babylonian captivity after the destruction of the temple. The destruction of Jerusalem and the temple was in 586 BC. This scroll was probably written after this time frame because of the events detailed at the end of 2 Kings. The time frame written about in 2 Kings was from the 800s BC until the destruction of the temple. Later in the days of Jesus the Pharisees were deeply religious Jews from various tribes, the Sadducees were descendants of Aaron and the Levites, and the Essenes were the scribes that meticulously oversaw the writings such as The Book and Acts of Solomon (1 Kings 11:41), The Book of the Chronicles of the Kings of Judah (1 Kings 14:29), The Book and Chronicles of the Kings of Israel (1 Kings 14:19), the books of Jasher, Jubilees, Enoch, and scrolls like Isaiah and Jeremiah. It was from sources like these that 1 and 2 Kings was comprised.

At the beginning of 2 Kings, Elijah was taken alive into heaven. He is the second man recorded in the Bible to have been raptured straight into heaven alive. The other man was Enoch. This is a picture and type of those that are alive and remain at the second coming of Christ that will be changed in the twinkling of an eye as described in 1 Corinthians 15:52-58.

In 2 Kings, what God was doing in the earth was done through the prophet Elisha, in the same way Elijah was used in 1 Kings. Elisha was powerfully used by God among the common people of Israel as he walked in a double-portion anointing from Elijah. The ten northern tribes called Israel (capital city Samaria), were carried away into exile by the vicious nation of Assyria in 722 BC. The king of that time was Hoshea (17:6).

The southern nation of Judah had some righteous kings like Hezekiah. Therefore, they lasted longer before judgment came. In fact, the famous story of the angel delivering Judah from Assyria by killing 100,000 of their military took place shortly after the northern kingdom had been exiled. This is why Hezekiah was so afraid. Isaiah the prophet told Hezekiah God would deliver him and Judah. This deliverance happened because Hezekiah, a righteous king and descendent of David, cried out to God in prayer. Eventually Judah came under judgment as well. In 586 BC Judah began to be broken up and conquered by the Babylonian army as seen in chapter 24. Nebuchadnezzar conquered Judah, eventually destroyed Jerusalem, destroyed the temple, and carried off 10,000 captives, all the national wealth, and mighty men of valor as chapter 25 details.

At times it might seem a little confusing because Israel and Judah are two separate nations. The wicked kings of Israel had their capital in Samaria, and there was not one righteous king Israel had since the days of Jeroboam. The southern kings of Judah had a mix of some righteous, but mostly wicked kings, that reigned as descendants of David from Jerusalem. Second Kings picks up at King Ahaziah, the eighth ruler of the northern kingdom of Israel.

A BASIC OUTLINE FOR 2 KINGS

1. Alliance between Israel and Judah. Chapters 1-9
2. Israel's prosperity, apostacy, and fall. Chapters 10-17
3. Judah survives Assyrian attack in the days of Hezekiah and Isaiah. Chapters 18-23
4. Judah eventually falls to Babylonian conquest. Chapters 23-25

MEMORABLE SCRIPTURES IN 2 KINGS:

2 Kings 2:11 "As they continued walking and talking, a chariot of fire and horses of fire separated the two of them, and Elijah went up by a whirlwind into heaven."

2 Kings 2:13-14 "He picked up the robe of Elijah that fell from him, and he returned and stood on the bank of the Jordan. [14]And he took the robe of Elijah that fell from him, and struck the water, and said, "Where is the Lord, God of Elijah?" When he had struck the water, it parted from one side to the other, and Elisha crossed over."

2 Kings 17:18-20 "Therefore the LORD was very angry with Israel and removed them from His presence. None remained except the tribe of Judah. [19]Judah also did not keep the commandments of the Lord their God, but walked in the statutes of Israel which they made. [20]The Lord rejected all the seed of Israel, afflicted them, and

gave them into the hand of plunderers until He had cast them out of His presence."

2 Kings 25:20-21 "Nebuzaradan captain of the bodyguard took them, and brought them to the king of Babylon at Riblah. [21]Then the king of Babylon struck them down and killed them at Riblah in the land of Hamath. Thus he exiled Judah from their land."

1 CHRONICLES

This is a supplemental writing to the Samuel and Kings account. First Chronicles begins with the dawn of the human race and gives the complete genealogy from Adam and the eleven chiefs of Edom are mentioned. Much of the same information given in the Samuel and Kings account are given as it covers the history of the nation of Israel from around 1010 BC (around the death of Saul) to around 970 BC (the death of King David). First Chronicles focuses on King David's reign. King David's reign is not only detailed in this account, but it is analyzed, and the emphasis seems to be on God's promise to David to have an eternal reigning bloodline which is fulfilled in Jesus Christ. It is worthy of mentioning that 1 Chronicles doesn't spend time on David's moral failings with adultery and murder as Samuel's writings did. It seems this writing is meant to encourage Israel of God's eternal plan from the beginning to have special people with a descendant of David on the throne. Of course, this promise will ultimately find its fulfillment during the millennial reign of Christ on the throne of David in Jerusalem.

In chapter 20 we see that David's men killed the remaining Nephilim that were among the Philistines.

A BASIC OUTLINE FOR 1 CHRONICLES:

1. Genealogy from Adam. Chapters 1-9

2. David's Reign. Chapters 10-29

MEMORABLE SCRIPTURES IN 1 CHRONICLES:

1 Chronicles 16:34-36 "Oh, give thanks to the LORD, for He is good; for His mercy endures forever. [35]Now say, 'Save us, O God of our salvation, and gather us and deliver us from the nations, that we may give thanks to Your holy name, to glory in Your praise. [36]Blessed is the LORD, the God of Israel, from everlasting to everlasting.'"

1 Chronicles 17:14 "I will assign him a place in My house and in My kingdom forever, and his throne will be established for all time."

2 CHRONICLES

God promised David that his seed would reign forever. For 513 years David's descendants reigned over Judah. Jesus is a direct descendant of David, and is really the true fulfillment of this prophecy. In fact, that is what Gabriel specifically told Mary when he spoke with her concerning her pregnancy (see Luke 1:26-38).

This was written at the same time 1 Chronicles was written. Ezra has traditionally been accepted as the author, but no one can say for certain. Ezra was a scribe who would have been well acquainted with the Essenes of Jesus' day. The history covered in 2 Chronicles spans 970 BC (rise of Solomon to power) to the 500s BC (when the exile to Babylon took place). It is noteworthy that Cyrus was specifically mentioned in Chronicles. He was a Persian king who allowed the Jews to return and rebuild the temple.

Like 1 Chronicles this book focuses on God's eternal plan for Israel, and His love for this special nation. We see the emphasis and focus put on the righteous kings and their acts over the wicked kings. We see Solomon and the building of the temple as a focal point in 2 Chronicles.

Chapter 20 details an amazing victory over Moab and Ammon during the reign of Jehoshaphat. The remarkable aspect to this victory is that Jehoshaphat put his faith in the true prophets for victory and sent the priestly worshippers in front of the army. As praise and worship went forth, the enemy was confused and destroyed each other. When Israel came upon the landscape full of dead bodies, it was obvious God had simply fought the battle for Israel, and now all that was left was taking all the spoils of war.

A BASIC OUTLINE FOR 2 CHRONICLES:

1. The reign of Solomon and building of the temple. Chapters 1-9
2. The kings of Judah. Chapters 10-36

MEMORABLE SCRIPTURES IN 2 CHRONICLES:

2 Chronicles 6:14 "O Lord God of Israel, there is no God like You in the heavens or on the earth, who keeps covenants and mercy with Your servants who walk before You with all their heart."

2 Chronicles 7:14 "If My people, who are called by My name, will humble themselves and pray, and seek My face and turn from their wicked ways, then I will hear from heaven, and will forgive their sin and will heal their land."

2 Chronicles 20:15 "And he said, 'Pay attention all Judah, and those dwelling in Jerusalem, and King Jehoshaphat: Thus says the Lord to you, 'Do not fear, nor be dismayed because of this great army, for the battle is not yours, but God's.'"

EZRA

Traditionally this book was written by Ezra himself. Chapters 7-10 have frequent references made to Ezra that were in the first person.

Ezra was a scribe. In the days of Jesus, these men were called scribes and were part of an elite group called the Essenes. It is important to point out that the Bible is not necessarily laid out in chronological order. After Israel was in Babylonian captivity for seventy years, Daniel was reading the scroll of Jeremiah. Jeremiah the prophet predicted Israel would only be captive for seventy years (Jeremiah 25:11-12; 29:10). Daniel was alive during these seventy years as Babylon lost power to the Persians. The Persian King Cyrus allowed the exiles to return to Israel and rebuild the temple. The first group to return was under the leadership of Zerubbabel (descendent of David) and Joshua the high priest (descendent of Aaron) in 537-516 BC. This first group rebuilt the altar, resumed sacrifices, and started to rebuild the temple. They were delayed eighteen years by armies of the north. The prophets sent to encourage them in their difficult labor were Haggai and Zechariah.

Later, the events of the book of Esther took place in Persia around 473 BC. The second return to Israel from Persia was under the leadership of Ezra around 458-457 BC. Ezra teaches the law to the people who have fallen away from God to the point of intermarrying with the idolatrous pagans around them. Ezra started helping the people move into obedience to the law during the fall feasts. This might be why to this day Israel begins their civil new year during the fall feasts instead of the Biblical new year which is in the spring. Traditionally it is believed Ezra set in place the weekly readings in synagogues, the Amidah prayer, and put in place the Sanhedrin.

The third return took place in 445-437 BC in the days of Nehemiah who rebuilt the wall. The book of Nehemiah shows the great resistance Israel was facing by the heathen around them. The prophet Malachi is believed to have been ministering during the days of Nehemiah.

A BASIC OUTLINE FOR EZRA:

1. The first return to the land. Chapters 1-2
2. The temple finished being rebuilt. Chapters 3-6
3. Finally Ezra's return and ministry influence. Chapters 7-10

A MEMORABLE SCRIPTURE IN EZRA:

Ezra 7:10 "Ezra had prepared his heart to seek the Law of the Lord, he was doing so and teaching the statutes and judgments in Israel."

NEHEMIAH

Nehemiah's name means "God has comforted." Nehemiah was the king's cupbearer (Nehemiah 1:11) in Shushan, Persia. When he learned of the breached, dilapidated walls around Jerusalem, he came under a great burden to return and help the work.

It is believed that Ezra actually wrote the book of Nehemiah. After the ten northern tribes were exiled by Assyria, the capital city of Samaria became filled with foreigners (2 Kings 17:24) who intermarried with the remaining Jews in the land. Into the days of Jesus, these were the Samaritans who were looked down upon by the Jews in Jerusalem.

When Nehemiah was rebuilding the wall, some of these Samaritans tried to offer their assistance. Nehemiah knew these people were deeply involved in idolatry and pagan beliefs. If he had accepted their help, they would have tried to push their beliefs into the temple worship, therefore their help was denied (Ezra 4:1-3; Nehemiah 2:19-20). This denial was met with hostility. God revealed to the prophet Daniel that the walls of Jerusalem would be rebuilt in troublesome times (Daniel 9:25).

Sanballat and others ridiculed and resisted the work of rebuilding the walls. Even in the midst of resistance and hostility, the reconstructing of the walls took place in fifty-two days. The people worked day and night in shifts with a trowel in one hand, and sword in the other. Because of how quickly the work took place, the people acknowledged that God helped them in their endeavor (Nehemiah 6:16). It is very likely that the prophet Malachi was alive and ministering during the days of Nehemiah.

A BASIC OUTLINE FOR NEHEMIAH:

1. Nehemiah rebuilds the walls. Chapters 1-6
2. The ministry of Ezra. Chapters 7-10
3. Nehemiah's ministry. Chapters 11-13

A MEMORABLE SCRIPTURE IN NEHEMIAH:

Nehemiah 5:19 "Remember me, O my God, for good, according to all that I have done for this people."

ESTHER

The author of the scroll of Esther is not stated, but some have believed it to either be Mordecai or Ezra the scribe. It was written in the middle of the great restoration taking place in Jerusalem. Esther's name comes from the word "stara" which is Persian for star. Her Hebrew birth name was Hadassah which means "myrtle."

It is obvious Satan was trying to stop Israel from reforming as a nation, instituting offerings and worship at the temple in Jerusalem, and the stage being set for the coming Messiah. The events of the book took place from 486-465 BC, and Esther became queen around 479 BC. The book of Daniel gives insight into the spiritual warfare in the heavens, mentioning the princes of Persia and Greece (Daniel 10:20). Today the land under the Prince of Persia is Iran. Iran is currently one of Israel's greatest enemies. Israel is still facing spiritual warfare from the Prince of Persia to this day. In a very similar way, the Gaza strip was the ancient land of the Philistines. Israel today is still facing great warfare from that land mass. Ancient principalities are still at work to destroy Israel and to try to stop the coming of Christ to Israel.

What is interesting and worth noting is that prayer and fasting brought the breakthrough in this spiritual battle written of in the book of Esther. A national beauty contest resulted in Esther becoming queen. A plan to exterminate the Jews by Haman was exposed by Mordecai to Esther. Esther risked her life to approach the king about this plot. God turned the situation around, causing Haman to be hung on his own gallows that he had built for Mordecai the Jew.

This great victory is still celebrated by the Jewish community to this day. Many Christians also celebrate Purim. It is common during Purim celebrations to have costume parties, eat hamantaschen cookies, read the story written in the scroll of Esther, and even put on a play of the events.

Some believe Haman is a picture and type of the antichrist, and Haman's ten sons prophetically foreshadow the ten kings that will align with the antichrist. The antichrist and the ten kings are pictured in Revelation with the beast that had ten horns.

The message of Esther is one of courage and the power of prayer and fasting to turn impossible situations around.

A BASIC OUTLINE FOR ESTHER:

1. The Jews that were in the Shushan Persian court. Chapters 1-2
2. The threat of annihilation of the Jews. Chapters 3-5
3. The Jews overcome, and God turns an impossible situation around. Chapters 6-10

MEMORABLE SCRIPTURES IN ESTHER:

Esther 2:15 "When the turn came for Esther, the daughter of Abihail the uncle of Mordecai, who had taken her as his own daughter, to go in to the king, she asked for nothing except what the king's eunuch Hegai, who had charge of the women, advised. Now Esther obtained favor in the sight of all who saw her."

Esther 4:14 "For if you remain silent at this time, protection and deliverance for the Jews will be ordained from some other place, but you and your father's house shall be destroyed. And who knows if you may have attained royal position for such a time as this?"

Esther 9:23-28 "So the Jews accepted what had begun as tradition as Mordecai had written to them. 24Haman, the son of Hammedatha, the Agagite, the enemy of all the Jews, had plotted against the Jews to destroy them, and had cast Pur (that is, cast lots), to crush and destroy them. 25But when Esther came before the king, he ordered by letter that the wicked plot which Haman had devised against the Jews should come upon his own head, and that he and his sons should be hanged on the gallows. 26Therefore, they call these days Purim on the basis of the name Pur. Furthermore, based on all the information of this letter, along with what they had seen in this regard and what had happened to them, 27the Jews instituted and accepted as tradition for themselves, for their descendants, and for all joining with them not to fail in observing the celebration of these two days as prescribed and as specified in each and every year. [28]These days should be remembered and celebrated throughout every generation, every family, province, and city, so that these days of Purim will not lose their significance among the Jews, and the commemoration of these days will not cease among their descendants."

JOB

Job was most likely written in the days of Solomon by scribes who were the keepers of the Word of God. The story itself is one of the oldest stories in the Bible. The story most likely took place around 2000 BC. If this is true, it is probable that Nimrod was the world leader of the Middle East of this time, and Canaan and Egypt were both populating and growing in their wicked idolatry and occult practices.

In these days God had a priesthood that was in the order of Melchizedek (Genesis 14:18-20). Moses' father-in-law Jethro, whom the Bible calls a priest in Midian (Exodus 18:1), also had a similar priesthood in the order of Melchizedek. Job would offer sacrifices to God on the altar he had built unto the Lord. Job's priesthood over his family was so powerful that Satan himself admitted he could not touch Job because of a hedge of protection around him, his family, and all he had (Job 1:9-11). If the blood of Job's sacrifices could have that much spiritual power to cause purification and protection for his family from Satan, how much more does the blood of Jesus cleanse and protect us today?

God is impressed with Job and speaks of him as blameless and upright. God then calls Satan's attention to Job and allows Satan to attack him. Once God lifted His protection, Satan attacked Job in:

- His livelihood—his farm animals were killed.
- His family—his ten children were killed.
- His health—Job developed painful boils.

• His friends—turned into accusers.

In all of Job's suffering, he never "cursed God and died" as his own wife suggested. Job never sinned against the Lord, nor did he abandon his faith in God. In fact, Job, through his suffering, saw the future Redeemer of mankind. This is revealed when he stated, "For I know that my Redeemer lives, and He will stand at last on the earth; [26]and after my skin is destroyed, yet in my flesh I will see God" (Job 19:25-26). This is an obvious reference to the resurrection of the dead in Christ.

It is also interesting to note that Leviathan is revealed in the book of Job in great detail. This spirit is also seen as the beast with seven heads and ten horns in the book of Revelation. Leviathan is the spirit of pride that brings great destruction. Job probably has the greatest description of this spirit in the entire Word of God. Because of what Job went through, it would have been such a great test of human pride to endure this, not curse God, and to not abandon faith in Him. It is therefore little wonder that the spirit of pride would be exposed so thoroughly in this writing. Isaiah also exposes Leviathan in Isaiah 27:1, "In that day the Lord with His fierce and great and strong sword shall punish Leviathan the fleeing serpent, even Leviathan the twisted serpent; and He shall slay the dragon that is in the sea." Some believe that the Leviathan of Revelation prophetically speaks of Israel's last great battle with the antichrist and his kingdom right before Jesus comes.

A BASIC OUTLINE OF JOB:

1. Background, historical setting, and Satan's activity. Chapters 1-3
2. Job's conversations with his three accusing friends. Chapters 4-31
3. Elihu presumes God's justice in punishing Job for his hidden sin. Chapters 32-37

4. God gives speeches of His vast knowledge and greatness. Chapters 38-41
5. Job's restoration. Chapter 42

MEMORABLE SCRIPTURES IN JOB:

Job 1:21 "He said, 'Naked I came from my mother's womb, and naked will I return there. The Lord gave, and the LORD has taken away; blessed be the name of the LORD.'"

Job 14:1 "Man who is born of a woman is of few days and full of trouble."

Job 16:2 "I have heard many such things; miserable comforters are you all!"

Job 42:6 "Therefore I abhor myself, and repent in dust and ashes."

PSALMS

This book is called Tehillim in Hebrew which is translated "praises." Most psalms are songs of praise and prayers of thanksgiving to God for His mighty work in Israel. It most likely began to be compiled in the days of Solomon and possibly was finished in the days of Ezra the scribe. There are 150 chapters that comprise around 100 songs. It was intended to be a songbook similar to a hymnal of today. Psalms is also filled with much prophetic symbolism. There are various authors of these psalms:

- David is attributed with 73 psalms (nearly half)
- Asaph (David's music director, a Levite, 1 Chronicles 6:29) is attributed with 12 psalms
- The Sons of Korah (Levites) attributed with 10 psalms
- Moses wrote a psalm
- Heman the Ezrahite wrote a psalm
- Ethan the Ezrahite wrote a psalm
- Solomon is also attributed with a few psalms

Varying authors over a span of time reflecting personal times of happiness, sorrow, tragedy, and divine inspiration cause the book of Psalms to be relatable and beloved down through the ages. To help in personal study, some Bible scholars have broken down Psalms in this way:

1. Liturgy: Chapters 120-130
2. Messianic prophecy: Chapters 2, 16, 22, 25, 69, 110
3. Repentance: Chapters 6, 32, 51
4. Personal: Chapters 23, 27, 37
5. Judgment on God's enemies: Chapters 69, 109
6. Historical: Chapters 78, 105, 106
7. Praise: Chapters 95, 100, 146-150
8. Alphabetical: Chapters 25, 111-112, 119
9. Supplications of God's righteous people: Chapters 17, 20, 40, 55

David had such a heart for the Lord and His presence. He went to great lengths to get the Ark of the Covenant moved to Jerusalem. Then David pitched a tent for it and established daily worship and prayer around the Ark. It is believed David made a reference to this in Psalm 91 when he stated "abiding in the shadow of His wings." When the rising sun would shine through the tent housing the Ark, it would cast a shadow of the wings of the cherubim onto those who were worshipping near the Ark.

Some highlights in Psalms are the shepherd psalm (23), David's remorse and deep repentance after his sin (51), a great psalm of praise (100), and the deep love of God's word (119).

Psalm 119:105 calls God's Word a lamp unto our feet and light unto our path. In Exodus 25:33 the menorah (lamp in the Tabernacle) had a total of 66 knops, buds, and bowls carved into it, if each is counted individually. Our canonized Protestant Bible has exactly 66 books of the Bible. Psalm 117 is exactly in the middle of the Bible, with 594 chapters before it and 594 chapters after it. Psalm 117:1-2 reads: "Praise the Lord, all you nations! Exalt Him, all you peoples! 2 For His merciful kindness is great toward us, and the faithfulness of the Lord endures forever. Praise the Lord!" God's word is truly a gift to the entire world.

A BASIC OUTLINE FOR PSALMS:

1. Psalms Chapters 1-41
2. Psalms Chapters 42-72
3. Psalms Chapters 73-89
4. Psalms Chapters 90-106
5. Psalms Chapters 107-150

MEMORABLE SCRIPTURES IN PSALMS:

Psalm 1:1-3 "Blessed is the man who walks not in the counsel of the ungodly, nor stands in the path of sinners, nor sits in the seat of scoffers; [2]but his delight is in the law of the Lord, and in His law he meditates day and night. [3]He will be like a tree planted by the rivers of water, that brings forth its fruit in its season; its leaf will not wither, and whatever he does will prosper."

Psalm 2:1-6 "Why do the nations rage, and the peoples plot in vain? [2]The kings of the earth set themselves, and the rulers take counsel together, against the Lord and against His anointed, saying, [3]'Let us tear off their bonds and cast away their ropes from us.' [4]He who sits in the heavens laughs; the Lord ridicules them. [5]Then He will speak to them in His wrath and terrify them in His burning anger: [6]'I have installed My king on Zion, My holy hill.'"

Psalm 8:1 "O Lord, our Lord, how excellent is Your name in all the earth!"

Psalm 23:1 "The Lord is my shepherd; I shall not want."

Psalm 51:10-11 "Create in me a clean heart, O God, and renew a right spirit within me.

11 Do not cast me away from Your presence, and do not take Your Holy Spirit from me."

Psalm 119:11 "Your word I have hidden in my heart, that I might not sin against You."

Psalm 121:1-2 "I will lift up my eyes to the hills, from where does my help come?

2 My help comes from the Lord, who made heaven and earth."

Psalm 133:1-3 "Behold, how good and how pleasant it is for brothers to dwell together in unity! [2]It is like precious oil upon the head, that runs down on the beard—even Aaron's beard—and going down to the collar of his garments; [3]as the dew of Hermon, that descends upon the mountains of Zion, for there the Lord has commanded the blessing, even life forever."

PROVERBS

Scholars agree that the Proverbs were primarily written by Solomon. Solomon had asked God for wisdom at the beginning of his reign over Israel (1 Kings 3:12), and God granted his request. The Hebrew title to this book is "The Proverbs of Solomon." Solomon took the throne in 970 BC after the death of his father David. Not much is known about King Lemuel (31:1) or Agur (30:1), but they did contribute to what we have in the book of Proverbs. First Kings 4:32 states that Solomon wrote 3,000 proverbs, but we only see a total of 560 proverbs in the book of Proverbs. Not all of Solomon's wisdom was contained in what we have today. The Hebrew word for Proverbs is *mishile*, taken from the Hebrew word *mashal*, which means "to rule."

There was always an ongoing process of compiling what we have today as the Bible. Much of this compiling happened in the days of Solomon and later with Ezra. We read in the days of Hezekiah (25:1) that some of these proverbs were copied and added. Hezekiah's scribes would have added these around 730 BC. There were scribes, later known in the days of Jesus as the Essenes, that meticulously guarded these writings to keep their integrity through the ages. Scribes were specially trained to handle the copying of manuscripts with perfect detail. This is why the Dead Sea Scrolls are exactly what we hold in our hands today.

James is the wisdom book of the New Testament. James 1:5 teaches us to ask God if we need wisdom, because He will give it to us liberally. Proverbs 4:7 teaches us that "wisdom is principal; therefore get wisdom and with all your getting, get understanding." As we understand each proverb, we learn the truth that "the fear of the Lord is the beginning of wisdom" (1:7). The book of Proverbs is a practical book intended to impart skillful and godly wisdom to the reader. An example of this is in chapters 1-9, as we see the contrast between wisdom and folly. Folly is seen connected with immorality and violence.

In Proverbs, Solomon discusses issues like hard work ethics, handling money well, the importance of sexual purity, overcoming temptation, advice in child rearing, the folly of drunkenness, and the danger of laziness.

A BASIC OUTLINE OF PROVERBS:

1. Contrasting wisdom and foolishness. Chapters 1-9
2. Contrasting right and wrong. Chapters 10-22:16
3. The words of the wise. Chapters 22:17-24
4. Proverbs that were by Hezekiah's scribes. Chapters 25-29
5. The Proverbs of Agur and Lemuel. Chapters 30-31

MEMORABLE SCRIPTURES IN PROVERBS:

Proverbs 3:5-6 "Trust in the Lord with all your heart, and lean not on your own understanding; [6]in all your ways acknowledge Him, and He will direct your paths."

Proverbs 6:6 "Go to the ant, you sluggard! Consider her ways and be wise."

Proverbs 10:1 "A wise son makes a glad father, but a foolish son is the grief of his mother."

Proverbs 11:22 "As a jewel of gold in a swine's snout, so is a fair woman who is without discretion."

Proverbs 13:24 "He who spares his rod hates his son, but he who loves him disciplines him early."

Proverbs 15:1 "A soft answer turns away wrath, but grievous words stir up anger."

Proverbs 16:3 "Commit your works to the Lord, and your thoughts will be established."

Proverbs 17:28 "Even a fool, when he holds his peace, is counted wise; and he who shuts his lips is esteemed a man of understanding."

Proverbs 20:1 "Wine is a mocker, strong drink is raging, and whoever is deceived by it is not wise."

Proverbs 22:1 "A good name is rather to be chosen than great riches, and loving favor rather than silver and gold."

Proverbs 27:6 "Faithful are the wounds of a friend, but the kisses of an enemy are deceitful."

Proverbs 28:1 "The wicked flee when no man pursues, but the righteous are bold as a lion."

Proverbs 31:10-11 "Who can find a virtuous woman? For her worth is far above rubies. [11]The heart of her husband safely trusts in her, so that he will have no lack of gain."

ECCLESIASTES

The book of Ecclesiastes was written sometime in the 900s BC by Solomon. Even though Solomon's name is not mentioned, the author is identified as the "son of David" (1:1), "king over Israel in Jerusalem (1:12), and says he had "more wisdom than all they that have been before him" (1:16). This seems to be referring to Solomon. The Hebrew title Ecclesiastes actually means "one who convenes and speaks at an assembly." The Greek word means "preacher."

Solomon had backslidden by disobeying the Bible in marrying foreign women who led him astray into worshipping their gods and idols. Ecclesiastes shows Solomon's miserable condition. It teaches us that apart from God, life is ultimately meaningless, empty, and unsatisfying. The central themes seem to be "under the sun" and "vanity."

Solomon looks at life through his backslidden condition and sees that all is vanity. He states that human wisdom, human labor, human design, envy, riches, popularity, and greed are all vanity. His attitude becomes that people simply live, work hard, die, and another inherits their wealth. He saw times that the wicked prospered over the righteous, the poor were oppressed by the rich, and all learning and pleasure led to emptiness. In the end, Solomon concludes all that will matter when your life is over is to "fear God, and keep His commandments: for this is the whole duty of man" (12:13). Sometimes it will seem that life isn't fair, or circumstances simply don't make sense, but Ecclesiastes teaches us there is still a God who understands all things.

A BASIC OUTLINE FOR ECCLESIASTES:

1. A look at how fleeting life is. Chapter 1:1-11
2. The limitations of wisdom. Chapters 1:12-2:26
3. There is a season for all things. Chapter 3
4. Being content and dealing with disappointment. Chapters 4-5
5. No satisfaction in this life. Chapters 6-8
6. Applying wisdom to life. Chapters 9-10
7. The fear of God is true wisdom. Chapters 11-12

MEMORABLE SCRIPTURES IN ECCLESIASTES:

Ecclesiastes 3:1 "To everything there is a season, a time for every purpose under heaven."

Ecclesiastes 4:9-10 "Two are better than one, because there is a good reward for their labor together. [10]For if they fall, then one will help up his companion. But woe to him who is alone when he falls and has no one to help him up."

Ecclesiastes 9:10 "Whatever your hands find to do, do with your strength; for there is no work or planning or knowledge or wisdom in Sheol, the place where you are going."

Ecclesiastes 12:1 "Remember your Creator in the days of your youth."

Ecclesiastes 12:13-14 "Now all has been heard. Let us hear the conclusion of the matter: Fear God and keep His commandments, for this is the whole duty of man. [14]For God will bring every deed into judgment, including every secret thing, whether good or evil."

SONG OF SOLOMON

Because of the first verse in Song of Solomon, we can conclude that the author is Solomon himself. The Hebrew *Shir Ha Shirim* literally translated "Song of Songs." This was written between 970-930 BC during his reign as king. It is interesting that Song of Solomon is read by the Jews every year during Passover just as Ruth is read every Pentecost. The Jews feel that God betrothed Himself to Israel at Sinai, and Passover is a renewal of the blood covenant God has established with His true people. The Song of Solomon is made up of seven poems written by Solomon. They are not in chronological order. Solomon's poems share intimate thoughts and conversations that took place between him and this simple peasant girl at their initial meeting, betrothal period, marriage, and consummation of marriage.

Song of Solomon is a very unique book of the Bible. It has some layered meanings in it. The most accepted interpretation is that Solomon is a type of Christ, and the Shulammite is a type of the bride of Christ. Many believe Abishag was actually the Shulammite. Abishag was chosen to take care of King David during his failing health before he died (1 Kings 1:3).

David's son Adonijah tried to take the throne (1 Kings 1-2), and after David's death, Adonijah asked for Abishag as his wife (1 Kings 2:13-18). Solomon felt this was part of a conspiracy to usurp the throne and had Adonijah killed for this request (1 Kings 2:13-46). It could also be that Solomon had a great love for Abishag, and Adonijah's attitude was that since Solomon took the throne from him, at least he should be given Abishag as his wife. Solomon had many wives in his harem. Many of them were probably obtained through political means since alliances between kings of nations involved giving of a daughter as a wife. With that said, it is obvious in Song of Solomon that he had a great love for Abishag above the others in his harem.

An alternate view that is very interesting is that Solomon is a picture and type of the antichrist. The Shulammite actually is in love with a shepherd (picture of the true Christ), but King Solomon (antichrist) pursues her and puts her into his harem (false church) thus separating her from her true love.

Song of Solomon also shows the love story between two people who fall in love and get married. There is a lot of godly wisdom about love and marriage that can be gleaned from Song of Solomon.

So we see that this collection of poems can be an allegory of the love between a man and woman, God's relationship to Israel, or Christ's relationship to the church. It can even have a deeper revelation of a battle for God's remnant bride in regard to the antichrist, and his false church, trying to seduce God's people away from Him.

A BASIC OUTLINE FOR SONG OF SOLOMON:

1. The king's court and the Shulammite. Chapters 1-2:7
2. The Shulammite thinking of her country lover. Chapters 2:8-3:5
3. The king's appeal. Chapters 3:6-4:7
4. The shepherd lover. Chapters 4:8-6:3
5. The kingly lover. Chapters 6:4-7:9
6. The Shulammite and her lover. Chapters 7:10-8:14

MEMORABLE SCRIPTURES IN SONG OF SOLOMON:

Song of Solomon 1:2 "Let him kiss me with the kisses of his mouth! For your love is better than wine."

Song of Solomon 2:4 “He brought me to the banquet house, and his banner over me was love.”

Song of Solomon 8:7 “Many waters cannot quench love, neither can floods drown it.”

ISAIAH

Isaiah was a prophet who lived during the period of the kings in Israel. He started his ministry around the time King Uzziah died (Isaiah 6:1). You can read about the time period he prophesied from 2 Kings 15 through 2 Kings 20. It is important to understand the spiritual condition of Israel during the time of Isaiah. Isaiah's name means “Salvation of Yahweh.” Isaiah was the author of this book of the Bible. The scroll of Isaiah would have been written between 740-680 BC (around sixty years). Isaiah resided in Jerusalem during a time of great spiritual and political upheaval in Israel. Other prophets who lived during this time were Hosea, Amos, Micah, and possibly Joel. Isaiah prophesied during the reigns of kings Uzziah, Jotham, Ahaz, and Hezekiah. Tradition states that Isaiah was sawed in half under Manasseh, the wicked son of Hezekiah, who reigned from 696-642 BC. Isaiah was no doubt one of those the writer of Hebrews had in mind when he stated the world was not worthy of these righteous ones: “They were stoned, they were sawn in two, were tempted, and were slain with the sword” (Hebrews 11:37). When King Uzziah died, God's judgment came to the northern kingdom of Israel as Assyria conquered Damascus in 732 BC and their capital city of Samaria in 722 BC. The northern ten tribes of Israel were taken captive to Assyria, and the land came under Assyrian control and domination. From Isaiah's perspective, the fate of both Judah and Israel were to ultimately go into captivity because of their sin. The few righteous kings of Judah simply delayed this inevitability.

Isaiah had some incredible insight into the coming Messiah, judgments Israel would face for their sin, and encouraging words to the righteous. One of Israel's great enemies during the days of Isaiah was

Assyria. Even secular researchers have mentioned how brutal Assyria was. The prophet Jonah had such strong negative feelings toward the Assyrians, he refused to go minister to them in their capital city of Nineveh until God allowed circumstances that changed his mind.

One of the most incredible stories of deliverance in the entire Bible took place during the days of Hezekiah. According to the word of the Lord through Isaiah, an angel was sent to destroy the Assyrian army that came to destroy and exile Judah. In one night, around 100,000 men of the Assyrian army were killed by this angel. Josephus records this took place because of a plague, though the Bible doesn't give the details of how they died. Josephus goes on to state that the military commanders were afraid the plague would kill the rest of the men so they retreated to their homeland where the king was assassinated. This incredible deliverance was written about in three different places in the Bible: 2 Kings 18-19, 2 Chronicles 32:1-23, Isaiah 36-37.

Isaiah had a specific prediction concerning Cyrus of Persia, saying he would be the one to allow the Jews to return to their homeland (Isaiah 44-45). Daniel had read in the scroll of Jeremiah that the exile would only last seventy years. Daniel realized the seventy years were over, so he began to pray and fast for the return of the Jews in Daniel chapter 9. This set off a series of events that ultimately led to the return of the Jews, the rebuilding of the temple, and the repairing of the wall around Jerusalem. The fact the Isaiah had predicted Cyrus by name shows the incredible accuracy of Isaiah's prophecies.

Some call Isaiah the fifth gospel because of his incredible prophecies concerning the birth, life, and death of Jesus some seven hundred years earlier. These encouraging prophecies of the ultimate redemption of all Israel were balanced by the stern warnings Isaiah gave to Israel and Judah because of their sin. Isaiah ends with a long section of chapters 40-66 describing God's ultimate restoration of Israel, the coming salvation, and the Messiah's eternal kingdom. Isaiah balanced his prophecies with God's love and sternness. The apostle Paul mentioned this balance when he wrote to consider both the kindness and sternness of God in Romans 11:22.

Jesus began His public ministry in Nazareth by reading the scroll of Isaiah (the Haftarah portion read in synagogue every Sabbath) in 61:1-2: "The Spirit of the Lord God is upon me because the Lord has anointed me to preach good news to the poor; He has sent me to heal the broken-hearted, to proclaim liberty to the captives, and the opening of the prison to those who are bound; 2 to proclaim the acceptable year of the Lord and the day of vengeance of our God; to comfort all who mourn."

Concerning end-time prophecy, Isaiah wrote of the fall of Babylon in chapter 47. It is very interesting to read this chapter, then read about the fall of Babylon in Jeremiah 51, and finally Revelation chapter 18. The correlation between the scriptures is amazing. Babylon is a picture and type of Satan's rebellious rival kingdom here on the earth. It is spiritual, but encompasses the nations of the world until Jesus comes. It seems the final manifestation of this Babylonian kingdom will be when the antichrist rules the world for a short time until Jesus comes. When God uses Babylon as a descriptive term for Satan's kingdom, it seems to always denote dark occult activity at work in conjunction with secular politics. There is a mystery Babylon that speaks of the dark arts of the occult.

A BASIC OUTLINE FOR ISAIAH:

1. Early prophecies concerning Judah. Chapters 1-35
2. Hezekiah's deliverance from Assyrian invasion. Chapters 36-39
3. The coming eternal kingdom of God to Israel. Chapters 40-66

MEMORABLE SCRIPTURES IN ISAIAH:

Isaiah 4:4-6 "When the Lord has washed away the filth of the daughters of Zion and has purged the blood of Jerusalem from the midst by the spirit of justice and by the spirit of burning, [5]then the LORD will create upon every dwelling place of Mount Zion, and upon her assemblies, a cloud and smoke by day and the shining of a flaming fire by night. For over all the glory shall be a covering. [6]There shall be a tabernacle for a shadow in the daytime from the heat, and for a place of refuge, and for a shelter from storm and from rain."

Isaiah 6:3 "One cried to another and said: 'Holy, holy, holy, is the LORD of Hosts; the whole earth is full of His glory.'"

Isaiah 7:14 "Therefore the Lord Himself shall give you a sign: The virgin shall conceive, and bear a son, and shall call his name Immanuel."

Isaiah 9:6-7 "For unto us a child is born, unto us a son is given, and the government shall be upon his shoulder. And his name shall be called Wonderful Counselor, Mighty God, Eternal Father, Prince of Peace. [7]Of the increase of his government and peace there shall be no end, upon the throne of David and over his kingdom, to order it and to establish it with justice and with righteousness, from now until forever."

Isaiah 40:31 "But those who wait upon the Lord shall renew their strength; they shall mount up with wings as eagles, they shall run and not be weary, and they shall walk and not faint."

Isaiah 41:14-16 "Do not fear, you worm Jacob, and you men of Israel. I will help you, says the LORD and your Redeemer, the Holy One of Israel. [15]See, I will make you a new sharp threshing instrument with double edges; you shall thresh the mountains, and beat them small, and shall make the hills as chaff. [16]You shall fan them, and the wind shall carry them away, and the whirlwind shall scatter them; and you shall rejoice in the LORD, and shall glory in the Holy One of Israel."

Isaiah 49:15-16 "Can a woman forget her nursing child, and have no compassion on the son of her womb? Even these may forget, yet I will not forget. [16]See, I have inscribed you on the palms of My hands; your walls are continually before Me."

Isaiah 53:1-7 "Who has believed our report? And to whom has the arm of the Lord been revealed? [2]For he grew up before Him as a tender plant and as a root out of a dry ground. He has no form or majesty that we should look upon him nor appearance that we should desire him. [3]He was despised and rejected of men, a man of sorrows and acquainted with grief. And we hid, as it were, our faces from him; he was despised, and we did not esteem him. [4]Surely he has borne our grief and carried our sorrows; Yet we esteemed him stricken, smitten of God, and afflicted. [5]But he was wounded for our transgressions, he was bruised for our iniquities; the chastisement of our peace was upon him, and by his stripes we are healed. [6]All of us like sheep have gone astray; each of us has turned to his own way, but the Lord has laid on him the iniquity of us all. [7]He was oppressed, and he was afflicted, yet he opened not his mouth; he was brought as a lamb to the slaughter, and as a sheep before its shearers is silent, so he opened not his mouth."

Isaiah 54:17 "No weapon that is formed against you shall prosper, and every tongue that shall rise against you in judgment, you shall condemn. This is the heritage of the servants of the Lord, and their vindication is from Me, says the LORD."

Isaiah 66:18-24 "For I know their works and their thoughts. The time shall come to gather all nations and tongues. And they shall come and see My glory. [19]I will set a sign among them, and send from them survivors to the nations: to Tarshish, Pul, and Lud—who draw the bow—to Tubal, and Javan, to the coastlands afar off who have not heard My fame nor seen My glory. And they shall declare My glory among the nations. [20]They shall bring all your brothers out of all nations as an offering to the Lord on horses, and in chariots, and in litters, and on mules, and on swift beasts to My holy mountain Jerusalem, says the Lord, as the sons of Israel bring an offering in a clean vessel into the house of the Lord. [21]I will also take some of them for priests and for Levites, says the Lord. [22]For as the new heavens and the new earth which I will make shall remain before Me, says the Lord, so shall your descendants and your name remain. [23]From one New Moon to another, and from one Sabbath to another, all flesh shall come to worship before Me, says the Lord. [24]And they shall go forth and look on the corpses of the men who have transgressed against Me. For their worm shall not die, nor shall their fire be quenched. And they shall be an abhorrence to all flesh."

JEREMIAH

Jeremiah's ministry took place the years right before Judah was taken captive to Babylon. Jeremiah was of the priestly bloodline. He was the son of Hilkiah, a priest who lived in the area of Benjamin. Jeremiah was the author of this book, with the help of the scribe named Baruch who was his assistant. Jeremiah probably spoke and Baruch documented in detail what was said. This book was written approximately 585 BC. Jeremiah is known as the weeping prophet, as he had such a love for God's people and land. The writings of Jeremiah are not in chronological order. One needs to understand that in reading it. The Assyrian kingdom declined after the destruction of Nineveh in 612 BC. Then Babylon under Nebuchadnezzar became the strongest military force of that day.

Jeremiah experienced the great revival and reform under Josiah who ruled from 640-609 BC. Jeremiah began his ministry around 627 BC which was right in the middle of this great revival under Josiah. Josiah was later killed in 609 BC. Jeremiah was Josiah's friend, but after his death, the wicked kings and leaders of the land strongly opposed Jeremiah's message of calling for repentance and predicting judgment.

God gave Judah forty years of Jeremiah's ministry to repent, but they did not. Jeremiah was called from birth (1:6), predicted a nation from afar coming to bring judgment (5:15), and was mocked, beaten, and imprisoned in a muddy well (chapter 38) for his true prophecies. Nevertheless, his prophecies came to pass as Babylon invaded (chapter 52). Jeremiah told the people to submit to the Babylonians as this was God's will and judgment, but the people rebelled. This rebellion resulted in the complete destruction of Jerusalem and the temple. Jeremiah took inventory of everything Nebuchadnezzar took from the temple. Even though there was no canonized Bible at this time, the prophet Daniel obtained a scroll of Jeremiah that he took very seriously. While reading it, he realized Jeremiah predicted the captivity in Babylon would only last seventy years (25:11). The seventy years were up, so Daniel committed himself to prayer and fasting to see Israel return and rebuild. Matthew also points to Jeremiah's prophecy being fulfilled regarding infants being killed in Bethlehem in Matthew 2:17. When Jesus asked the disciples "who do people say that I am?" some said he was Jeremiah the prophet in Matthew 16:13-14.

Jeremiah followed the ministry of Isaiah about sixty years. Jeremiah's ministry took place during the kings Josiah (very righteous king), Jehoahaz, Jehoiakim, Zedekiah, and Gedaliah (who was assassinated). Zephaniah and Habakkuk were also prophets during the beginning of Jeremiah's ministry, but Jeremiah was most likely the only true prophet right before the exile. Like Elijah, Jeremiah seemed to feel isolated, discouraged, and depressed at what was happening in Israel. These feelings were written down in Lamentations. Daniel followed Jeremiah's ministry in Babylon.

Right before the exile, Jeremiah seemed to be the only true prophet alive prophesying. Yet there were many false prophets predicting the opposite of what Jeremiah was saying. The Bible seems to indicate that this is the same pattern right before Jesus returns. There would be some true prophetic voices, but there would also be many false prophets and great deception. Jeremiah was rejected by his neighbors (11:19-21), his own priestly family (12:6), the unfaithful priests and the false prophets (20:1-2), his friends (20:10), the people (26:8), and finally the king (36:23). Jeremiah adamantly prophesied judgment for the sin of the people, and gave admonitions of hope and restoration as God would not completely abandon His people even though He judges them. Jeremiah foretold of the coming Messiah (23:5-6), spoke of the good and false shepherd (23:18-40), the seventy years in Babylon (25:11), taught prophetic insight into the New Covenant (31:31-34), and predicted the restoration of the Jews (chapters 30-33). Traditionally some believe Jeremiah hid the Ark of the Covenant so that Nebuchadnezzar could not take it to Babylon.

Paul stated the gifts of God are without repentance in Romans 11:29. This means God does not change His mind about it. Jeremiah shows us we are called even from birth for a purpose and we have a destiny. After the destruction of Jerusalem, Jeremiah chose to stay with the remnant of the land, and fled with them when they eventually went into Egypt.

A BASIC OUTLINE FOR JEREMIAH:

1. Jeremiah's call from birth. Chapter 1
2. The sinful condition of Judah. Chapters 2-6
3. The temple, the Law of God, and the Covenant. Chapters 7-12
4. Predictions of coming captivity. Chapters 13-18
5. Confrontations with the wicked leaders of the land. Chapters 19-29
6. The ultimate promise of restoration. Chapters 30-33
7. Babylon's invasion and destruction of Judah. Chapters 34-39
8. Moving to Egypt. Chapters 40-45
9. Foreign nations in prophecy. Chapters 46-51
10. The fall of Jerusalem and destruction of the temple. Chapter 52

MEMORABLE SCRIPTURES IN JEREMIAH:

Jeremiah 1:4-10 "Now the word of the Lord came to me, saying,
5'Before I formed you in the womb I knew you; and before you were
born I sanctified you, and I ordained you a prophet to the nations.'
6Then I said, 'Ah, Lord God! Truly, I cannot speak, for I am a youth.'

7But the LORD said to me, 'Do not say, 'I am a youth.' For you shall go
everywhere that I send you, and whatever I command you, you shall
speak. 8Do not be afraid of their faces. For I am with you to deliver
you,' says the LORD. 9Then the LORD put forth His hand and touched
my mouth. And the LORD said to me, "Now, I have put My words in
your mouth. 10See, I have this day set you over the nations and over
the kingdoms, to root out and to pull down, to destroy and to throw
down, to build and to plant."

Jeremiah 6:16 "Thus says the LORD: Stand in the ways and see, and ask for the old paths where the good way is and walk in it, and you shall find rest for your souls. But they said, 'We will not walk in it.'"

Jeremiah 17:5-8 "Thus says the LORD: Cursed is the man who
trusts in man and makes flesh his strength, and whose heart departs
from the Lord. 6For he will be like a bush in the desert and will not
see when good comes, but will inhabit the parched places in the wilderness, in a salt land and not inhabited. 7Blessed is the man who
trusts in the LORD, and whose hope is the LORD. 8For he shall be as a
tree planted by the waters, and that spreads out its roots by the river,
and shall not fear when heat comes, but its leaf shall be green, and it
shall not be anxious in the year of drought, neither shall cease from
yielding fruit."

Jeremiah 17:9 "The heart is more deceitful than all things and desperately wicked; who can understand it?"

Jeremiah 18:6 "O house of Israel, can I not do with you as this potter? says the LORD. As the clay is in the potter's hand, so are you in My hand, O house of Israel."

Jeremiah 29:11 "For I know the plans that I have for you, says the Lord, plans for peace and not for evil, to give you a future and a hope."

Jeremiah 30:8 "For it shall come to pass in that day, says the LORD of Hosts, that I shall break his yoke from off their neck and tear away their bonds, and strangers shall no longer make them their slaves."

Jeremiah 31:3 "The LORD has appeared to him from afar, saying: Indeed, I have loved you with an everlasting love; therefore with lovingkindness I have drawn you."

Jeremiah 33:3 "Call to Me, and I will answer you, and show you great and mighty things which you do not know."

LAMENTATIONS

Most scholars believe Baruch wrote down what Jeremiah was saying in this book entitled Lamentations (2 Chronicles 35:25). It was probably written around the same time Jeremiah was written. Lamentations is a word for a dirge, which is a funeral song. It is a sorrow-filled poem from Jeremiah's heart about the destruction of Jerusalem. In the original Hebrew text, the first four chapters are acrostically arranged. The twenty-two verses in each of these (sixty-six in chapter 3) use the twenty-two letters of the Hebrew alphabet. This shows that it is poetic. This is not much different from the outline of Psalm 119 which uses ascending Hebrew letters in its text. It broke Jeremiah's heart to see the great revival under Josiah, and now see things end the way it did. Lamentations teaches us that God gives us space to repent, but if we do not truly repent of our sins, judgment will certainly come.

Lamentations truly gave Jeremiah the name "the weeping prophet." The sight of the destruction of Jerusalem caused Jeremiah to weep profusely (1:16). Jeremiah wept seeing the children taken into captivity (1:5) as he cried to the Lord, "Restore us to Yourself, O Lord, that we may return! Renew our days as of old, 22 unless You have utterly rejected us, and are very angry with us" (5:21-22).

Let us remember that God will chastise His people. Hebrews 12:11 "No discipline seems to be joyful at the time, but grievous. Yet afterward it yields the peaceful fruit of righteousness in those who have been trained by it." Also, we understand from God's Word that He promises restoration after His discipline. Hosea 6:1 "Come, let us return to the Lord, for He has torn, and He will heal us. He has struck, and He will bind us up." Along those lines, Joel shows us that God allows the enemy to come in to destroy and devour like locusts because of our sin, but if we repent, He will drive the enemy away and restore the years the locusts have eaten (Joel 1-2).

God allowed this destruction and captivity for a time, but the days came when God restored Israel to the land, restored Jerusalem, restored the wall, and restored the temple.

A BASIC OUTLINE OF LAMENTATIONS:

1. Jerusalem's destruction. Chapter 1
2. God's judgment has come. Chapter 2
3. Suffering and finding hope in God. Chapter 3
4. Remembering the glory of Jerusalem and her present destruction. Chapter 4
5. A desperate cry for God's mercy. Chapter 5

MEMORABLE SCRIPTURES IN LAMENTATIONS:

Lamentations 3:22-24 "It is of the LORD's mercies that we are not consumed; His compassions do not fail. [23]They are new every morning; great is Your faithfulness. [24]'The LORD is my portion,' says my soul, 'therefore I will hope in Him.'"

Lamentations 5:19-21 "You, O LORD, remain forever; Your throne endures from generation to generation. [20]Why do You forget us forever, and forsake us for so long a time? [21]Restore us to Yourself, O LORD, that we may return! Renew our days as of old."

EZEKIEL

Like the prophet Jeremiah, Ezekiel was of the bloodline of Aaron. He was a priest and a prophet of God. Ezekiel, along with Daniel, were God's prophets while Israel was in exile. This book was probably written between 590-570 BC.

Ezekiel offered hope of restoration while reminding the people that it was their sin that led them into exile in the first place. Ezekiel speaks clearly of personal sin when he states: "All souls are Mine. The soul of the father, so also the soul of the son is Mine. The soul who sins shall die. 5 But if a man is righteous and does that which is lawful and right… 9 has walked in My statutes, and has kept My judgments to deal truly, he is righteous and shall surely live, says the Lord God" (Ezekiel 18:4-5, 9).

Ezekiel had amazing and at times bizarre visions and revelations from the Lord. Ezekiel had an incredible vision of God, His throne, and the cherubim that guard the throne (1:1-25). He taught us the incredible importance of spiritual watchmen whose prayers create a hedge of protection and avert judgment and destruction (3:17-21). He received a powerful revelation of the prince of Tyre in 28:1-19 that has an obvious dual reference to Lucifer along with the aforementioned prince. Many believe that the valley of dry bones Ezekiel saw was a reference to the Holocaust that took place under Hitler. Ezekiel reveals in 38-39 the next great difficulty Israel will face is the Gog war. The Gog war will be a coalition of various nations like Russia, Iran, Turkey, and others that will attack Israel. God Himself will defend and deliver Israel in that day. From a historical perspective, the First World War freed up the land of Israel from Turkish rule. The Second World War caused the birth of the nation of Israel. The Gog war will probably be considered the Third World War, and will most likely cause Israel to sign a peace treaty with the antichrist, thus starting the tribulation time also known as the "days of Jacob's trouble."

Ezekiel prophetically saw the Messiah come to Israel and the millennial temple he would both live in and reign from (chapters 40-48). In the last eight chapters of Ezekiel, he goes into great detail describing the Millennial temple. Ezekiel revealed to those in oppression in exile that God, the great Shepherd, will eventually regather all of Israel from the ends of the earth in their homeland (see Matthew 24:31,

Zechariah 12:10). The nations that oppressed Israel's return will be defeated and judged (see Matthew 25:31-46).

A BASIC OUTLINE FOR EZEKIEL:

1. Ezekiel's call and commissioning. Chapters 1-3
2. Israel's exile, the destruction of Jerusalem, and the reason for it. Chapters 4-24
3. God will judge nations on how they treat Israel. Chapters 25-32
4. Israel in the last days before Christ returns. Chapters 33-39
5. The millennial temple and reign of Christ on the throne of David. Chapters 40-48

MEMORABLE SCRIPTURES IN EZEKIEL:

Ezekiel 18:4 "All souls are Mine. The soul of the father, so also the soul of the son is Mine. The soul who sins shall die."

Ezekiel 36:26-27 "Also, I will give you a new heart, and a new spirit I will put within you. And I will take away the stony heart out of your flesh, and I will give you a heart of flesh. [27]I will put My Spirit within you and cause you to walk in My statutes, and you will keep My judgments and do them."

Ezekiel 37:1 "The hand of the LORD was upon me, and He carried me out in the Spirit of the Lord and set me down in the midst of the valley which was full of bones."

DANIEL

Daniel was taken captive into Babylon and became the leading prophet among the wise men of Babylon. This book was written between 605-538 BC. Daniel, along with Shadrach, Meshach, and Abednego, were chosen to be among the wise and exceptional in the Babylonian kingdom who would serve in the king's court. An interesting note is that the book of Daniel was written in Aramaic and Hebrew, not just Hebrew alone like the rest of the Old Testament.

Daniel lived through the Babylonian period into the Persia rule. Gabriel told Daniel that the Prince of Persia (fallen angel over the Persian empire) resisted him twenty-one days. Then Michael came to help in the fight. After the Prince of Persia would come the Prince of Greece (see 10:12-14; 10:20-21).

Isaiah (39:5-8) and Jeremiah (20:4) had warned for years that Babylon would come and destroy Jerusalem and the temple. Now Daniel was living in the fulfillment of those prophecies.

The book of Daniel has many incredible stories like Shadrach, Meshach, and Abednego being thrown into a fiery furnace and coming out unscathed. The next Babylonian king, Belshazzar, throws a party while drinking from holy vessels previously stolen from the temple in Jerusalem; he sees the writing on the wall which Daniel interprets as meaning Belshazzar is weighed in the balance and found wanting. Daniel goes on to predict the Medes and Persians coming to conquer. After the conquest of the Medo-Persian alliance, Daniel is chosen by Darius their king to continue to serve in the king's court as leader of the wise men. The Median king is tricked into passing a law designed by other jealous officials to hurt Daniel. This causes Daniel to end up in a den of lions, but the angel of the Lord shuts the mouth of the lions, and Daniel escapes unharmed. The final six chapters of Daniel deal with incredible revelation of future days for Israel, including the coming Messiah, and the seventy weeks. The last week of the seventy weeks is the seven-year tribulation.

Daniel received great insight directly from Gabriel. Daniel understood through Nebuchadnezzar's dream of the statue, and the revelation of the beasts, that Babylon (head of gold and lion), would eventually be conquered by the Medes and Persians (chest and arms of silver, the ram, and the bear). Then Greece led by Alexander the Great (loins of bronze, the shaggy goat, and leopard with four heads and four wings) would conquer the Medes and Persians. The Medes and Persians were huge in number, that is why God chose the bear to represent them. Greece, more than any predecessors, was able to reproduce their culture, and that is why God chose the loins of the statue to represent them. Also Greece swiftly conquered the world, and that is why the leopard with wings spoke of this kingdom. The four heads of the leopard reveals that after Alexander the Great's death, his kingdom was split four ways and given to his four generals. Finally, the legs of iron represent Rome (terrible unknown beast with ten horns) which had an eastern branch in Constantinople (left leg), and a western branch in Rome, Italy (right leg).

It is interesting that Daniel saw sixty-nine weeks from the second temple period to the Messiah being cut off (killed). It was as though a pause took place in the revelation after Christ died, and the Jews were scattered. Then Daniel saw the seventieth week which is the "days of Jacob's trouble" we call the seven-year tribulation. The ten toes of the statue are connected to these last days. They represent a "revived Rome," also known as "Babylon," which will be led by the Antichrist and his ten main kingdoms which each have an evil ruler that aligns with him. This is the seventh and final kingdom that will unsuccessfully try to destroy Israel and stop the coming of Christ to Jerusalem. The stone that struck the toes speaks of Christ's return to crush the Antichrist and his Babylonian kingdom.

Gabriel brought Daniel very precise information in 9:25-27: "Know therefore and understand that from the going forth of the command to restore and to rebuild Jerusalem until the Prince Messiah shall be seven weeks, and sixty-two weeks. It shall be built again, with plaza and moat, even in times of trouble. [26]After the sixty-two weeks Messiah shall be cut off and shall have nothing. And the troops of the prince who shall come shall destroy the city and the sanctuary. The end of it shall come with a flood. And until the end of the war desolations are determined. [27]And he shall make a firm covenant with many for one week. But in the middle of the week he shall cause the sacrifice and the offering to cease. And on the wing of abominations shall come one who makes desolate, until the decreed destruction is poured out on the desolator."

Sir Robert Anderson calculated Gabriel's specific words that from the time of the decree to restore Jerusalem until the day Jesus rode in on the donkey (see Zechariah 9:9; Luke 19:38; Psalm 118) in Jerusalem was exactly 173,880 days (69 X 7 years). He took into account God uses 360-day years in the Bible, and considered leap years in the equation. So from the decree of Artaxerxes Longimanus on March 14, 445 BC until April 6, 32 AD was exactly 173,880 days. This is 173,740 days, plus 24 days between March 14 to April 6, and adding the 116 days for leap years. Gabriel's prophecy was perfect down to the day Christ rode in on a donkey presenting Himself as king.

All the revelation Daniel received was no doubt well documented. Many believe Daniel had a following among these wise men of the east. When the Medes and Persians conquered Babylon, the Magi were a hereditary group of wise men among the Medes. Daniel was placed by Darius over the magi, and they were jealous of Daniel (an outsider) and tried to get him killed in the lion's den.

The "wise men" of these nations studied the science of that day (astrology/alchemy-sorcery), mixed with the occult (witchcraft), and dream/omen interpretations (divination). These wise men brought in a dark counterfeit "priestly" type of ministry to the secular king's court. They were very similar to what we would call a witch doctor or shaman of today. These wise men brought the spiritual together with the politics of the king's court. Daniel brought something very holy and pure into something very dark and evil. Daniel dealt with this battleground in Babylon, and now he was going to have to face it again with the magi of the Medo-Persian empire.

It could be that the group of magi "wise men" that came from the east were descendants of the devout followers of Daniel's ministry in the east. They studied Daniel's prophecies. In particular, they were counting the sixty-nine weeks and knew the Messiah was about to come. When they saw the star over Bethlehem, they concluded it was a sign of this great Jewish Messiah/King coming into the world. Could the star have been the shekinah glory over Bethlehem? The group of wise men that came would have been a very large number, not just three as tradition says. Because there were three main gifts mentioned, people assume there were only three men.

Years prior to Jesus' birth and the visit of the magi, the Maccabees freed Israel from the tyranny of the Seleucid Greek empire, and a Parthian revolt broke the Medo-Persia area free from Greece as well. The Parthians were a rival group to Rome. So when this large entourage came in from the east, it made Herod nervous and wondering if they were coming in peace.

THE SILENT YEARS: THE STORY OF HANUKKAH

There is a period from Malachi to Matthew that scholars call the silent years but, in fact, God was at work. This was during the time of the Greeks which were eventually conquered by Rome. During the Grecian period, Alexander died young and left his empire to his four generals. Seleucus took the middle east area, and Ptolemy took over the Egyptian territory. Israel was in the middle of this conflict. There arose a Greek tyrant named Antiochus Epiphanes who was a picture and type of the Antichrist. Here is a little history about Hanukkah for us as Christians today:

John 10:22-23 "At that time the Feast of the Dedication [Hanukkah] took place at Jerusalem; 23 it was winter, and Jesus was walking in the temple in the portico of Solomon."

Jesus thought enough of Hanukkah to keep this festival. Hanukkah lasts eight days, and we would not have Jesus or the New Testament if God had not intervened during the days of the Hasmonean Maccabees.

Antiochus Epiphanes was a delusional Greek ruler over the area of Syria and most of the Middle East. He wanted to conquer Israel fully and sought to do away with God's word and culture and make all Jews become Greek. He tried to prevent things like circumcision, Sabbath observance, celebrating feasts, keeping a kosher diet, study of Torah, or going to synagogue. He was successful at temporarily stopping the temple rituals, erecting a statue of Zeus, sacrificing a pig on the altar, then pouring the pig's broth over things like Torah scrolls etc. He desperately wanted to defile the temple area. He erected shrines and altars throughout the land, and the people were forced to offer sacrifices as tokens of their acceptance of the new religion. Some Jews were fine with this transition, but most were deeply troubled and stayed totally devoted to God. Those who were disobedient to the Greeks were either tortured or killed or both. Many that were tortured, their bodies were mutilated, and while they were still alive and breathing, they were crucified. Some wives, and sons whom they had circumcised, were strangled to death. Some were crucified with the dead bodies of their children made to hang around their necks. Hebrews chapter 11 talks about those who were martyred and tortured. Some Biblical scholars say this reference included those who died taking a stand for the Lord against Epiphanes and his violent assault 167 years before Christ was born. They remained faithful to God even unto death.

If Epiphanes had been successful long-term in extinguishing God's people and culture and replacing it with his own, the stage for the appearing of Christ would have been destroyed. Just as Herod was trying to kill all the male babies in an attempt to kill the Christ child, so Satan stirred up Epiphanes in an attempt to stop the coming of the future Messiah.

The Maccabees were a family of faithful priests. The king Epiphanes sent representatives throughout the land. In a particular city there was to be a sacrifice and the representative asked the influential priestly leader Mattathias to do the sacrifice as a pledge of his allegiance to the Greek king Epiphanes. He stated "far be it from us to desert the law and the ordinances. We will not obey the king's words by turning aside from our religion neither to the right or the left." Another Jew came forward in the sight of all to offer a sacrifice on the altar, and like his ancient ancestor Phineas, Mattathias burned with zeal for the Lord and killed the Jew right there on the spot. This started a war.

The Maccabees (name derived from the Hebrew word for hammer) became a group of warrior priests that rallied for war, and God gave them victory though they were very small in number. Biblical scholars believe the Maccabees were the "little help" the prophet Daniel saw and wrote about in Daniel 11:34. After the death of their father Mattathias, Judah, his son, took charge. In a three-year bloody war, they pushed back the king and his large army (which was a supernatural victory). Then they proceeded to rededicate and cleanse the temple as holy unto God. They had to build a new bronze altar because the previous had been defiled. After realizing there was only enough oil for one day of the menorah being lit, they lit it anyway (it was supposed to burn night and day), and God gave them another miracle in that the oil did not run out for eight consecutive days. This was a great encouragement after such a horrific trial they had just been through. The eight days the menorah miraculously stayed lit was enough time to make more oil. This is why there are the eight candles lit on the Hanukkah menorah.

So on Kislev 25th in 165 BC, exactly three years after the altar to Zeus had been set up, the temple was cleansed, and the daily burnt offerings and other religious ceremonies resumed.

The Hanukkah celebration involves lighting a light each night of the eight-day period. So the light gets brighter every night until the final night when all eight are lit along with the shamash (servant) candle totaling nine. For Christians this is an extremely powerful time to remember. We obviously have Christmas around this same time as well, but without Hanukkah there would be no Christmas. Yes, it was that serious. The temple could have been destroyed and the Hebrew culture done away with. But God brought a miracle for His people! Below I list how we can apply Hanukkah to our lives as followers of the Messiah.

THE GREAT WARNING OF HANUKKAH

The king Epiphanes was trying to force God's people to become like the sinful world around them. He wanted them to assimilate into the evil world's idolatrous system of that day. As followers of Christ, there should be a huge difference in our lives compared to the sinful world around us. We should stick out like a star in the night sky. People should take note about us that we talk differently, dress differently, and act differently than the sinful world we live in. We are truly a new creation in Christ. This is a time to honestly examine our lives before the Lord. Antiochus Epiphanes is a picture and type of the coming Antichrist. Hanukkah can help us understand the abomination that causes desolation Jesus prophesied would come.

For us today as followers of our Messiah Jesus:

1. This is a time for rededicating our lives unto the Lord and deeply consecrating ourselves unto Him since we are the temple of the Holy Spirit. Also, consecrate your home as holy unto the Lord.

2. Seek the Lord for major breakthroughs in warfare. Are there stubborn situations that truly need change? Like in the days of the Maccabees, Moses, Gideon, or Hezekiah, God can give great breakthroughs in the most dire of situations.

3. Seek the Lord for a fresh anointing and a move of revival in your life. The Lord is coming for wise virgins with extra oil (Matt 25). Hanukkah speaks of supernatural oil.

4. Like the lighted menorah, we are called to be a light in this world. Live a life that is truly righteous and causes people to know there is a God in heaven. The middle candle is called the shamash or servant candle from which all others get their fire. It represents Jesus being the source of all light and fire. With that candle, all the other candles are lit. Jesus is our source of life, light, truth, revelation, and victory in all warfare.

5. Just like the Maccabees had to do, and Elijah had to do on Mt. Carmel, we need to rebuild the altar of the Lord. Let's get our personal prayer lives where they need to be again.
6. This is a time of tipping the scales of justice. The Lord promised us that if an evil judge would give a persistent widow justice, how much more would our heavenly Father give justice unto His children (Luke 18)? Over this last year, we have sown much into the kingdom, but has Satan stolen anything from you? Petition the Lord for justice! Proverbs 6:31 states when a thief is caught, he must restore sevenfold what he has stolen.
7. It is also customary to read from Psalm 30 during this time. There is a beautiful Jewish poem called *Maoz Tzur* that is read at Hanukkah each year.

Maoz Tzur (fortress rock)

Rock and fortress of my salvation, to you it is fitting to give praise. May the house of my prayer be built, and there we will bring an offering of thanks. When you prepare a place of slaughter for the blaspheming enemy, then will I lift my voice with a song of dedication of the altar.

My soul was satiated with tribulations, my strength was sapped with sadness. My life was embittered with difficulty of the enslavement to the kingdom of the calf [Egypt]. But with his great hand, he extricated the beloved treasured nation. The army of Pharaoh, and all his descendants sunk like a stone into the depths.

He brought me to the sanctuary of his holiness, but there, too, I had no rest. The oppressor [Nebuchadnezzar] came and exiled me, for I had worshipped foreign gods, and the poisonous wine [of sin] I did taste. I had barely left my land when the end of the Babylonian exile came, with Zerubabbel and at the end of the seventy years, I was emancipated.

> Cut down the towering cypress [of Mordechai], the Agagite son of Hamdata [Haman] requested. But it has become an entrapment for him, and his arrogance was silenced. You raised the head of Mordechai—and the enemy—his name you erased. His many sons, his possessions, you hanged on the tree.
>
> The Syrian-Greeks gathered upon me [story of Hanukkah] in the days of the Hasmonians. They broke through the walls of my towers, and defiled all the oils of the temple. But from the remnant of the flasks, a miracle was wrought for the roses [Israel]. The men of wisdom [the sages] instituted eight days of song and praise.
>
> Unleash your holy arm, and bring near the final salvation. Avenge your servants from the evil nation. For it has been too long already, and there is no end to the days of evil [possible prophecy of the end times with the antichrist]. Repel the red one [descendants of Edom—possible reference to Palestians], and raise up for us the seven shepherds [coming true Messiah with his righteous ones after the Tribulation].

To better understand Bible prophecy, listen to Pastor Scott Boyd's teachings entitled *The Spine of Prophecy*, which are a very comprehensive study of end-time prophecy throughout all of Scripture. To better understand the book of Revelation, listen to Pastor Scott Boyd's teachings entitled *Revelation: The Final Days,* which is a word-for-word study of the book of Revelation. These can be found on the media page of www.fnirevival.com under the playlist entitled *End Time Prophecy.* These are free resources with corresponding notes.

A BASIC OUTLINE FOR DANIEL:

1. During Nebuchadnezzar's reign. Chapters 1-4
2. Daniel on trial. Chapters 5-6
3. Revelation Daniel receives during Belshazzar's reign. Chapters 7-8

4. Daniel's prayer for Israel's restoration and revelation of seventy weeks. Chapter 9
5. The final revelations Daniel receives. Chapters 10-12

MEMORABLE SCRIPTURES IN DANIEL:

Daniel 3:17-18 "If it be so, our God whom we serve is able to deliver us from the burning fiery furnace, and He will deliver us out of your hand, O king. [18]But even if He does not, be it known to you, O king, that we will not serve your gods, nor worship the golden image which you have set up."

Daniel 6:22 "My God has sent His angel and has shut the lions' mouths so that they have not hurt me, because innocence was found in me before Him; and also before you, O king, I have done no harm."

Daniel 9:18-19 "O my God, incline Your ear and hear. Open Your eyes and look at our desolations and the city which is called by Your name, for we do not present our supplications before You for our righteousness, but for Your great mercies. [19]O Lord, hear! O Lord, forgive! O Lord, listen and act! Do not defer, for Your own sake, O my God. For Your city and Your people are called by Your name."

HOSEA

Most scholars agree that Hosea wrote this book although it is written in both first and third person. It could be that Hosea had a scribe write what was dictated, just as Jeremiah the prophet had Baruch. Hosea's name means "salvation." It was most likely written between 750 BC to 722 BC. Around 750 BC is when Hosea began prophesying against the sin of Israel, and in 722 BC Israel was taken captive to Assyria. Actually, it is possible Hosea began prophesying in 753 BC right before the death of Jeroboam II. Hosea had a very long ministry as he prophesied for 72 years spanning four kings in Israel and four kings in Judah. He continually refers to the ten northern tribes of Israel as "Ephraim." The northern kings of Israel during Hosea's tenure were Menahem, Pekahiah, Pekah, and Hoshea. Some prophets alive and ministering during Hosea's time were Amos, Isaiah, and Micah. The southern kings alive during Hosea's prophetic ministry were Uzziah (Azariah), Jotham, Ahaz, and Hezekiah.

What most people remember about Hosea was that God called him to marry an unfaithful prostitute (1:2) which gave him nothing but grief. This was a prophetic act, because God was showing Israel how they were an unfaithful wife to Him. The prostitute Hosea married was named Gomer, and when she returned to her life of sin, Hosea had to buy her back from the slave market. She had three children that might have been his or maybe they were of another father because of her unfaithfulness. Hosea gave each of the three children prophetic names. He named the oldest son Jezreel implying a "massacre." He named the daughter Lo-ruhamah which means "not loved (pitied)." Finally, he named the other son Loammi which means "not my people." In Hosea we see a picture of God being a good and faithful husband while Israel was playing the harlot with other gods.

A BASIC OUTLINE FOR HOSEA:

1. Hosea's personal family life. Chapters 1-3
2. The outcry against the sins of unfaithful Israel. Chapters 4-6
3. The punishment coming to Israel. Chapters 6-10
4. God's judgment and mercy. Chapters 11-14

MEMORABLE SCRIPTURES IN HOSEA:

Hosea 4:6 "My people are destroyed for lack of knowledge. Because you have rejected knowledge, I will reject you from being My priest. And because you have forgotten the law of your God, I will also forget your children."

Hosea 6:1-2 "Come, let us return to the Lord, for He has torn, and He will heal us.

He has struck, and He will bind us up. 2 After two days He will revive us. On the third day He will raise us up, that we may live before Him."

Hosea 6:6 "For I desired mercy, and not sacrifice, and the knowledge of God more than burnt offerings."

Hosea 8:7 "For they sow the wind, and they will reap the whirlwind."

Hosea 11:1 "When Israel was a child, I loved him, and out of Egypt I called My son."

JOEL

The book of Joel is an incredible book full of wisdom and revelation to be gleaned for us today. It was written by Joel himself, the son of Pethuel (1:1). Joel's name means "Yahweh (Jehovah) is God." Little else is known about him, and there is a lot of speculation about the actual date Joel was written. It seems to be a prophecy about the invasion of the Assyrians into northern Israel, but it could have been written much later concerning the Babylonian invasion. So the dates of Joel range from the ninth to the fifth century, but traditionally most scholars believe it was written around 830 BC as the condition of the nation seems to reflect this time frame the most. Not to mention that Amos indicates an awareness of Joel in his writings.

Joel didn't spend any time calling out specific sins in the nation, but rather, he simply called for humility, prayer, fasting, and deep repentance.

The picture Joel paints for us today in his writings is simple. When we allow sin in our lives, or nation, the enemy begins to invade like locusts. The enemy comes in to steal, kill, and destroy. If we will humble ourselves in prayer, fasting, and deep repentance, God promises to drive away the enemy and restore the years the locusts have eaten. Also, there is a promise of revival connected with the restoration. We see a pattern in Scripture (Isaiah 58, Joel 2, and 2 Chronicles 7:14) that God pours out His Spirit and restores the ancient ruins the enemy has destroyed. The revival and restoration brings healing to our land. Those who pray and fast will be among those rebuilding the ancient ruins, raising up age-old foundations, repairing breaches in the walls, and creating streets to dwell in (Isaiah 58:12).

It is very interesting that Joel has references to the Tribulation (1:15-20), the Antichrist and final battle of Armageddon (2:2-11), the final restoration of Israel in the end (2:21-27), and world-wide outpouring of the Holy Spirit (2:28-29). Also, Peter quoted Joel in Acts 2:16-21 while preaching on the day of Pentecost.

A BASIC OUTLINE OF JOEL:

1. God's rebuke—the plague of locust (invading army). Chapter 1:1-12
2. Call for repentance, prayer, and fasting. Chapters 1:13-2:11
3. God's promise of restoration and revival. Chapter 2:12-32
4. The final restoration of Israel and reign of the Messiah. Chapter 3

MEMORABLE SCRIPTURES IN JOEL:

Joel 2:1 "Blow the ram's horn in Zion, sound the alarm on My holy mountain! All the inhabitants of the earth will tremble, because the day of the Lord has come, because it is near."

Joel 2:28-29 "And it will be that, afterwards, I will pour out My Spirit on all flesh; then your sons and your daughters will prophesy, your old men will dream dreams, and your young men will see visions. [29]Even on the menservants and maidservants in those days I will pour out My Spirit."

Joel 2:32 "And it will be that everyone who calls on the name of the Lord will be saved."

Joel 3:14 "Multitudes, multitudes, in the valley of decision! For the day of the Lord is near in the valley of the decision."

AMOS

Amos, whose name means "burden," was a mighty prophet of God, but he was also a humble, lowly shepherd. God chose this humble man of low socioeconomic status to prophesy against the corrupt, wealthy, powerful elite of Israel's society of his time. The book of Amos was written approximately in the 760s BC. Amos was from Tekoa near Bethlehem. Amos was from the southern tribe of Judah, but was called by God to prophesy to the northern tribe of Israel.

After the mighty prophetic ministries of Elijah and his successor Elisha, God raised up a group of powerful prophets like Isaiah, Micah, Amos, Hosea, and probably Joel during the era from King Uzziah until the righteous King Hezekiah. Amos prophesied for two years before a great earthquake struck Jerusalem in the days of Uzziah (1:1).

Amos strongly condemned the sins of idol worship, persecuting God's prophets, and of oppressing the poor. God gave Amos a vision of a plumb line that Israel was not measuring up to God's standard of righteousness. Amos also saw a basket of ripe fruit indicating Israel had become ripe for God's judgment.

Amos 3:11-12 gives prophetic insight that is relevant for us today. The picture is a lamb that wandered off from the shepherd. A vicious lion jumped on the lamb, devouring it and leaving only two limbs and a piece of an ear. Sometimes, for various reasons, people don't really stay faithful to a powerful praying local church. Maybe they took for granted the good shepherd over that church? Maybe they stopped appreciating the spiritual protection they have lived under for years? When they get out into the world, Satan pounces on them and devours their lives. At times these will find their way back into that fold, but the shepherd has to help undo a lot of the bondages put on them, and repair the damage inflicted on them by the enemy. Make sure you are led by the Lord into a powerful church. Stay faithful under that covering of spiritual protection for you and your family.

SPIRITUAL FAMINE AND DROUGHT

Amos 8:11-12 "The time is coming, says the LORD GOD, when I will send a famine on the land, not a famine of bread, nor a thirst for water, but of hearing the words of the LORD. [12]They will wander from sea to sea, and from north to east; they will run back and forth to seek the word of the LORD, but they will not find it."

Amos 4:7-8 "I also withheld the rain from you, when there were still three months to the harvest. I would send rain on one town, and send no rain on another town. One field would receive rain, but another field without rain would wither. [8]So two or three towns wandered to one town to drink water, but they were not satisfied; yet you did not return to Me, says the LORD."

In these two passages we see God's judgment brought a famine of the word of God and a drought of rain. We are living in times that one may have to drive a good distance to find a place that will preach the true word of God and see a genuine move of the Holy Spirit. When we find that type of a church, we need to stay there, be faithful in our giving, and help earnestly pray that God's purposes for that church will be fulfilled.

A BASIC OUTLINE FOR AMOS:

1. Prophecies against nations. Chapters 1-2
2. Israel's sin condemned. Chapters 3-6
3. A series of five prophetic visions warning Israel. Chapters 7-9:10
4. God's promise of restoration. Chapters 9:11-15

MEMORABLE SCRIPTURES IN AMOS:

Amos 4:7 "I also withheld the rain from you, when there were still three months to the harvest. I would send rain on one town, and send no rain on another town. One field would receive rain, but another field without rain would wither. [8]So two or three towns wandered to one town to drink water, but they were not satisfied; yet you did not return to Me, says the LORD."

Amos 4:12 "Prepare to meet your God, O Israel!

Amos 5:14-15 "Seek good and not evil, so that you may live; then the LORD, the God of Hosts, will truly be with you, as you claim. [15]Hate evil and love good, and establish justice at the gate. It may then be that the Lord God of Hosts will be gracious to the remnant of Joseph."

Amos 5:24 "But let justice roll down like water, and righteousness like an ever-flowing stream."

Amos 8:11-12 "The time is coming, says the LORD GOD, when I will send a famine on the land, not a famine of bread, nor a thirst for water, but of hearing the words of the LORD. [12] hey will wander from sea to sea, and from north to east; they will run back and forth to seek the word of the LORD, but they will not find it."

OBADIAH

The author was Obadiah (1:1), or this could have been an unknown prophet that used the title Obadiah which means "servant of God." The date this was written is not very clear, but it seems to be approximately thirty years after Babylon invaded Judah in 586 BC.

The Edomites are the descendants of Esau. The kingdom of Edom consisted of Mount Seir (see Joshua 24:4), Bozrah (see Isaiah 63:1), and Sela (see 2 Kings 14:7). Edom was prophetically called Seir many times. The reference to the heights of their pride was because of their security of their mountain strongholds in Seir, just south of the Dead Sea. Sela is today known as Petra in Jordan. Many believe there will be a Jewish remnant that flees from the Antichrist to Petra and finds refuge during the second half of the Tribulation.

The Jewish Midrash states that when Esau was getting old, he called in his grandson Amalek and said: "I tried to kill Jacob but was unable. Now I am entrusting you and your descendants with the important mission of annihilating Jacob's descendants—the Jewish people. Carry out this deed for me. Be relentless and do not show mercy."

Obadiah prophesies that Edom will suffer for participating in the destruction of Jerusalem and the temple. The Edomites hated Israel so much that when Babylon invaded the land, they were cheering at the destruction of God's people. Obadiah reveals God's faithfulness to His people in that God promised the seed of Abraham that He would "bless those that bless you, and curse those that curse you" (Genesis 12:3).

The first king of Israel, Saul, was given a command by God to completely exterminate the Amalekites. He did not do as he was commanded. It is interesting to note that in the days of Esther, Haman almost destroyed the Jews still in Persia, and the Bible calls him an Agagite (Esther 3:1). Agag was the king of the Amalekites that Saul let live. Apparently some of the household of Agag survived because of Saul's disobedience. God saw the future, and this would explain the anger of the Lord at Saul for not fulfilling his mission. Esther 2:5 calls Esther a descendant of Kish who was the father of King Saul. The message we can take from this is that if we do not win the battles in our generation, we will leave those battles for our children and descendants to have to face in their generation. If Saul had truly fulfilled his mission, Esther would not have had to fight this battle.

EDOM BECOMES IDUMEA

Revelation 2:9 "I know your afflictions and your poverty—yet you are rich! I know about the slander of those who say they are ***Jews and are not, but are a synagogue of Satan***" (emphasis mine).

Edom infiltrated the land of Israel, and then became false Jews. Most people only see a very basic Bible map at the end of your Bible, but many times these leave out a significant change. Edom is southeast of the Jordan, but history records the Arab Nabateans, who were an ancient powerful group that was at war with Edom, forced them out of their mountainous strongholds to move western into Israel's border around Hebron. This defeat of Edom by the Nabateans was the fulfillment of Obadiah's prophecies, and it brought this ancient enemy right into God's land.

Edom was the one cheering as Jacob's descendants were being destroyed by Babylon. When Babylon, under Nebuchadnezzar, destroyed Jerusalem in 586 BC, neighboring citizens (Edomites) shouted with joy, "Raze it! Raze it! Dash their little children against the stones and wipe out the Jews!" This is what Psalm 137:7-9 is speaking of. The Edomites participated in at least four episodes of plundering Jerusalem.

They became known later as the Idumeans, and they intermarried with the inhabitants of Samaria after the Assyrian exile. Early Roman maps show Idumea. The Samaritans persecuted those rebuilding the second temple and walls (see Ezra and Nehemiah). These inhabitants of Samaria were a mixed race (part Jewish) that practiced a great deal of paganism and superstition.

Later in history Judas Maccabaeus retook the city of Hebron in 164 BC. Even though it came under Jewish control, the Idumites had intermarried with Samaria and other areas. When the Jews regained control, the Idumites either fled or were forced into Judaism. So some assumed the Idumeans were Jews, but they were not. This is very significant for us today. Satan not only attacks from without, but he will infiltrate, and attack from within. Some of the greatest church problems come from the tares (false Christians) among the wheat.

Later in 47 BC when Julius Caesar promoted an Idumean named Antipater as procurator over Judea, Samaria, and Galilee, he just assumed he was a Jew, but he wasn't. He was an Idumean. In 37 BC the Romans named Herod, the son of Antipater, as king over Israel. The Idumeans had five centuries of history in the land of Israel up to the point Jesus came on the scene. One Herod killed the children of Bethlehem trying to kill Jesus. Another killed John the Baptist, and another killed James the brother of Jesus and tried to kill Peter. The ancient hatred Esau had toward Jacob was evident. This everlasting hatred is called by the Jews "olam ebah."

Many believe, in a metaphoric sense, the modern-day Palestinians are prophetically seen as the tents of Edom (Psalm 83). The continual war with Israel's neighbors has similarities to the battles with Edom of ancient times. Edom (and Amalek) is a picture and type of anti-Semitism in the world down through the ages. This attack to destroy Israel is Satan's attempt to stop the coming of Jesus to the earth. Satan knows Jesus is returning to Jerusalem. Another interesting fact is that Jewish rabbis today call the worldwide financial cabal cult a modern-day Esau. There are those who people would think are Jews because of their heritage, but they are a part of great wealth that funds what opposes God and His purposes in the earth (see Psalm 2:1-6).

In reading Obadiah there is a stark contrast between the prideful Edomites (1-16), and the faithful true worshippers in the house of Jacob (17-21).

A BASIC OUTLINE FOR OBADIAH:

1. Foretelling Edom's destruction. Chapters 1-9
2. Edom's arrogant attitude toward Jerusalem. Chapters 10-14
3. Edom in the day of the Lord. Chapters 15-21

MEMORABLE SCRIPTURES IN OBADIAH:

Obadiah 1:2-4 "See, I will make you small among the nations; you will be greatly despised. [3]The pride of your heart has deceived you, you who live in the clefts of the rock, whose dwelling is high; you say in your heart, 'Who will bring me down to the ground?' [4]Though you ascend high like the eagle, and though you set your nest among the stars, I will bring you down from there, says the Lord."

Obadiah 1:6-9 "How the things of Esau have been ransacked! How his hidden treasures hunted out! [7]All your confederates have driven you to the border; your allies have deceived and prevailed against you. Those who eat your bread have set a trap for you. You will not detect it. [8]On that day, says the Lord, I will destroy the wise out of Edom, and understanding out of Mount Esau. [9]Your mighty men shall be shattered, O Teman, so that everyone from Mount Esau will be cut off."

JONAH

The story of Jonah is written in third person, so it is unclear who actually wrote the story. The story took place around 560 BC during the reign of Jeroboam II. Jonah son of Amittai was mentioned in 2 Kings 14:23-25. In his early ministry, he predicted Jeroboam II would retake land in the north that Hazael, king of Syria, took years prior. The name Jonah means "dove."

Assyria was one of the most brutal nations of this era in history. It would similar to the extreme violence displayed by Muslim terrorists today against Jews. Jonah hated Assyria because of the brutality they were showing toward Israel and other nations. Nineveh was the capital city of Assyria. The fact that God sent a prophet to this heathen nation shows that He loves all people, and desires that none perish, but all come unto repentance.

Jewish writings indicate that the Shunammite's son spoken of in 2 Kings grew up to be Jonah. This could be true as the timing would fit even though the Bible does not specifically say this. It also stands to reason this could be true because the Shunammite was barren until Elisha prophesied over her. Therefore, she had a supernatural aspect to her pregnancy. Later, the son died mysteriously as though Satan was trying to kill him before his mission to serve God as a prophet. God used Elisha to then lie on him and raise him from the dead (see 2 Kings 4). A lot of supernatural activity surrounded this child of destiny. The anointing on Jonah was strong enough to bring repentance to all of Nineveh. It is possible that Jonah might have received an impartation of the anointing when Elisha laid on him and prayed over him, raising him from the dead. Elisha imparted life into him, prophetic vision into his eyes, prophetic words into his mouth, and authority and power into his hands. It is also very possible that Jonah was one of the sons of the prophets that sat under Elisha's ministry (see 2 Kings 2).

Jesus referred to Jonah as historical fact in Matthew 12:39-40 and Luke 11:29-30.

A BASIC OUTLINE OF JONAH:

1. Jonah's rebellion against God's call. Chapter 1
2. Jonah brought to repentance and deliverance. Chapter 2
3. Jonah goes to Ninevah and judgment was averted. Chapter 3
4. Jonah upset at God's mercy. Chapter 4

MEMORABLE SCRIPTURES IN JONAH:

Jonah 2:9 "But I will sacrifice to You with the voice of thanksgiving; I will pay what I have vowed. Salvation is of the Lord!"

Jonah 4:11 "Should I not, therefore, be concerned about Nineveh, that great city, in which there are more than a hundred and twenty thousand people, who do not know their right hand from their left, and also many animals?"

MICAH

The scroll of the prophet Micah the Morasthite was written around 700 BC. The name Micah means "who is like the Lord." He lived in southern Judah near Gath of the Philistines. As with other prophets, Micah either wrote this with his own hand or dictated it to a scribe. Micah lived in the days of Isaiah the prophet along with Hosea. He prophesied during the reign of Jotham, Ahaz, and Hezekiah. Like Isaiah, Micah eventually witnessed the northern kingdom of Israel being taken into captivity to Assyria.

Micah predicts that both the northern and southern kingdoms would be invaded and their capitals destroyed because of their sin. He also pointed out that the leaders of Israel were sinful. The priests, prophets, and kings did not fear the Lord and practiced wickedness.

His message exposed the wealthy oppressing the poor, corruption of the priesthood, and the greed of merchants in swindling customers.

We see in Micah 2:12 that Micah still predicts the restoration of Israel, even though both the northern and southern nations would go into captivity because of their sin.

Centuries before Jesus was born, Micah predicted He would be born in Bethlehem (see 5:2). This was referenced in Matthew 2:6.

A BASIC OUTLINE OF MICAH:

1. Judgment coming to capitals Samaria and Jerusalem. Chapter 1
2. Sin of Israel's leaders exposed. Chapters 2-3
3. God will restore. Chapters 4-5
4. God's judgment and mercy. Chapters 6-7

MEMORABLE SCRIPTURES IN MICAH:

Micah 2:12-13 "I will indeed assemble Jacob—all of you; I will indeed gather the remnant of Israel. I will place them together like sheep in a fold, like a herd in its pasture—thronging with people. 13 He who breaks through has gone up before them; they will break through and pass the gate and go out by it. Then their king will pass on before them, the Lord at their head."

Micah 5:2 "But you, Bethlehem Ephrathah, although you are small among the tribes of Judah, from you will come forth for Me one who will be ruler over Israel. His origins are from of old, from ancient days."

Micah 6:8 "He has told you, O man, what is good—and what does the Lord require of you, but to do justice and to love kindness, and to walk humbly with your God?"

Micah 7:18-19 "Who is a God like You, bearing iniquity and passing over transgression for the remnant of His inheritance? He does not remain angry forever, because He delights in benevolence. [19]He will again have compassion upon us. He will tread down our iniquities, and cast all of our sins into the depths of the sea."

NAHUM

As with other prophets, Nahum either wrote this himself or dictated it to a scribe that wrote it for him. Nahum ministered sometime between 663 BC to 612 BC. The name Nahum means "consolation" or "comfort." His native city Elkosh is uncertain, but is thought to be a small city in southwest Judah.

Jonah had already been to Nineveh (100-150 years prior) which caused a temporary revival in the capital of Assyria, but Assyria went on to brutally attack northern Israel and take them into captivity. Nahum shows that Israel's judgment was inevitable, and it was only delayed by their temporary repentance. The Assyrians took the ten northern tribes captive in 722 BC (2 Kings 17:3-6). Assyrian King Sennacherib planned to also take Jerusalem but was stopped when God sent an angel to deliver Judah because of the prayers of the righteous King Hezekiah's prayers (2 Kings 18:3-19:37).

Assyria was known for its cruelty even among secular historians. Nahum condemns Assyria's cruelty, idolatry, and occult practices. His prophecy comes true in 612 BC when Babylon conquered Assyria. In 3:13-15 there is a prediction of both water and fire as a judgment. A canal of the Tigris flowed through Nineveh which overflowed and caused large breeches in the walls of the city for the Babylonian army to enter. The King of Nineveh knew he was doomed and set fire to his own palace, thus fulfilling the words of the prophet.

Nahum 3:1-7 "Woe to the bloody city! It is full of lies and plunder. The prey never departs. [2]The noise of the whip and the noise of the rattling of the wheels, galloping horses, and rushing chariots! [3]Horsemen charging with flashing sword and glittering spear. Multitude of slain, great number of corpses, dead bodies without end—they stumble on the corpses—[4]because of the countless harlotries of the seductive harlot, the mistress of sorceries, who sells

nations through her harlotries and families through her sorceries.
[5]I am against you, says the Lord of Hosts; I will lift your skirts over your face, and I will show the nations your nakedness, and the kingdoms your shame. [6]I will throw filth on you, and make you vile, and make you a spectacle. [7]All who look at you will flee from you, and say, 'Nineveh is devastated! Who will lament for her?' Where shall I seek comforters for you?"

A BASIC OUTLINE FOR NAHUM:

1. How awesome is our God. Chapter 1
2. Nineveh will fall. Chapter 2
3. The reason for God' judgment on Nineveh. Chapter 3

MEMORABLE SCRIPTURES IN NAHUM:

Nahum 1:3 "The Lord is slow to anger and great in power, and the Lord will in no way acquit the guilty."

Nahum 1:7 "The Lord is good, a stronghold in the day of distress; and He knows those who take refuge in Him."

HABAKKUK

There is nothing known about Habakkuk's background. His name seems to come from a root word that implies "embrace." He lived in the days right before the Babylonian invasion. He probably ministered around 600 BC. It seems by the time Jerusalem fell to Babylon, Jeremiah was the only true prophet left. Habakkuk lived and ministered a little before the writings of Jeremiah.

This book is a dialogue between the prophet and God Himself. Habakkuk has a problem with God's justice. He felt that God sending the Babylonians was not the solution, but God told Habakkuk He was using the Babylonians as an instrument of His judgment and would later punish them for their sins. Habakkuk also felt God's character was being brought into question because of His judgments. When God explained things to Habakkuk, the prophet ultimately submitted to God's justice. It is similar to the way Job did not understand why things had to happen the way they did, but he submitted himself to God's will.

Sometimes we don't understand why God allows certain things to happen, but we have to trust Him. The apostle Paul quoted Habakkuk in Romans chapter 1 as he gives a powerful gospel presentation.

Habakkuk 2:15-17 "Woe to him who makes his neighbor drink, pouring out your poison until they are drunk, that you may look on their nakedness! 16 You will be filled with shame instead of glory. You yourself—drink and show your uncircumcision! The cup of the Lord's right hand will be turned against you, and utter shame will come on your glory! 17 The violence done to Lebanon will cover you, as will the plunder of beasts that terrified them, because of the bloodshed of men and violence of the land, of the cities and all who live in them."

Just like tattoos and yoga, the Bible does not speak well of alcoholic drinks. The word for wine was a general term used for even the grapes still clustered on the vine. The old wine would have been fermented, but the preferred new wine was grape juice. With that said, nothing good ever happened in the Bible associated with strong drink. It is implied strong drink influenced Nadab and Abiju to burn unauthorized incense before the Lord, and God had to strike them dead. We read right after this incident that God told Moses to tell the priests not to drink strong drink when ministering before the Lord (see Leviticus 10:8-11). Noah was drunk which resulted in his shame and a curse placed upon his son named Ham (Genesis 9:21-25). Lot was drunk and his two daughters committed incest with him (Genesis 19:35-38). Isaiah spoke of priests and prophets getting into error because of strong drink (Isaiah 28:7). Today we see so many families destroyed, and criminal acts committed, that are directly connected to strong drink. As the Bible warns us, "Wine is a mocker, strong drink is raging, and whoever is deceived by it is not wise" (Proverbs 20:1). The Nazarite vow in the Bible was connected to consecrating one's life unto God. A Nazarite was not allowed strong drink during his time of consecration (Numbers 6:3). Our Christian spiritual mothers and fathers of the faith taught us to avoid alcohol, and Jesus' parables seem to warn against drunkenness in the last days. We read this in Matthew 24:45-51:

"Who then is a faithful and wise servant, whom his master has made ruler over his household to give them food at the appointed time? [46]Blessed is that servant whom his master will find so doing when he comes. [47]Truly, I say to you that he will make him ruler over all his goods. [48]But if that evil servant says in his heart, 'My master delays his coming,' [49]and begins to strike his fellow servants and eat and drink with the drunkards, [50]the master of that servant will come on a day when he does not look for him and in an hour he is not aware of [51]and will cut him in pieces and appoint him his portion with the hypocrites, where there shall be weeping and gnashing of teeth."

You will do well to avoid alcohol and teach your children to do the same.

In Habakkuk 3:1 we see the Hebrew word *Shigionoth* which means "a wild passionate song with rapid changes of rhythm." There are seven Hebrew words for praise, and they imply loud, wild, exuberant dance and song. This is similar to the way David praised the Lord with all his might and was criticized by his wife for it.

A BASIC OUTLINE FOR HABAKKUK:

1. Habakkuk asks why God is allowing injustice. Chapter 1:1-4
2. The Babylonians (Chaldeans) will be used to punish the wicked. Chapter 1:5-11
3. The Babylonians are worse than the wicked Jews. Chapters 1:12-2:1
4. Having faith in God. Chapter 2:2-4
5. God assures Habakkuk the Babylonians will eventually be punished. Chapter 2:5-20

6. Habakkuk's psalm of thanks. Chapter 3:1-19

MEMORABLE SCRIPTURES OF HABAKKUK:

Habakkuk 2:4 "Look, his soul is lifted up; it is not upright in him; but the just shall live by his faith."

Habakkuk 3:18 "Yet I will rejoice in the Lord; I will exult in the God of my salvation."

ZEPHANIAH

In verse 1, Zephaniah identifies himself as the great-great-grandson of Hezekiah who was probably the godly king of Israel (see 2 Chronicles 29). If this is the case, Zephaniah is a prophet of kingly lineage of the line of David. His name means "he whom the Lord has hidden." Zephaniah prophesied during the great revival that took place in the days of Josiah (640-609 BC). The other prophets during this time were Jeremiah, Nahum, and possibly Habakkuk. Even though revival was happening, Zephaniah knew judgment would still eventually come. Josiah led the most intense revival in the history of Israel since his ancestor David. He found the book of the Law and swept the land clean from any idolatry or spiritual uncleanness (see 2 Kings 22-23).

Zephaniah prophetically foresaw the invasion of the Babylonians (Chaldeans) who brought utter devastation to Judah, Jerusalem, and the temple in the years 605-586 BC. Zephaniah calls Judah to repentance (2:1-3) and predicts this destruction will also affect other surrounding nations. Just like all other prophets, Zephaniah also predicts restoration will eventually come.

A BASIC OUTLINE FOR ZEPHANIAH:

1. Predicting God's judgment. Chapters 1:1-2:3

2. How far God's judgment will extend. Chapters 2:4-3:7

3. Predicting restoration and God's final kingdom. Chapter 3:8-20

MEMORABLE SCRIPTURES IN ZEPHANIAH:

Zephaniah 1:14 "The great day of the LORD is near, near and hastening quickly. The sound of the day of the LORD is bitter; the mighty man shall cry out there."

Zephaniah 3:8-9 "Therefore wait for Me, declares the Lord, until the day when I rise up to seize the plunder; for My decision is to gather nations, to assemble kingdoms, to pour on them My indignation, all My fierce anger; for all the earth will be devoured with the fire of My jealousy. [9]For then I will restore to the peoples a pure speech that all of them may call on the name of the LORD, to serve Him with one accord."

Zephaniah 3:13 "The remnant of Israel will do no unrighteousness, nor speak lies; nor will a deceitful tongue be found in their mouth; for they will feed and lie down, and no one will make them afraid."

Zephaniah 3:14-17 "Sing, O daughter of Zion! Shout, O Israel! Be glad and rejoice with all your heart, O daughter of Jerusalem! [15]The LORD has taken away your judgments, He has cast out your enemies. The King of Israel, the LORD, is in your midst; you will see evil no more. [16]On that day it will be said to Jerusalem: Fear not, O Zion; let not your hands be slack. [17]The LORD your God is in your midst, a Mighty One, who will save. He will rejoice over you with gladness, He will renew you with His love,

He will rejoice over you with singing."

HAGGAI

Haggai wrote his scroll during the days of Zechariah, Zerubbabel, and Joshua the high priest of Israel. He and Zechariah were used of God to bring some correction, but also encouragement to the remnant God sent back to rebuild the temple by the decree of Cyrus. The book of Haggai would have been written around 520 BC. The name Haggai means "my festival." Haggai is mentioned in Ezra 5:1 and 6:14. There is little known about Haggai other than what is written in this book.

Haggai encouraged the people to continue rebuilding the temple as he was seeing how distracted they were with building their own houses. The people were focused on getting their families established back in the land, but God told the people, through Haggai, to build the temple first in order to break a drought that was affecting the land. God was trying to teach these returning to the land to put him first in all things. If they would do this, he would bring a blessing on them.

A BASIC OUTLINE FOR HAGGAI:

1. God calls the people to rebuild the temple. Chapter 1
2. Desire for a new temple. Chapter 2:1-9
3. God's promise to bless their endeavor. Chapter 2:10-19
4. God's final victory. Chapter 2:20-23

MEMORABLE SCRIPTURES IN HAGGAI:

Haggai 1:5-8 "Now, therefore, thus says the Lord of Hosts: Consider your ways. [6]You have sown much, and harvested little. You eat, but you do not have enough; you drink, but you are not filled with drink; you clothe yourselves, but no one is warm; and he who earns wages earns wages to put them into a bag with holes. [7]Thus says the Lord of Hosts: Consider your ways. [8]Go up to the mountain and bring wood and rebuild the house, that I may take pleasure in it and be glorified, says the Lord."

Haggai 2:4-5 "Yet now be strong, O Zerubbabel, says the Lord, and be strong, O Joshua, son of Jehozadak, the high priest. Be strong all you people of the land, says the Lord. Work, for I am with you, says the Lord of Hosts. [5]According to the covenant that I made with you when you came out of Egypt, so My Spirit remains among you. Do not fear."

Haggai 2:6-7 "For thus says the Lord of Hosts: Once more, in a little while, I will shake the heavens and earth, the sea and dry land. [7]And

I will shake all the nations, and they will come with the wealth of all nations, and I will fill this house with glory, says the LORD of Hosts."

Haggai 2:9 "The glory of this latter house will be greater than the former, says the LORD of Hosts. And in this place I will give peace, says the LORD of Hosts."

ZECHARIAH

Zechariah lived during the rebuilding of the Second Temple under the leadership of Zerubbabel the governor and Joshua the high priest. Both Haggai and Zechariah prophesied correction and great encouragement to those assigned to see this restoration. Zechariah was the author although some believe chapters 9-14 might have been added by an unknown author at a later time. Zechariah is the author of all fourteen chapters, but it could be that all of it was compiled at a later time by someone like Ezra. Zechariah's name means "he whom Jehovah remembers."

Zechariah, like Haggai, urged the people to be busy with the rebuilding of the temple and Jerusalem. He gives powerful apocalyptic prophecies about the coming Messiah, including the final battle over Jerusalem. Zechariah saw that during the millennial reign of the Messiah, the Feast of Tabernacles was required to be observed by the whole world (Zechariah 14:16-19).

Zechariah prophesied Christ would be betrayed with thirty pieces of silver (see 11:10-14). He also saw that the Messiah would come riding a donkey (9:9) which was fulfilled at the triumphal entry (Matthew 21:1-11). He foresaw that the Jews would one day "look to Me, whom they have pierced through" (12:10). This will be fulfilled at Christ's second coming when he enters Jerusalem to reign over all Israel for a thousand years.

Zechariah had nine major visions: 1. The rider of the red horse among the myrtle trees (1:7-17) 2. Four horns that scattered Jerusalem (1:18-19) 3. Four carpenters making the four gentile horns (1:20-21) 4. The measuring line that measured Jerusalem (2:1-13) 5. The confrontation with Satan regarding Joshua the high priest (3:1-10) 6. The two olive trees pouring into the menorah (4:1-14) 7. The flying scroll of the curse (5:1-4) 8. The evil woman in a basket carried to Shinar (Babylon) (5:5-11) 9. The four chariots and horses (6:1-8).

Zechariah chapters 9-14 introduce a humble Messiah King who will be rejected by His people. These chapters focus more on a long-range work of God, end-time prophecy, leading to the final kingdom under Christ. Zechariah saw that in the last days before Christ returns, Jerusalem would become a burdensome stone to the nations (12:3). He also saw the second coming of Christ when His feet would touch the Mount of Olives (chapter 14) which will fulfill what the angels told the onlookers at Christ's ascension (Acts 1:11).

The book of Zechariah corresponds with the book of Revelation. It is a mini-apocalyptic writing full of revelation concerning the end times. Here are some scriptural links between Zechariah and Revelation:

1. Both saw an angel measuring Jerusalem (Zechariah 2:1-3) and the temple (Revelation 11:1).
2. The two olive trees representing Zerubbabel and Joshua (Zechariah 4:1-14) which John sees again in Revelation, this time as the two witnesses (Revelation 11:3-4).
3. Zechariah saw a flying scroll (5:1) and John saw a scroll sealed with seven seals (Revelation 5:1).
4. Zechariah 6:1-3 shows four chariots with the same colors John saw with his four horsemen of the apocalypse (Revelation 6:2-8).
5. Zechariah 5:5-11 speaks of an evil woman (Jezebel—whore of Babylon) being placed in a basket and carried to Shinar which is another name for Babylon. We see her rise to power in John's writings of Revelation 17-18.

A famous portion of scripture in Zechariah states, "This is the word of the Lord to Zerubbabel, saying: Not by might nor by power, but by My Spirit, says the Lord of Hosts. [7]"Who are you, O great mountain? Before Zerubbabel you will be made level ground, and he will bring out the top stone amidst shouting of 'Grace! Grace to the stone!'" (Zechariah 4:6-7).

What was happening during this time frame was that great pressure from the Samaritans caused Darius the Mede, back in Babylon, to mandate that the rebuilding of the temple be stopped (Ezra 4). Darius became the "great mountain" that was standing in their way (Zechariah 4:7). Could this have been on the mind of Jesus when He stated, "For truly I say to you, whoever says to this mountain, 'Be removed and be thrown into the sea,' and does not doubt in his heart, but believes that what he says will come to pass, he will have whatever he says" (Mark 11:23)? The Lord used Zechariah to reveal that Zerubbabel and Joshua had been anointed by God, and this task would be accomplished by the power of the Holy Spirit—not just human effort.

A BASIC OUTLINE FOR ZECHARIAH:

1. A call for obedience. Chapter 1:1-6
2. The series of nine visions. Chapters 1:7-6:15
3. Obeying God verses legalism. Chapters 7-8
4. A humble Messiah King will come and be rejected. Chapters 9-13
5. The Messiah King reigning. Chapters 14:1-21

MEMORABLE SCRIPTURES IN ZECHARIAH:

Zechariah 1:3 "So you will say to them, Thus says the Lord of Hosts: Return to Me, and I will return to you, says the Lord of Hosts."

Zechariah 4:6 "This is the word of the Lord to Zerubbabel, saying: Not by might nor by power, but by My Spirit, says the Lord of Hosts."

Zechariah 9:9 "Rejoice greatly, O daughter of Zion! And cry aloud, O daughter of Jerusalem! See, your king is coming to you; he is righteous and able to deliver, he is humble and riding on a donkey, a colt, the offspring of a donkey."

Zechariah 12:10 "And I will pour out on the house of David and over those dwelling in Jerusalem a spirit of favor and supplication so that they look to Me, whom they have pierced through. And they will mourn over him as one mourns for an only child and weep bitterly over him as a firstborn."

Zechariah 14:4 "On that day His feet will stand on the Mount of Olives, which is to the east of Jerusalem. And from east to west the Mount of Olives will be split in two halves by a very great valley so that one half moves to the north and the other to the south."

MALACHI

Zechariah and Haggai were the two prophets ministering during the first wave of exiles returning home under Zerubbabel and Joshua. Malachi prophesied later during the days of Nehemiah, probably around 450 BC. It is little wonder God sent these great prophets during this period of restoration. The people needed the correction they brought, but they also needed their encouragement. Malachi means "my messenger." Malachi brings strong correction to the people, letting them know God will not tolerate their sins any more than he did the sins of their forefathers. The temple had already been rebuilt, but the people were allowing apostasy, intermarriage with heathen women, and neglecting their tithes and offerings. The people were bringing sickly and lame animals for offerings, divorcing their wives for pagan women, and neglecting the temple. Malachi exposes these sins and calls the people to repentance.

There are several things we can learn from Malachi. Israel was bringing blind and lame offerings God despised (1:6-12), and they were breaking the hearts of their godly wives by divorcing them for pagan women (2:10-16). It is possible for us to give of our time and resources, but God not be pleased with it. We must make sure we are doing the right things with the right motives. Things can be done out of just religious routine, but not really from the heart. If we are not careful, our mouths can praise God, but our hearts become distant from Him. We must also always put God first in giving Him our first and best. If we are hurting our spouses, or are unfaithful to them, God tells us it hinders our prayers (1 Peter 3:7). So we can learn that God wants our first and best. He is also concerned with the way we treat others. If we are not living right, He does not accept our offerings and will not answer our prayers.

Malachi 3:1 directly refers to John the Baptist coming as a forerunner to Christ's ministry. John the Baptist was the last Old Testament prophet. His ministry was pivotal to leaving the Old Covenant and moving into the New Covenant in Christ.

Malachi 3:7-12 teaches us how important our tithes and offerings really are. They honor God and put Him first in our lives. Many times one can look at where money is spent to see what is most important in someone's life. If someone really loves the Lord with all their heart, you will see that they are tithers and givers. We also see that God desired to be tested in giving. God clearly states He would rebuke what is devouring our finances, open the heavens over our lives, and pour out abundance. An open heaven is not only a reference to financial prosperity, but it also refers to revival in our lives.

Malachi 3:16-17 also teaches us that God has books. We know from Revelation that there is a Lamb's book of life (Revelation 21:27). Malachi reveals to us that there is also a book of remembrance. Malachi states that those written in the book of remembrance are those that fear the Lord, speak to one another about the Lord, and think upon His name. It is also noteworthy that this book is mentioned right after tithes and offerings were discussed. During the flood God placed Noah and his family in the ark. Later, God remembered Noah to cause the flood to recede and bring him out of the ark. This book seems to document those who are God's remnant. God will remember them in days of trouble to protect and deliver them. Could this book also include those who will be remembered at the rapture? Like Noah, some will float up (in the future rapture) while the wrath of God comes upon the earth, then will return to the earth after the wrath of God subsides. Are God's remnant recorded in a book of remembrance?

Malachi 3:16-17 "Then those who feared the Lord spoke to one another. The Lord listened and heard them, and a book of remembrance was written before Him for those who fear the Lord and who esteem His name. [17]They shall be Mine, says the Lord of Hosts, on the day when I make up My jewels. And I will spare them as a man spares his son who serves him."

A BASIC OUTLINE FOR MALACHI:

1. God speaks of His love for Israel. Chapter 1:1-5
2. Israel offends God by their sin. Chapters 1:6-2:17
3. God's righteous requirements. Chapter 3:1-15
4. God's judgment coming to distinguish between the righteous and the wicked. Chapters 3:16-4:6

MEMORABLE SCRIPTURES IN MALACHI:

Malachi 3:1 "I will send My messenger, and he will prepare the way before Me. And the Lord, whom you seek, will suddenly come to His temple, even the messenger of the covenant, in whom you delight. He is coming, says the Lord of Hosts."

Malachi 3:7 "From the days of your fathers you have gone away from My ordinances and have not kept them. Return to Me, and I will return to you, says the Lord of Hosts."

Malachi 3:10-12 "Bring all the tithes into the storehouse, that there may be food in My house, and test Me now in this, says the Lord of Hosts, if I will not open for you the windows of heaven and pour out for you a blessing, that there will not be room enough to receive it. [11]I will rebuke the devourer for your sakes, so that it will not destroy the fruit of your ground, and the vines in your field will not fail to bear fruit, says the LORD of Hosts. [12]Then all the nations will call you blessed, for you will be a delightful land, says the LORD of Hosts."

Malachi 4:1-6 "Surely the day is coming, burning like an oven; all the proud, yes, all evildoers will be stubble. The day that is coming will burn them up, says the LORD of Hosts, so that it will leave them neither root nor branch. [2]But for you who fear My name, the sun of righteousness will rise with healing in its wings. You will go out and grow up like calves from the stall. [3]And you will tread down the wicked, for they will be ashes under the soles of your feet, on the day when I do this, says the LORD of Hosts. [4]Remember the Law of Moses, My servant, the statutes and judgments which I commanded him at Horeb for all Israel. [5]See, I will send you Elijah the prophet before the coming of the great and dreaded day of the LORD. [6]He will turn the hearts of the fathers to their children, and the hearts of the children to their fathers, lest I come and strike the earth with a curse."

Section Six: Understanding the New Testament Synopsis

MATTHEW

The word synoptic means "seeing together." Scholars believe Mark originally wrote the first Gospel, Matthew read it and added to it, and finally Luke added even more. These three Gospels are described as the Synoptic Gospels. The Gospel of John is altogether a very different rendering of the life and ministry of Christ.

The author is traditionally Matthew, who was a tax collector, called by Jesus to be one of His twelve main disciples. These twelve later became known as apostles. The word apostle means "one sent with a special message." Matthew is also known as Levi (see Mark 2:14) which could imply that he had a Levitical or priestly heritage.

The Gospel of Matthew speaks to more of the Jewish population than gentile. Matthew references numerous Old Testament prophesies and their fulfillment in Christ. He also gives a genealogy that shows Jesus' ancestry through King David and Abraham. Therefore, he presents Jesus as the king of the Jews, who is the long-awaited Messiah of Israel. This book was probably written around 70 AD. This was around the time of the destruction of the temple by Vespasian and his son Titus. It is possible that Matthew wrote his Gospel in Antioch, which was a very Jewish center of Christianity in the first century. The word gospel means "good news." It is interesting that Matthew is the only Gospel to use the word "church" and also the phrase "kingdom of heaven."

It seems that Matthew focuses a lot on the teaching ministry of Jesus. You can see this in these scriptures: 5:3-7:27; 10:5-42; 13:3-52; 18:3-35; and 24:4-25:46.

A BASIC OUTLINE FOR MATTHEW:

1. Genealogy and preparation. Chapters 1-4:11
2. Jesus ministers in Galilee. Chapters 4:12-18:35
3. Jesus goes to Jerusalem to minister and die on the cross. Chapters 19-28

MEMORABLE SCRIPTURES IN MATTHEW:

Matthew 1:21 "She will bear a Son, and you shall call His name JESUS, for He will save His people from their sins."

Matthew 5:13-16 "You are the salt of the earth. But if the salt loses its saltiness, how shall it be made salty? It is from then on good for nothing but to be thrown out and to be trampled underfoot by men.
[14]You are the light of the world. A city that is set on a hill cannot be hidden. [15]Neither do men light a candle and put it under a basket, but on a candlestick. And it gives light to all who are in the house. [16]Let your light so shine before men that they may see your good works and glorify your Father who is in heaven."

Matthew 5:44 "But I say to you, love your enemies, bless those who curse you, do good to those who hate you, and pray for those who spitefully use you and persecute you."

Matthew 7:1-2 "Judge not, that you be not judged. [2]For with what judgment you judge, you will be judged. And with the measure you use, it will be measured again for you."

Matthew 7:7-8 "Ask and it will be given to you; seek and you will find; knock and it will be opened to you. [8]For everyone who asks receives, and he who seeks finds, and to him who knocks, it will be opened."

Matthew 28:19-20 "Go therefore and make disciples of all nations, baptizing them in the name of the Father and of the Son and of the Holy Spirit, [20]teaching them to observe all things I have commanded you. And remember, I am with you always, even to the end of the age. Amen."

MARK

Even though it is not specifically mentioned, the author is traditionally John Mark, the cousin of Barnabas, who traveled with Paul and Barnabas for a short time (Acts 12:25). John Mark was a close associate of the apostle Peter (1 Peter 5:13). It could have been during Peter's lifetime, or shortly after his death (55-65 AD), that Mark wrote his Gospel. Mark would have been one of the original seventy Jesus sent out to go before Him (Luke 10:1). Mark might have been a spiritual son to Peter as Peter calls him his son (1 Peter 5:13).

It is traditionally seen as the first Gospel to ever have been written. Mark wrote the Gospel putting an emphasis on the suffering that Christ endured for us. This Gospel was written for both a Jew and gentile audience showing Jesus' power to heal, drive out demons, to control the forces of nature, and overcome Satan. Mark shows us how much Jesus suffered and was rejected by the Jewish leaders (9:31), rejected by His hometown of Nazareth (6:1-3), and even His own family members (3:21). The Gospel of Mark is the only Gospel that shows this rejection by Jesus' immediate family as they seemed to think He was crazy.

Mark was the son of a woman named Mary, who lived in Jerusalem (Acts 12:12). He ministered for a time with Barnabas, his cousin (Acts 4:36-37). He went with Barnabas to one of the centers of Christianity which was in Antioch in Syria (Acts 12:25). Then he went with Paul and Barnabas on their first missionary journey, but he departed in Cyprus, and returned to his hometown of Jerusalem (Acts 13:13). Many years later, John Mark went to see Paul in Rome (2 Timothy 4:11; Colossians 4:10). It is believed that after he left Paul in Rome, Mark went to Alexandria, Egypt, where he planted a church. Mark would have received the information he included in his Gospel directly from people like Mary the mother of Jesus, Peter, and other disciples. Barnabas was a Levite (Acts 4:36). Therefore, it is likely that John Mark had Levitical blood as well, since they were cousins.

Mark 14:51-52 "A young man followed Him, wearing a linen cloth around himself. And the young men laid hold of him, [52]so he left the linen cloth, and fled from them unclothed." These two verses are only mentioned in Mark's Gospel. Most scholars agree that this was John Mark himself who was present at the Passover meal and when Jesus was arrested.

The first recorded miracle of Jesus before entering the ministry was turning the water into wine. Mark 1:23 shows us the first miracle after Jesus enters his ministry was casting out a demon. Jesus had direct confrontation with demon powers. The deliverance ministry was unique to Him up to this point. All previous prophets did miracles, and some raised the dead, but Jesus was the first to cast out demons. This was, and is today, a powerful aspect of the ministry of Jesus Christ. He has truly come to set the captives free.

A BASIC OUTLINE OF MARK:

1. Introduction to John the Baptist and calling of Jesus. Chapter 1:1-13
2. Jesus enters His public ministry. Chapters 1:14-8:26
3. Jesus calls and teaches His disciples. Chapters 8:27-10:45
4. Jesus ministers in Jericho and on into Jerusalem. Chapters 10:46-13:37
5. The death of Jesus. Chapters 14:1-15:47

6. The resurrection of Jesus and the great commission. Chapter 16:1-20

MEMORABLE SCRIPTURES IN MARK:

Mark 1:17 "Jesus said to them, "Come, follow Me, and I will make you fishers of men."

Mark 10:14 "But when Jesus saw it, He was very displeased and said to them, 'Allow the little children to come to Me, and do not forbid them, for of such is the kingdom of God.'"

Mark 10:25 "It is easier for a camel to go through the eye of a needle than for a rich man to enter the kingdom of God."

Mark 12:17 "Then Jesus answered them, 'Render to Caesar the things that are Caesar's, and to God the things that are God's.'"

Mark 14:38 "Watch and pray, lest you enter into temptation. The spirit indeed is willing, but the flesh is weak."

Mark 16:15-18 He said to them, "Go into all the world, and preach
the gospel to every creature. [16]He who believes and is baptized will be
saved. But he who does not believe will be condemned. [17]These signs
will accompany those who believe: In My name they will cast out demons; they will speak with new tongues; [18]they will take up serpents;
if they drink any deadly thing, it will not hurt them; they will lay
hands on the sick, and they will recover."

Mark 16:20 "Then they went forth and preached everywhere, the Lord working with them and confirming the word through the accompanying signs. Amen."

LUKE

Even though the Bible does not state this clearly, it is traditionally believed that Luke (a gentile physician) wrote both Luke and Acts. Some of this is derived from the "we" passages beginning in Acts 16:10. His education is brought out in his writings, since they are very thorough and well written. It is interesting to note that not one time in Luke or Acts is there a mention of his medical practices in use, even though he probably helped bandage Paul's wounds. The early church seemed to understand the power of God to heal, and they leaned heavily upon the supernatural healing from the Lord. In fact, James, the brother of Jesus, stated that if someone is sick among you, have the elders anoint him with oil and the prayer of faith will bring healing to him (see James 5:14).

Luke was called the beloved physician (Colossians 4:14). Luke traveled at times with the apostle Paul, including during his first missionary journey. Even though a gentile, some suggest Luke was one of the original seventy sent out by Jesus (10:1-20). The book of Luke was probably written in 60-80s AD as the gospel was spreading throughout the Roman Empire. If he is Lucius (as some scholars believe he is) who is mentioned in 16:21, then he is related to Paul. This Lucius could be the Lucius of Cyrene mentioned in Acts 13:1. Paul mentioned his beloved travelling companion in Philemon 24, while imprisoned in Rome (2 Timothy 4:11).

Matthew was written to a Jewish audience, but Luke seems to be writing to more of a gentile audience. Luke goes to great lengths to show Jesus' love and compassion for all people, whether Jew or gentile. He mentioned the Roman centurion (7:1-10), widows (7:11-17), sinners (7:36-50), the sick (8:43-48), lepers (17:11-19), as well as many others, including the sinners who died on the cross to his right and left (23:40-43).

Since Luke is the only Gospel to mention the road to Emmaus event, some scholars believe Luke to be one of the two disciples Jesus appeared to (Luke 24:13-31). Luke must have spent considerable time speaking with Mary, the mother of Jesus, as well as others, because he gives details about Christ's conception, birth, and details of His sufferings that the other Gospels do not have. For example, Luke is the only Gospel that shares about Christ's childhood and words spoken as a child (see chapter 2).

There is much debate as to who Theophilus was. It could just be a generic term for all readers, as it is simply translated "friend of God."

Some scholars believe since Luke wrote more to a gentile audience, even showing Jesus' genealogy going back beyond Abraham to Adam (the son of God), that perhaps Theophilus was an actual person. This same greeting is used in Acts, and that is how we know Luke wrote both of these books. Luke is the only Gospel that shares the parables of the good Samaritan (10:25-37), the prodigal son (15:11-32), and the story of Lazarus and the rich man (16:19-31).

The overall message of Luke and Acts is that no matter if you are a Jew, gentile, rich, or poor, Christ loves you, and came to seek and to save the lost.

A BASIC OUTLINE FOR LUKE:

1. Introduction. Chapter 1:1-4
2. Christ's birth and childhood stories. Chapters 1:5-2:52
3. John the Baptist. Chapter 3:1-20
4. Jesus revealed by John the Baptist and enters ministry. Chapters 3:21-4:44
5. Jesus ministers. Chapters 5-6:16
6. Jesus teaches, heals, and delivers. Chapters 6:17-9:50
7. Jesus fulfilling his mission. Chapters 9:51-18:30
8. Jesus' suffering, death, burial, resurrection, ascension. Chapters 18:31-24:53

MEMORABLE SCRIPTURES IN LUKE:

Luke 12:34 "For where your treasure is, there will your heart be also."

Luke 15:7 "Likewise, I tell you, there will be more joy in heaven over one sinner who repents than over ninety-nine righteous men who need no repentance."

Luke 17:33 "Whoever seeks to save his life will lose it, and whoever loses his life will preserve it."

Luke 18:17 "Truly, I say to you, whoever will not receive the kingdom of God as a little child will in no wise enter it."

Luke 19:10 "For the Son of Man has come to seek and to save that which was lost."

JOHN

John is traditionally the author of this book. The book was probably written in John's old age as he was living in Ephesus close to the end of the first century. John also authored 1, 2, and 3 John, and the book of Revelation.

He was a Galilean fisherman (Mark 1:19-20). He is referred to as the "disciple whom Jesus loved" four times (John 13:23; 20:2; 21:7; 21:20). Jesus entrusted to John the task of looking after his mother, Mary, as He was hanging on the cross. John's brother was James, the son of Zebedee (Matthew 4:21). James and John were called the "Sons of Thunder" by Jesus (Mark 3:17). It is believed John was also the youngest disciple since he sat on Jesus' right hand at the Passover meal, and leaned left onto the breast of Jesus. The youngest would sit on the right in a traditional seder and recline left at a certain point as part of the seder meal. It is believed that John and Andrew were disciples of John the Baptist before following Jesus (John 1:40). It is possible James and John were related to Jesus as Salome (James and John's mother) was probably the sister of Mary, the mother of Jesus (Matt 27:56; Mark 15:40; John 19:25). It is also possible that James and John, like John the Baptist, were of the Levitical and/or priestly bloodline. We derive this from the fact that John was able to easily attend the trial of Jesus where only people of Levitical or priestly lineage would have had access (John 18:28-19:42).

John was the disciple Jesus predicted would live the longest (see John 21:21-25). In Christian tradition, Rome tried to kill John by boiling him in oil, but they were unsuccessful. This is only tradition, and we have no way of knowing if this is true. John ended up exiled, as a prisoner, to the Isle of Patmos (penal colony) where he received the book of Revelation. Later in life, he was released from Patmos, and was an overseer of the church of Ephesus. It is believed John died of old age in Ephesus. Early church writings reference John as being an overseer in the church in Ephesus and his tomb being there.

The Synoptic Gospels (Mark, Matthew, Luke) have great similarities, but John is a very different rendering of the life of Christ. John doesn't share one parable, and only a few miracles, but rather, he focuses on Jesus being the Son of God, and the reason why Jesus came into the world. John shows us Jesus came to be a light in darkness and give abundant life. He emphasizes the deity of Christ. John gives details of the gentle treatment Jesus gave Thomas for doubting (20:24-29), and how Jesus reinstates Peter after Peter denied Him (21:15-23).

It is interesting that Jesus' first miracle of turning water into wine, and the raising of Lazarus from the dead, are only mentioned in John's Gospel. Other stories only recorded in John are the healing of the man born blind (9:1-38), the healing of the nobleman's son (4:46-54), and the story of Nicodemus, who was a Jewish religious leader (John 3).

John emphasizes Jesus as the great I AM. We see Jesus revealed as I AM the:

1. Bread of Life 6:35
2. Light of the World 8:12
3. Door 10:7
4. Good Shepherd 10:11-14
5. Resurrection and the Life 11:25
6. Way, the Truth, and the Life 14:6
7. True Vine 15:1

A BASIC OUTLINE FOR JOHN:

1. Introduction. Chapter 1:1-18
2. Jesus is introduced. Chapters 1:19-4:54

3. Jesus' ministry as the Son of God. Chapters 5:1-10:42

4. Jesus in Jerusalem. Chapters 11:1-12:50

5. Jesus with His disciples before His arrest. Chapters 13:1-17:26

6. Jesus' trial, death, burial, resurrection. Chapters 18-21:25

MEMORABLE SCRIPTURES IN JOHN:

John 1:1-5 "In the beginning was the Word, and the Word was with God, and the Word was God. [2]He was in the beginning with God. [3]All things were created through Him, and without Him nothing was created that was created. [4]In Him was life, and the life was the light of mankind. [5]The light shines in darkness, but the darkness has not overcome it."

John 3:16-18 "For God so loved the world that He gave His only begotten Son, that whoever believes in Him should not perish, but have eternal life. [17]For God did not send His Son into the world to condemn the world, but that the world through Him might be saved. [18]He who believes in Him is not condemned. But he who does not believe is condemned already, because he has not believed in the name of the only begotten Son of God."

John 6:35 "Jesus said to them, "I am the bread of life. Whoever comes to Me shall never hunger, and whoever believes in Me shall never thirst."

John 10:11 "I am the good shepherd. The good shepherd lays down His life for the sheep."

John 14:6-7 "Jesus said to him, 'I am the way, the truth, and the life. No one comes to the Father except through Me. [7]If you had known Me, you would have known My Father also. From now on you do know Him and have seen Him.'"

John 20:31 "But these are written that you might believe that Jesus is the Christ, the Son of God, and that believing you may have life in His name."

John 21:25 "There are also many other things which Jesus did. Were every one of them to be written, I suppose that not even the world itself could contain the books that would be written. Amen."

ACTS

Even though the Bible does not clearly state the author, scholars agree that Luke wrote Acts as well as the Gospel of Luke. Luke was a missionary companion of the apostle Paul (2 Timothy 4:11), as well as a gentile physician (Colossians 4:14). By the fact that Luke and Acts are addressed to Theophilus, and the "we" chapters in Acts (16:11-17; 20:5-21:18; 27-28), we conclude that Luke was the author of this book as well as his Gospel. They were both probably written together as one continuous writing (one scroll).

After writing his Gospel, Luke continues in Acts to write about the activity of the early church in the years 30-60s AD. Acts was most likely written between 62-80 AD. It is likely that after Luke and Acts were written, the apostle John settled in Ephesus and wrote his Gospel, letters, and the book of Revelation.

Luke begins the book of Acts with the same introduction to Theophilus, and writes of the ascension of Christ from the Mount of Olives. Ten days after Jesus ascends from the Mount of Olives, the Holy Spirit was poured out at the upper room of the temple area. There were one hundred and twenty present when this happened. It is interesting to point out that the angels prophesied that Christ will return exactly as He left. This means upon His return to Israel, His feet will touch the Mount of Olives. The Bible predicts this in Zechariah 14:4, which states that the Mount of Olives will split in two when Christ stands on it at His return.

Through the baptism in the Holy Spirit, the church gains boldness and power to speak the gospel fearlessly. The book of Acts centers more around Peter at the beginning, but then it moves more into the life of Paul. Acts shows all three of Paul's missionary journeys. This is the basis for understanding the epistles Paul wrote to the churches he planted on these journeys.

The supernatural aspect of Christianity really shines forth in the book of Acts. God has not changed. The church today should be seeing right now everything we read in the book of Acts. The book of Acts tells the story of the stoning of Stephen and the conversion of Paul. Acts shows the transition from the period of the Gospels into the period of the epistles written by Peter, John, and Paul.

Jesus' words that the gospel would begin in Jerusalem, then Judea, after that Samaria, and finally the ends of the earth are shown to take place here in the book of Acts (1:8). We see it begin in Jerusalem when Peter preached on the day of Pentecost. The gospel quickly spread through Judea. Philip takes the gospel to Samaria, and finally Paul takes it to the gentiles. We see how the gospel began among the Jews, but ends up going to the gentiles.

As Paul ends up in Roman confinement, history records Nero had him beheaded. Paul's times of imprisonment allowed him to write epistles and letters.

A BASIC OUTLINE FOR ACTS:

1. Christ ascends. Chapter 1:1-11
2. The birth of the church on Pentecost. Chapters 1:12-2
3. The church in Jerusalem. Chapters 3-7
4. The spreading of the gospel. Chapters 8-12:23
5. Apostle Paul's first missionary journey. Chapters 12:24-14:28
6. Central church in Jerusalem has council meeting. Chapter 15:1-35
7. Apostle Paul's second missionary journey. Chapters 15:36-18:22
8. Apostle Paul's third and final missionary journey. Chapters 18:23-20:2
9. Apostle Paul in Jerusalem and Caesarea Chapters 20:3-26:32

10. Paul's witness and final days in Roman imprisonment Chapters 27:1-28:31

MEMORABLE SCRIPTURES IN ACTS:

Acts 1:8 "But you shall receive power when the Holy Spirit comes upon you. And you shall be My witnesses in Jerusalem, and in all Judea and Samaria, and to the ends of the earth."

Acts 1:11 "They said, 'Men of Galilee, why stand looking toward heaven? This same Jesus, who was taken up from you to heaven, will come in like manner as you saw Him go into heaven.'"

Acts 2:38-39 "Peter said to them, 'Repent and be baptized, every one of you, in the name of Jesus Christ for the forgiveness of sins, and you shall receive the gift of the Holy Spirit. [39]For the promise is to you, and to your children, and to all who are far away, as many as the Lord our God will call.'"

Acts 4:12 "There is no salvation in any other, for there is no other name under heaven given among men by which we must be saved."

Acts 9:4 "He fell to the ground and heard a voice saying to him, 'Saul, Saul, why do you persecute Me?'"

Acts 10:38 "How God anointed Jesus of Nazareth with the Holy Spirit and with power, who went about doing good and healing all who were oppressed by the devil, for God was with Him."

ROMANS

The apostle Paul wrote this book of the Bible to the church in Rome probably after his third missionary journey around 57 AD. It was probably written in Corinth where Paul spent three months (Acts 20:3). The letter was sent by Phoebe (Romans 16:1), who was a deaconess in Cenchrea, which is located near Corinth.

The book of Romans teaches us about the true life found in Christ. It starts by showing God's anger at sin in the first two chapters. Then in chapter 3 we start seeing how we find righteousness in God through faith in Christ alone. The theme throughout this letter is righteousness by faith in Christ alone. Then Paul discusses the battle between the flesh and spirit in chapter 7. This leads into the life that God's Spirit quickens within us in chapter 8. Paul helps the gentile church understand God's ultimate calling and purpose for the nation of Israel in chapters 9-11. In chapter 12 we are taught to offer our bodies as a living sacrifice, and renew our minds with the Word of God, so we can live an overcoming life. Finally, we see how believers need to be like-minded toward one another, and not be judgmental based on personal convictions, as we see in chapters 14 and 15.

The overall theme of Romans is that both Jew and gentile are only made righteous through the cross. It is a comprehensive look at the significance of the death, burial, and resurrection of Christ. There is no salvation or righteousness apart from the blood of Jesus. The focus of Romans is the new covenant found in the sacrifice of Jesus on the cross. We are only justified before God by faith, never by works.

A LITTLE ABOUT THE EARLY CHURCH

It is important to understand that churches met in homes during this time. The book of Romans would have been a letter (scroll), which would have circulated through Rome to these various house churches. Later in history, around 300 AD, Constantine took over Christianity and "Romanized" it to look like what they wanted. The church was forced to move out of homes into cathedrals. This was the birth of Roman Catholicism which perverted Christianity and led to the Dark Ages. Roman Catholicism deliberately removed anything that would appear Jewish, and replaced it with worship similar to the pagan Roman temple worship that Constantine would have been familiar with.

The early church was led by the fivefold ministry in homes. It was very family based, and focused on spreading the gospel. They operated in gifts of the Spirit and walked in the power of the anointing. A typical church service during this time would look almost nothing like what we see today.

Here is an example of what a service would have looked like in the early church:

Arriving at a house on a Saturday evening, there is a host that warmly welcomes you in. Then it would appear there is a lively party going on with music playing and people singing, dancing, and clapping their hands. There would be loud shouts of joy. As worship played, some would flow in the gifts of the Spirit like tongues, interpretation of tongues, or prophecy. The church at this time would have had a very Hebrew flavor to it. This would include Jewish dancing in circles like the Hora. There were early church writings from authors like Clement of Alexandria that described these dances in the early church by the young ladies. The instruments would be lyres, flutes, and tambourines. After much singing and dancing, food would be brought out for the "love feasts." These feasts served the purpose of fellowship and feeding the less fortunate as well.

After the food is brought out, a woman of the house would light the candles, saying a special prayer and blessing unto the Lord. This is a Hebrew custom that would have been taught to the churches. The head of the house would then lead communion with those present as the fruit of the vine and bread was passed out. During the feasting, stories of testimonies were given of what the Lord has been doing in the lives of the people. One of the leaders would give a sermon, possibly read part of a letter Paul wrote to them, or maybe some other portion of Old Testament scripture.

After the meal, worship would begin again. As the presence of God filled the house, the elders would ask anyone who needed healing or special prayer to come forward. Demonstrations of the Spirit's power would take place as some may have fallen on the ground under the power of God. Many healings took place, people were baptized in the Holy Spirit, and some were possibly delivered of a demon. These moves of God continued weekly in the life of the early church. People were taught the Word, experienced the power of the Holy Spirit, and were out sharing their faith with those around them.

For a new believer, the books of Romans would be a wonderful study, but it also may be a little hard to understand. This is why good Bible teachers are so important to the body of Christ. Peter acknowledged this in his writings:

2 Peter 3:14-16 "Therefore, beloved, since you are waiting for these things, be diligent that you may be found by Him in peace, spotless and blameless. 15 Keep in mind that the patience of our Lord means salvation, even as our beloved brother Paul has also written to you according to the wisdom given to him. 16 As in all his letters, he writes about these things, in which some things are hard to understand, which the unlearned and unstable distort, as they also do the other Scriptures, to their own destruction."

A BASIC OUTLINE FOR ROMANS:

1. Introduction by Paul. Chapter 1:1-17
2. God's anger at the sin of mankind. Chapters 1:18-3:20
3. God's righteousness is only found in Christ. Chapters 3:21-5:21
4. Righteousness given to man. Chapters 6-7
5. The life of the Holy Spirit in the believer. Chapter 8
6. Understanding Israel. Chapters 9-11
7. How to practically live out a righteous life. Chapters 12-15:13
8. Conclusion. Chapters 15:14-16:27

MEMORABLE SCRIPTURES IN ROMANS:

Romans 3:23 "For all have sinned and come short of the glory of God."

Romans 5:1 "Therefore, since we have been justified by faith, we have peace with God through our Lord Jesus Christ."

Romans 5:8 "But God demonstrates His own love toward us, in that while we were yet sinners, Christ died for us."

Romans 6:23 "For the wages of sin is death, but the gift of God is eternal life through Jesus Christ our Lord."

Romans 7:24-25 "O wretched man that I am! Who will deliver me from the body of this death? [25]I thank God through Jesus Christ our Lord. So then, with my mind, I serve the law of God, but with my flesh, the law of sin."

Romans 8:14-17 "For as many as are led by the Spirit of God, these are the sons of God. [15]For you have not received the spirit of slavery again to fear. But you have received the Spirit of adoption, by whom we cry, 'Abba, Father.' [16]The Spirit Himself bears witness with our spirits that we are the children of God, [17]and if children, then heirs: heirs of God and joint-heirs with Christ, if indeed we suffer with Him, that we may also be glorified with Him."

Romans 8:26-27 "Likewise, the Spirit helps us in our weaknesses, for we do not know what to pray for as we ought, but the Spirit Himself intercedes for us with groanings too deep for words. [27]He who searches the hearts knows what the mind of the Spirit is, because He intercedes for the saints according to the will of God."

Romans 8:28 "We know that all things work together for good to those who love God, to those who are called according to His purpose."

Romans 13:8 "Owe no one anything, except to love one another, for he who loves another has fulfilled the law."

Romans 13:10 "Love works no evil to a neighbor. Therefore love is the fulfillment of the law."

1 CORINTHIANS

The author of 1 and 2 Corinthians is the apostle Paul. He was writing to a gentile church he had planted. This book of the Bible was probably written around 55-57 AD. The one carrying this scroll to the church in Corinth might have been Timothy (16:10).

Crete and Corinth were known for their sin. Being a port city off the Mediterranean, many transient people trafficked through this area, creating a climate for immorality and dishonest trade. Sinful attractions would have marked this area. Many of the people who were attending the church in Corinth had come out of deep, dark sin, as the phrase "such were some of you" would imply (see 1 Corinthians 6:7-11). Thus, Paul was having to deal with church problems from people who were still spiritual babes within the church.

All the churches of this time period were Spirit-filled, speaking in tongues, operating in the gifts, and seeing the miraculous. In that respect, this church was no different than any other church. A few have erroneously tried to state that the church in Corinth was a "charismatic" church, therefore full of problems. All churches were speaking in tongues. The problem was not with the fact the church in Corinth was Spirit-filled, but rather, the problem was the church was still worldly and carnal (1 Corinthians 3:1-3).

The apostle Paul also defends his apostleship in his writings to the Corinthians (2 Corinthians 5:20-6:10). It is as though his authority was being challenged by some of the rebellious at Corinth.

The greatest revival of Paul's ministry that we know of took place in Asia Minor in the city of Ephesus. While Paul was in Ephesus, he wrote to the Corinthians to correct some problems in that church caused by people who were still carnal and worldly. There are issues of strife, immorality, lawsuits among believers, sanctity of marriage, idolatry, pagan customs, and how to administer the Lord's Supper. Some of these issues can be found below:

1. Disunity and strife. 1 Corinthians 3:1-9
2. Sexual immorality. 1 Corinthians 5
3. Lawsuits among believers. 1 Corinthians 6:1-6
4. Sinfulness in the lives of believers. 1 Corinthians 6:9-10
5. Understanding order in the home and spiritual covering. 1 Corinthians 11:1-16

6. How to properly administer the Lord's Supper. 1 Corinthians 11:17-22

7. Not reverencing what is holy. 1 Corinthians 11:27-34

8. Not properly using spiritual gifts. 1 Corinthians 14

A basic understanding of spiritual gifts is clearly laid out in 1 Corinthians 12. The understanding of all the gifts can be summed up in this simple manner:

- Gifts of the Father given at salvation: (Romans 12:6-8) prophecy, serving, instructing, encouraging, giving, administration, or showing mercy.
- Gifts of the Holy Spirit activated by the baptism in the Holy Spirit (1 Corinthians 12)
    - o Vocal gifts: tongues, interpretation, and prophecy
    - o Revelation gifts: words of knowledge, words of wisdom, and discerning of spirits
    - o Power gifts: faith, healing, and working of miracles
- Gifts given to us by Jesus for the church: (Ephesians 4:11) apostles, prophets, evangelists, pastors, and teachers.

First Corinthians shows how much the Hebrew culture was brought into the gentile church. Paul clearly spoke of these gentiles celebrating Passover when he wrote: "Do you not know that a little yeast leavens the whole batch? [7]Therefore purge out the old yeast, that you may be a new batch, since you are unleavened. For even Christ, our Passover, has been sacrificed for us. [8]Therefore let us keep the feast, not with old yeast, nor with the yeast of malice and wickedness, but with the unleavened bread of sincerity and truth" 1 Corinthians 5:6-8.

A BASIC OUTLINE FOR 1 CORINTHIANS:

1. Introduction. Chapter 1:1-9

2. Dealing with strife within the church. Chapters 1:10-4:21

3. Dealing with immorality, lawsuits, and righteous living. Chapters 5:1-6:20
4. Honoring the sanctity of marriage. Chapter 7:1-40
5. Foods offered to idols. Chapter 8
6. Apostle Paul defends his apostleship. Chapter 9
7. Warning against idolatry. Chapter 10
8. Understanding spiritual covering, order in the home, and worship. Chapter 11
9. Understanding spiritual gifts. Chapters 12-14
10. Understanding the resurrection. Chapter 15
11. Conclusion. Chapter 16

MEMORABLE SCRIPTURES IN 1 CORINTHIANS:

1 Corinthians 1:18 "For to those who are perishing, the preaching of the cross is foolishness, but to us who are being saved it is the power of God."

1 Corinthians 1:25 "For the foolishness of God is wiser than men, and the weakness of God is stronger than men."

1 Corinthians 3:11 "For no one can lay another foundation than that which was laid, which is Jesus Christ."

1 Corinthians 4:20 "For the kingdom of God is not in word, but in power."

1 Corinthians 8:9 "But take heed, lest by any means this liberty of yours becomes a stumbling block to those who are weak."

1 Corinthians 9:22 "To the weak, I became as weak, that I might win the weak. I have become all things to all men, that I might by all means save some."

1 Corinthians 11:26 "As often as you eat this bread and drink this cup, you proclaim the Lord's death until He comes."

1 Corinthians 12:12 "For as the body is one and has many parts, and all the many parts of that one body are one body, so also is Christ."

1 Corinthians 13:1 "If I speak with the tongues of men and of angels, and have not love, I have become as sounding brass or a clanging cymbal."

1 Corinthians 14:18 "I thank my God that I speak in tongues more than you all."

2 CORINTHIANS

The author of this book of the Bible is also the apostle Paul. It seems that this scroll would have been written shortly after the first letter to Corinth between 55-57 AD. The apostle Paul was in a major move of God taking place in Ephesus while having to write these two letters addressing the problems within the church at Corinth.

In this letter we see that the church in Corinth was listening to Paul's first letter and addressing some of the sinful issues in their midst, but there were some rebels that were questioning Paul's authority, causing him to have to defend his authority as an apostle of the Lord (2 Corinthians 11:16-13:5).

This writing also taught the gentile church the importance of sowing and reaping in regard to finances (8-9:15). There was a prediction that a famine was coming upon the land (Acts 11:27-30); Paul was teaching the gentile church to sow into blessing Israel and the poor beforehand. This would cause a blessing to be upon their finances when the famine came.

A BASIC OUTLINE FOR 2 CORINTHIANS:

1. Introduction. Chapter 1:1-11
2. The apostle Paul's travel plans and forgiveness to offender. Chapters 1:12-2:17
3. The ministry of the New Covenant. Chapters 3:1-6:13
4. Being holy and repentant. Chapters 6:14-7:16
5. Sowing and reaping. Chapters 8-9

6. Paul defends his apostleship and exposes false apostles. Chapters 10-13:10
7. Conclusion. Chapters 13:11-14

MEMORABLE SCRIPTURES IN 2 CORINTHIANS:

2 Corinthians 4:4 "The god of this world has blinded the minds of those who do not believe, lest the light of the glorious gospel of Christ, who is the image of God, should shine on them."

2 Corinthians 4:7 "But we have this treasure in earthen vessels, the excellency of the power being from God and not from ourselves."

2 Corinthians 5:21 "God made Him who knew no sin to be sin for us, that we might become the righteousness of God in Him."

2 Corinthians 6:16-18 "What agreement has the temple of God with idols? For you are the temple of the living God. As God has said: "I will live in them and walk in them. I will be their God, and they shall be My people." [17]Therefore, 'Come out from among them and be separate, says the Lord. Do not touch what is unclean, and I will receive you.' [13]"I will be a Father to you, and you shall be My sons and daughters, says the Lord Almighty.""

2 Corinthians 9:6-7 "But this I say: He who sows sparingly will also reap sparingly, and he who sows bountifully will also reap bountifully. [7]Let every man give according to the purposes in his heart, not grudgingly or out of necessity, for God loves a cheerful giver."

GALATIANS

The apostle Paul wrote this letter to the church in Galatia. Paul planted this church on his missionary journeys. Keep in mind that these letters were written on scrolls and passed around the house churches in and around Galatia. The book of Romans also spends time explaining that we are only justified before God by faith and not the letter of the law. It seems that Paul had used a scribe to write previous letters, but in this letter he specifically mentions that he wrote this with his own hand (6:11). Scholars believe this book was one of his earliest letters, probably written around 48-49 AD. After he left, Judaizers came from Judah to pervert the gospel. The dating of this time frame is probably true because the council in Jerusalem (Acts 15) had not yet convened to make a decision concerning the gentile churches in these matters. Most likely the churches Paul was addressing in this book were located in Pisidia, Iconium, Lystra, Derbe, and of course Galatia. These were churches he had established on his first missionary journey (Acts 13-14).

Apparently there were some Judaizers who crept into the churches, teaching people that they needed to be circumcised and live under the law of Moses to be saved. They were also challenging Paul's authority, which is probably why he opened his letter by calling himself an apostle. This false teaching had to be corrected and confronted. Our salvation is based on our faith in Christ alone. This is the gospel in its purest form. If the gospel is allowed to be perverted, these churches would have turned into cults with another spirit at work in their midst.

Some confusion exists in this area that shouldn't exist. When people keep the feasts from a New Testament (fulfilled in Christ) perspective, this is certainly a good thing. If people are keeping the feasts out of a legalistic view, that by doing so they are made right with God and saved by their works, this is a horrible deception that must be corrected. The early church would have been extremely Hebrew. The feasts were kept, but it was understood they were shadows of things to come. We see this in Paul's writings in Colossians 2:16-17: "Therefore let no one judge you regarding food, or drink, or in respect of a holy day or new moon or sabbath days. [17]These are shadows of things to come, but the substance belongs to Christ." The Jewish believers of this time still circumcised their children, but considered it a baby dedication, not a salvation. Paul even taught the gentile churches to keep the feasts as we see in 1 Corinthians 5:6-8: "Do you not know that a little yeast leavens the whole batch? [7]Therefore purge out the old yeast, that you may be a new batch, since you are unleavened. For even Christ, our Passover, has been sacrificed for us. [8]Therefore let us keep the feast, not with old yeast, nor with the yeast of malice and wickedness, but with the unleavened bread of sincerity and truth."

Unfortunately, when Rome took over the church in 300 AD through Constantine, there was a lot of anti-Semitism in the gentile world of Rome. So anything Hebrew was deliberately purged out of the church. Then, Constantine made the church meet in cathedrals and look like the Roman temple worship that he officiated at. This led to the Dark Ages over time. Since the Reformation, we are only now seeing a restoration to the Hebrew roots of our faith like the early church had.

As long as we understand that anything we do is done in faith in the finished work of Christ, and Jesus is the center of it, we can appreciate things considered Jewish properly. The apostle Paul understood the feasts from a fulfilled perspective as Jesus taught us that He came to fulfill the law, not do away with it (Matthew 5:17-20). We see that Paul tried to get to Jerusalem for the feast known as Shavuot (Pentecost) in Acts 20:16: "Paul had decided to sail by Ephesus, to avoid spending time in Asia. For he was hurrying so he could be in Jerusalem, if possible, on the day of Pentecost."

Unfortunately the Judaizers were a group that did not understand the gospel. Paul warned that this was another Jesus, another gospel, and another spirit (2 Corinthians 11:4; Galatians 1:6-9). Paul was shocked that the Galatians would so quickly turn away from the freedom of Christ to the rules of the law. Peter made the mistake of treating gentiles differently than Jews (2:11-13), and received a rebuke to his face from Paul. The apostle Paul strongly and clearly wrote in Galatians that no man is justified by the law in the sight of God, but the just shall live by faith (3:11).

A BASIC OUTLINE FOR GALATIANS:

1. Introduction. Chapter 1:1-9
2. Establishing the gospel. Chapters 1:10-2:21

3. God's grace versus adherence to the law (legalism and works). Chapters 3-4
4. The gospel practically lived out. Chapters 5-6:15
5. Conclusion. Chapter 6:16-18

MEMORABLE SCRIPTURES IN GALATIANS:

Galatians 3:1 "O foolish Galatians! Who has bewitched you that you should not obey the truth? Before your eyes Jesus Christ was clearly portrayed among you as crucified."

Galatians 5:16 "I say then, walk in the Spirit, and you shall not fulfill the lust of the flesh."

Galatians 5:22-23 "But the fruit of the Spirit is love, joy, peace, patience, gentleness, goodness, faith, [23]meekness, and self-control; against such there is no law."

EPHESIANS

The apostle Paul wrote this book of the Bible to a church he planted during a great revival that took place under his ministry. This revival took place over a two-year period, and it can be read about in Acts 19. This book was most likely written during Paul's two-year imprisonment in Rome which was around 60-62 AD. Tychicus was the courier of this letter (6:21). The revival taking place caused Ephesus to be a hub for many other churches. It could be that this scroll was intended to circulate to all the churches in the surrounding areas. There were no specific problems addressed to a single congregation like there was to the church in Corinth. This might indicate that this letter was intended for a wider audience than one single church.

Ephesians teaches us about our authority in Christ (chapters 1-2), how to grow up into Christ in all things (chapters 4-5), and victory in spiritual warfare (chapter 6). Ephesians chapters 5-6 speaks extensively about the order God requires in the home. We learn the husband is the head over the home. Wives are to submit in everything as unto the

Lord, and children are to honor and obey their parents. This teaching comes right before Paul begins to teach about spiritual warfare and the armor of God. For us to really have victory in spiritual warfare, we must first have our homes in order.

The apostle Paul also teaches that Jews and gentiles are reconciled to God and are made into one new man in Christ (2:11-18).

Paul first went through Ephesus on his first missionary journey, but nothing remarkable happened. It seemed he just passed through. On Paul's second missionary journey, God fell in a mighty way. Acts chapter 19 records that many put their faith in Christ during this revival. There was public repentance of sin, burning of occult paraphernalia, and extraordinary miracles taking place. Paul wrote of this revival in 1 Corinthians 16:7-9: "For I do not wish to see you now in passing. Instead, I trust to remain a while with you, if the Lord permits. [8]But I will remain at Ephesus until Pentecost. [9]For a great and effective door has opened to me, and there are many adversaries." We see that when God is moving in great revival, Satan will send much persecution, and there will be many adversaries. This is why Paul taught on our spiritual authority, the armor of God, and understanding spiritual warfare on the earth and in the heavens.

A BASIC OUTLINE FOR EPHESIANS:

1. Greetings. Chapter 1:1-2
2. Headship of Christ over the church. Chapter 1:3-23
3. Understanding who we are in Christ. Chapters 2-3
4. Christian living, homes in order. Chapters 4-6:9
5. Spiritual warfare and the armor of God. Chapter 6:10-20
6. Final words. Chapter 6:21-24

MEMORABLE SCRIPTURES IN EPHESIANS:

Ephesians 2:22 "In whom you also are being built together into a dwelling place of God through the Spirit."

Ephesians 2:8-10 "For by grace you have been saved through faith, and this is not of yourselves. It is the gift of God, [9]not of works, so that no one should boast. [10]For we are His workmanship, created in Christ Jesus for good works, which God prepared beforehand, so that we should walk in them."

Ephesians 6:11-12 "Put on the whole armor of God that you may be able to stand against the schemes of the devil. [12]For our fight is not against flesh and blood, but against principalities, against powers, against the rulers of the darkness of this world, and against spiritual forces of evil in the heavenly places."

Ephesians 6:18 "Pray in the Spirit always with all kinds of prayer and supplication."

PHILIPPIANS

The apostle Paul wrote this letter to the church in Philippi while in jail. Surprisingly, this is probably Paul's most upbeat letter. Timothy assisted in the writing of this scroll, probably around 61 AD. This is the fourth of his "prison letters" along with Ephesians, Colossians, and Philemon. The fact that Paul wrote these letters that became a part of God's canonized Word that has circled the globe and has transformed countless lives and churches, shows us that even in our darkest times of suffering, God can use us in the mightiest of ways. Surely the Lord becomes strong in our weaknesses (2 Corinthians 12:9-10). This letter was probably written during Paul's first imprisonment in Rome (59-61 AD), since there are references to Caesar's household (4:22), and to the imperial guard (1:13). These clues indicate Rome was the location where this letter was written.

The letter was addressed to a specific group. In fact, Paul urged two women, Euodias and Syntyche, to be of one mind in the Lord. The apostle Paul learned to be content in all things and rejoice in suffering. There are sixteen references to "joy" and "rejoicing" in his letter to the Philippians.

The church in Philippi sent a gift to Paul after hearing of his imprisonment. This gift was carried by Epaphroditus (4:18). Paul thanked the church for their support (1:5). Epaphroditus became ill, but after his recovery, Paul sent this letter with him back to the church in Philippi (2:25-29). Acts 16:12-40 speaks of the church of Philippi as having been established during Paul's second missionary journey. Philippi was a leading city in Macedonia which is today in northern Greece. Paul's second missionary journey took place because of a vision Paul had of a man asking him to come minister in Macedonia (Acts 16:9). This is the region where the psychic woman with a spirit of divination (Python spirit) was delivered (Acts 16:16-18). Paul was arrested, but as Paul and Silas sang praises to God, the jail shook and they were freed (Acts 16:25-34). These events caused a good foundation of faith to be laid for the church in Philippi. This church obviously had a deep love for the apostle Paul. Luke (author of Luke and Acts) was the pastor of this church for six years.

A BASIC OUTLINE FOR PHILIPPIANS:

1. Introduction. Chapter 1:1-11
2. The apostle Paul shares of his imprisonment and concerns. Chapter 1:12-30
3. Be servants as Christ was a servant. Chapter 2:1-18
4. Paul speaks of Timothy and Epaphroditus. Chapter 2:19-30
5. Encouragements. Chapters 3:1-4:20
6. Final words. Chapter 4:21-23

MEMORABLE SCRIPTURES IN PHILIPPIANS:

Philippians 1:21 "For to me, to continue living is Christ, and to die is gain."

Philippians 3:14 "I press toward the goal to the prize of the high calling of God in Christ Jesus."

Philippians 4:4-7 "Rejoice in the Lord always. Again I will say, rejoice! [5]Let everyone come to know your gentleness. The Lord is at hand. [6]Be anxious for nothing, but in everything, by prayer and supplication with gratitude, make your requests known to God. [7]And the peace of God, which surpasses all understanding, will protect your hearts and minds through Christ Jesus."

COLOSSIANS

The apostle Paul wrote this letter to the church of Colossae while Timothy was with him. This was probably written during his first imprisonment in Rome (59-61 AD), along with his writings to Philippi, Ephesus, and to Philemon. Colossae was a small town in Asia Minor (modern-day Turkey) about twelve miles from Laodicea. This letter has similarities to the letter to Ephesus and was written at the same time.

Even though Paul had not been to Colossae personally (2:1), this church was probably evangelized during the two-year revival Paul had while in Ephesus (Acts 19). Some evangelists probably went to this area and planted a church, reporting this back to Paul.

Apparently some false teaching had crept into this church that Paul describes as "enticing words" in 2:4. There were teachings of Gnosticism and Jewish teachings of legalism that were trying to creep into the church. Gnosticism teaches a philosophy that the physical realm is inherently evil while spirit is good. Judaizers were not only targeting Galatia with their deception, but they were creeping into the church in Colossae. These false doctrines were endangering the church. Therefore, the first half of the scroll deals with doctrinal issues, while the second half deals with Christian living.

The letter was written to show Christ's supreme authority over Satan as He "disarmed authorities and powers, He made a show of them openly, triumphing over them by the cross" (2:15). It also shows Christ's authority over all creation when Paul states: " For by Him all things were created that are in heaven and that are in earth, visible and invisible, whether they are thrones, or dominions, or principalities, or powers. All things were created by Him and for Him. 17 He is before all things, and in Him all things hold together (1:16-17)." This letter goes on to show Christ's authority over the Law of Moses: "Therefore let no one judge you regarding food, or drink, or in respect of a holy day or new moon or sabbath days. 17 These are shadows of things to come, but the substance belongs to Christ" (2:16-17).

Paul mentions a letter to the church of Laodicea which was never canonized (4:16).

A BASIC OUTLINE FOR COLOSSIANS:

1. Introduction. Chapter 1:1-8
2. The person and work of Christ. Chapters1:9-2:7
3. Confronting false doctrines. Chapters 2:8-3:4
4. Christian living. Chapters 3:5-4:6
5. Conclusion. Chapter 4:7-18

MEMORABLE SCRIPTURES IN COLOSSIANS:

Colossians 1:9 "For this reason we also, since the day we heard it, do not cease to pray for you and to ask that you may be filled with the knowledge of His will in all wisdom and spiritual understanding."

Colossians 1:15 "He is the image of the invisible God and the firstborn of every creature."

Colossians 2:8-9 "Beware lest anyone captivate you through philosophy and vain deceit, in the tradition of men and the elementary principles of the world, and not after Christ. [9]For in Him lives all the fullness of the Godhead bodily."

Colossians 3:2-3 "Set your affection on things above, not on things on earth. [3]For you are dead, and your life is hidden with Christ in God."

Colossians 3:15-17 "Let the peace of God, to which also you are called in one body, rule in your hearts. And be thankful. [16]Let the word of Christ dwell in you richly in all wisdom, teaching and admonishing one another in psalms and hymns and spiritual songs, singing with grace in your hearts to the Lord. [17]And whatever you do in word or deed, do all in the name of the Lord Jesus, giving thanks to God the Father through Him."

1 THESSALONIANS

This book of the Bible was most likely written in 51-52 AD by the apostle Paul who had Silas and Timothy with him. Paul was most likely in either Corinth or Athens (see Acts 17) on his second missionary journey. This could have been Paul's earliest canonized writing. This book was written to encourage God's people that Jesus will return to gather His true elect unto Him. Therefore, with this in mind, "walk in a manner worthy of God, who has called you to His kingdom and glory" (2:12).

The first three chapters of 1 Thessalonians are written to admonish the believers, but the last two were written to deal with doctrine.

1 Thessalonians contains two of the shortest verses in the entire Bible: "rejoice always" (5:16) and "pray without ceasing" (5:17).

A BASIC OUTLINE FOR 1 THESSALONIANS:

1. Greetings and encouragement to the church. Chapter 1:1-10
2. Paul's ministry in Thessalonica. Chapters 2-3
3. Dealing with doctrinal issues. Chapters 4-5:11
4. Final words. Chapter 5:12-28

MEMORABLE SCRIPTURES IN 1 THESSALONIANS:

1 Thessalonians 4:13-18 "But I would not have you ignorant, brothers, concerning those who are asleep, that you may not grieve as others who have no hope. [14]For if we believe that Jesus died and arose again, so God will bring with Him those who sleep in Jesus. [15]For this we say to you by the word of the Lord, that we who are alive and

remain until the coming of the Lord will not precede those who are asleep. [16]For the Lord Himself will descend from heaven with a shout, with the voice of the archangel, and with the trumpet call of God. And the dead in Christ will rise first. [17]Then we who are alive and remain shall be caught up together with them in the clouds to meet the Lord in the air. And so we shall be forever with the Lord. [18]Therefore comfort one another with these words."

1 Thessalonians 5:1-4 "Concerning the times and the seasons, brothers, you have no need that I write to you. [2]For you know perfectly that the day of the Lord will come like a thief in the night. [3]When they say, 'Peace and safety!' then sudden destruction will come upon them as labor upon a woman with child, and they shall not escape. [4]But you, brothers, are not in darkness so that this Day should overtake you as a thief."

2 THESSALONIANS

Apparently, there were some who were very troubled about the coming of the Lord. Not to mention, a false letter had been sent in Paul's name saying the Lord had already returned (2:2). So shortly after 1 Thessalonians was written, Paul had to send another letter to this church.

This gentile church was trying to learn what pleases the Lord since they had no Jewish upbringing. With that in mind, Paul was also establishing some doctrine concerning the end times. Chapter 2 goes into depth concerning end-time prophecy. Paul strongly taught that Christians should work until the Lord returns, and those refusing to work should not eat (3:10). We understand that we must be ready for the Lord's return at any moment, but we must also be faithful to be busy with the things of God here on the earth.

A BASIC OUTLINE FOR 2 THESSALONIANS:

1. Paul expresses his concerns. Chapter 1:1-12

2. Explaining what will happen before the Lord's return. Chapter 2:1-17

3. Final words. Chapter 3:1-18

MEMORABLE SCRIPTURES IN 2 THESSALONIANS:

2 Thessalonians 1:6-8 "It is a righteous matter with God to repay with tribulation those who trouble you, [7]and to give you who are troubled rest with us when the Lord Jesus is revealed from heaven with His mighty angels, [8]in flaming fire taking vengeance on those who do not know God and do not obey the gospel of our Lord Jesus Christ."

2 Thessalonians 2:3-4 "Do not let anyone deceive you in any way. For that Day will not come unless a falling away comes first, and the man of sin is revealed, the son of destruction, [4]who opposes and exalts himself above all that is called God or is worshipped, so that he sits as God in the temple of God, showing himself as God."

2 Thessalonians 3:13 "But you, brothers, do not be weary in doing good."

1 TIMOTHY

The apostle Paul wrote this letter around 63-65 AD to his spiritual son. Paul was older by this time, and his letters to Timothy were some of the last that he wrote before his death. Paul died a martyr, beheaded at Nero's command in Rome. First Timothy was written during Paul's imprisonment in Rome as described in Acts 28.

This writing is the first of the three pastoral epistles Paul wrote. Timothy was now pastoring in Ephesus. The church in Ephesus was a revival church of prominence during this time in church history. Jesus himself wrote a small epistle to Ephesus in Revelation chapter 2.

Paul teaches us to wage a good warfare in prayer concerning the true prophecies we have received. Paul understood that Satan would try to attack those prophecies, attempting to hinder or delay them from coming to pass (1:18). Paul then goes on to teach us when we gather together, we must pray for the right leadership over our countries so we can live in peace and righteousness. In chapter 2, Paul gives us four types of prayers. These are supplications, prayers, intercessions, and thanksgivings.

The overall theme of this letter was to give Timothy encouragement and instruction for his ministry and calling while he was pastoring in Ephesus. You can sense Paul's love for Timothy, his spiritual son, in this writing.

A BASIC OUTLINE FOR 1 TIMOTHY:

1. Introduction. Chapter 1:1-2
2. Confronting legalism and false doctrines. Chapter 1:3-20
3. Instructions on prayer. Chapter 2:1-15
4. Qualifications for leadership. Chapter 3:1-13
5. Exhortation and predictions. Chapters 3:14-6:10
6. Final words. Chapter 6:11-21

MEMORABLE SCRIPTURES IN 1 TIMOTHY:

1 Timothy 1:15-17 "This is a faithful saying and worthy of all acceptance, that Christ Jesus came into the world to save sinners, of whom I am the worst. [16]But I received mercy for this reason, that in me, first, Jesus Christ might show all patience, as an example to those who were to believe in Him for eternal life. [17]Now to the eternal, immortal, invisible King, the only wise God, be honor and glory forever. Amen."

1 Timothy 3:1 "This is a faithful saying: If a man desires the office of an overseer, he desires a good work."

1 Timothy 4:1 "Now the Spirit clearly says that in the last times some will depart from the faith and pay attention to seducing spirits and doctrines of devils."

1 Timothy 6:6-10 "But godliness with contentment is great gain. [7]For we brought nothing into this world, and it is certain that we can carry nothing out. [8]If we have food and clothing, we shall be

content with these things. [9]But those who desire to be rich fall into temptation and a snare and into many foolish and harmful lusts, which drown men in ruin and destruction. [10]For the love of money is the root of all evil. While coveting after money, some have strayed from the faith and pierced themselves through with many sorrows."

1 Timothy 6:12 " Fight the good fight of faith. Lay hold on eternal life, to which you are called and have professed a good profession before many witnesses."

2 TIMOTHY

This was the last known letter from the apostle Paul. Paul begs Timothy to come visit him as soon as possible as his time of death was drawing near (4:6). Paul wrote this letter to Timothy, his dear son in the faith (1:2). This letter was probably written around 66 AD. Paul encourages Timothy to stand against false teaching, live a pure life before God, endure hardships in life (3:12), and believe God to be faithful to deliver us out of trouble (4:18). Paul validates God's Word as given by inspiration of the Holy Spirit, calling it God-breathed (3:16). Paul wrote this letter knowing he was about to die. His parting words are an inspiration to us all to finish well as he wrote:

2 Timothy 4:6-8 "For I am already being poured out as a drink offering, and the time of my departure has come. 7 I have fought a good fight, I have finished my course, and I have kept the faith. 8 From now on a crown of righteousness is laid up for me, which the Lord, the righteous Judge, will give me on that Day, and not only to me but also to all who have loved His appearing."

A BASIC OUTLINE FOR 2 TIMOTHY:

1. Greetings. Chapter 1:1-2

2. Faithful to the gospel. Chapter 1:3-18

3. Being a good soldier. Chapter 2:1-26

4. The last days. Chapter 3:1-9

5. Final words to his spiritual son. Chapters 3:10-4:18

6. Final greetings. Chapter 4:19-22

MEMORABLE SCRIPTURES IN 2 TIMOTHY:

2 Timothy 1:6-7 "Therefore I remind you to stir up the gift of God, which is in you by the laying on of my hands. [7]For God has not given us the spirit of fear, but of power, and love, and self-control."

2 Timothy 2:3 "Endure hard times as a good soldier of Jesus Christ."

TITUS

Paul wrote to Titus around 63 AD after his release from his first imprisonment in Rome. Titus must have been a strong leader able to handle the difficult issues that would have arisen among the believers of Crete. Crete was infamous for its sin and corruption. Paul quotes a Cretan philosopher as he states, "One of them, a prophet of their own, said, 'The Cretans are always liars, evil beasts, and idle gluttons!' 13 This witness is true. So rebuke them sharply that they may be sound in the faith" (Titus 1:12-13). This letter to Titus seems to indicate the church in the area needed to be put in order, and the people needed correction.

Paul left Titus as a leader of the churches of the area of Crete to get things in order as he states in the fifth verse of the first chapter: "For this reason I left you in Crete, that you should set in order the things that are lacking, and appoint elders in every city." We must remember that churches met in homes, and there would have been several in this area. Titus had to be the type of leader who would be "holding firmly the trustworthy word that is in accordance with the teaching, that he may be able both to exhort with sound doctrine and to convince those who oppose it" (1:9).

A BASIC OUTLINE FOR TITUS:

1. Introduction. Chapter 1:1-4

2. Qualifications for elders and deacons. Chapter 1:5-15

3. Teaching sound doctrine and pastoral duties. Chapters 2:1-3:11

4. Final words. Chapter 3:12-15

MEMORABLE SCRIPTURES IN TITUS:

Titus 2:3-5 "Likewise, older women should be reverent in behavior, and not be false accusers, not be enslaved to much wine, but teachers of good things, [4]that they may teach the young women to love their husbands, to love their children, [5]and to be self-controlled, pure, homemakers, good, obedient to their own husbands, that the word of God may not be dishonored."

Titus 2:13-14 "As we await the blessed hope and the appearing of the glory of our great God and Savior Jesus Christ, [14]who gave Himself for us, that He might redeem us from all lawlessness and purify for Himself a special people, zealous of good works."

Titus 3:5 "Not by works of righteousness which we have done, but according to His mercy He saved us, through the washing of rebirth and the renewal of the Holy Spirit."

PHILEMON

The apostle Paul wrote to Philemon pleading with him to take back his slave Onesimus, who apparently ran away from him, but later accepted Christ through Paul's ministry (1:10). Paul calls Philemon a "fellow laborer," implying that he is a Christian (1:1). Philemon was apparently a member of the Colossian church. What we can learn from this letter from Paul is that as Christians we are called to forgive and allow reconciliation in relationships. Apparently Onesimus had stolen some of Philemon's goods when he ran away. Now that Onesimus was a Christian, Paul desired restoration in their relationship.

This is the shortest canonized letter the apostle Paul wrote. This letter was written at the same time Colossians and an unknown letter to Laodicea were written (59-61 AD).

A BASIC OUTLINE FOR PHILEMON:

1. Salutation. Chapter 1:1-3
2. Philemon's love and faith. Verses 4-7
3. Paul pleads for Onesimus. Verses 8-22
4. Final words. Verses 23-25

MEMORABLE SCRIPTURES IN PHILEMON:

Philemon 1:4-5 "I thank my God, always mentioning you in my prayers, [5]whenever I hear of your love and faith, which you have toward the Lord Jesus and for all the saints."

Philemon 1:21 "Being convinced of your obedience, I write to you, knowing that you will also do more than I say."

HEBREWS

The book of Hebrews was written to a very Jewish audience before the destruction of the temple in 70 AD. It was probably written between 66-67 AD, and it has no greeting or hint of its author. It is a bit of a mystery because no one is sure of the exact date or author of Hebrews. Scholars differ on who the author is. It is debated to either be Paul, Luke, Barnabas, Apollos, or an unknown believer. It is unlikely to be Luke. Since Luke was a gentile, he would not have known enough of the information contained in this letter to have written it. Barnabas was from a Levitical family, which would give him a lot of the information contained in this letter. This has led some to believe the writer was Barnabas. Although Paul might have written this letter since he was well versed in the Scriptures, the writing style is very different from Paul's other letters. This is why some don't believe Paul to be the author. Either way, it was written as though the sacrifices in the temple were still going on, so it was written before 70 AD. The writer was acquainted with Timothy, and was most likely in Paul's inner circle. All of this evidence could point to Barnabas as the writer of Hebrews.

The letter was written with the purpose of proving that Jesus has fulfilled the Law in every way, and he is superior to the prophets (1:1-3), angels (1:4-2:18), Moses (3:1-6), Joshua (3:7-4:13), Aaronic priesthood (4:14-8:6), and animal sacrifices under the Law. The book of Hebrews lays out perfect doctrine showing how the Law led up to the gospel, and now Christ has fulfilled the Law. There is a very healthy fear of God in the warnings given in this book of the Bible.

Hebrews 10:19-24 "Therefore, brothers, we have confidence to enter the Most Holy Place by the blood of Jesus, [20]by a new and living way that He has opened for us through the veil, that is to say, His flesh, [21]and since we have a High Priest over the house of God, [22]let us draw near with a true heart in full assurance of faith, having our hearts sprinkled to cleanse them from an evil conscience, and our bodies washed with pure water. [23]Let us firmly hold the profession of our faith without wavering, for He who promised is faithful. [24]And let us consider how to spur one another to love and to good works."

A BASIC OUTLINE FOR HEBREWS:

1. God has spoken by His Son. Chapters 1:1-4:13
2. Superior priesthood in Christ. Chapters 4:14-7:28
3. Superior covenant than the Law provided. Chapters 8:1-10:18
4. Final warnings. Chapters 10:19-13:25

MEMORABLE SCRIPTURES IN HEBREWS:

Hebrews 2:3 "How shall we escape if we neglect such a great salvation?"

Hebrews 4:9 "Therefore a rest remains for the people of God."

Hebrews 8:6 "But now He has obtained a more excellent ministry, because He is the Mediator of a better covenant, which was established on better promises."

Hebrews 9:11-14 "But Christ, when He came as a High Priest of the good things to come, by a greater and more perfect tabernacle, not made with hands, that is to say, not of this creation, [12]neither by the blood of goats and calves, but by His own blood, He entered the Most Holy Place once for all, having obtained eternal redemption. [13]For if the blood of bulls and goats, and the ashes of a heifer, sprinkling the unclean, sanctifies so that the flesh is purified, [14]how much more shall the blood of Christ, who through the eternal Spirit offered Himself without blemish to God, cleanse your conscience from dead works to serve the living God?"

Hebrews 9:27 "As it is appointed for men to die once, but after this comes the judgment."

Hebrews 10:25 "Let us not forsake the assembling of ourselves together, as is the manner of some, but let us exhort one another, especially as you see the Day approaching."

Hebrews 11:1 "Now faith is the substance of things hoped for, the evidence of things not seen."

Hebrews 12:1-2 "Therefore, since we are encompassed with such a great cloud of witnesses, let us also lay aside every weight and the sin that so easily entangles us, and let us run with endurance the race that is set before us. [2]Let us look to Jesus, the author and finisher of our faith, who for the joy that was set before Him endured the cross, despising the shame, and is seated at the right hand of the throne of God."

Hebrews 13:1-5 "Let brotherly love continue. [2]Do not forget to entertain strangers, for thereby some have entertained angels unknowingly. [3]Remember those who are in chains, as if imprisoned with them, and those who are ill treated, since you are also in the body. [4]Marriage is to be honored among everyone, and the bed undefiled. But God will judge the sexually immoral and adulterers. [5]Let your lives be without love of money, and be content with the things you have."

JAMES

The book of James is referred to as the "wisdom book" or "Proverbs" of the New Testament. It was written by James, the half-brother of

Jesus (see Matthew 13:55; Mark 6:3). James was a key figure and leader of the Apostolic church in Jerusalem (see Acts 15:12-34). Even though James is honored as the brother of Jesus (Galatians 1:19), he only refers to himself as a servant. Many gentiles would not know that James is really an English translation of Jacob. This book of the Bible was probably one of the earlier writings of the New Testament, written around 48 AD. This scroll was probably written in a similar time frame as the book of Galatians, and the purpose of the writing was to give wisdom, correction, and show how faith has corresponding good works. James encourages believers to show their faith by their good works, and to view every trial as an opportunity for spiritual growth. This book has very practical advice to help in our spiritual walk. An example of this is how James teaches us to watch what comes out of our mouths. No one has to apologize for something they never said in the first place. It is wisdom to be slow to speak and choose your words carefully.

James pastored the Jerusalem church for many years. He was martyred sometime between 62-67 AD. Some scholars debate as to whether this book was written in 48 AD or possibly right before his death around 60 AD or so. The content would suggest it was written earlier (48 AD) to help correct some errors about faith without corresponding action. Galatians was written around this time to correct some false teachings being introduced by Judaizers.

A BASIC OUTLINE FOR JAMES:

1. What is true religion. Chapter 1:1-27
2. Practical living. Chapters 2-3:12
3. Applying wisdom in Christian living. Chapters 3:13-5:20

MEMORABLE SCRIPTURES IN JAMES:

James 2:19 "You believe that there is one God; you do well. The demons also believe and tremble."

James 4:8 "Draw near to God, and He will draw near to you. Cleanse your hands, you sinners, and purify your hearts, you double-minded."

James 4:17 "Therefore, to him who knows to do good and does not do it, it is sin."

James 5:13-16 "Is anyone among you suffering? Let him pray. Is anyone merry? Let him sing psalms. [14]Is anyone sick among you? Let him call for the elders of the church, and let them pray over him, anointing him with oil in the name of the Lord. [15]And the prayer of faith will save the sick, and the Lord will raise him up. And if he has committed any sins, he will be forgiven. [16]Confess your faults to one another and pray for one another, that you may be healed. The effective, fervent prayer of a righteous man accomplishes much."

1 PETER

The author of this book was Peter, one of the twelve original apostles of Jesus Christ. Most scholars believe Peter wrote this in Rome, and it was probably written in the mid- to late 60s AD right before his martyrdom. First Peter is a more polished writing than 2 Peter. This leads some to believe Peter had a scribe (possibly Silvanus, see 5:12) helping him write 1 Peter. Christian history records that Peter died by crucifixion, but because he did not feel worthy to die the same way Jesus died, he requested to be crucified upside down on an X-shaped cross. Peter lived to be an old man, and he was the apostle to the Jewish branch of Christianity based out of Jerusalem. Paul was the apostle to the gentile branch of Christianity which was more centered out of Antioch and later Ephesus. Babylon was a word used to describe this sinful world we live in under the temporary dominion of Satan (see 5:13). Peter's writings were during the time of great persecution from Rome. Starting with Nero, through Diocletian, were many years spanning ten emperors, during which time persecution of Christians was very intense. These were the "ten days" Jesus spoke about to the church of Smyrna (Revelation 2:8-11). During this persecution, Christians were fed to lions in the colosseum for sport as thousands looked on and cheered. Many were dipped in oil, hung on a stick, and used to light the streets of Rome. Some were beheaded and others were crucified. Satan thought this would snuff out the church, but the church kept growing stronger. Peter's writings were to provide strength, instruction for holy living, and encouragement to those suffering.

A BASIC OUTLINE FOR 1 PETER:

1. Greetings. Chapter 1:1-2
2. Our great salvation and holy living. Chapters 1:3-2:10
3. Righteous living. Chapters 2:11-4:11
4. A message to the suffering church. Chapters 4:12-5:11
5. Final words. Chapter 5:12-14

MEMORABLE SCRIPTURES IN 1 PETER:

1 Peter 2:2 "As newborn babies, desire the pure milk of the word, that by it you may grow."

1 Peter 2:9 "But you are a chosen race, a royal priesthood, a holy nation, a people for God's own possession, so that you may declare the goodness of Him who has called you out of darkness into His marvelous light."

1 Peter 2:24 "He Himself bore our sins in His own body on the tree, that we, being dead to sins, should live unto righteousness. 'By His wounds you were healed.'"

1 Peter 3:5 "For in this manner, in the old times, the holy women, who trusted in God, adorned themselves, being submissive to their own husbands."

1 Peter 5:5-9 "Likewise you younger ones, submit yourselves to the elders. Yes, all of you be submissive one to another and clothe yourselves with humility, because 'God resists the proud, but gives grace to the humble.' [6]Humble yourselves under the mighty hand of God, that He may exalt you in due time. [7]Cast all your care upon

Him, because He cares for you. [8]Be sober and watchful, because your adversary the devil walks around as a roaring lion, seeking whom he may devour. [9]Resist him firmly in the faith, knowing that the same afflictions are experienced by your brotherhood throughout the world."

2 PETER

This book of the Bible was Peter's last writing, and would have most likely been written between 65-68 AD right before his crucifixion. The concept of this writing is to beware of false teachers within the church. Peter wrote this letter obviously knowing his death was near. We see this when he penned: "knowing that soon I will take off this body, even as our Lord Jesus Christ has shown me. [15]And I will also be diligent to make sure that after my death you will always remember these things (see 1:14-15)."

Peter taught that by living out a true Christian life, adding knowledge of scripture, we would be able to be protected from false teachers and heretical doctrines. He wrote "For this reason make every effort to add virtue to your faith; and to your virtue, knowledge; [6]and to your knowledge, self-control; and to your self-control, patient endurance; and to your patient endurance, godliness; [7]and to your godliness, brotherly kindness; and to your brotherly kindness, love. [8]For if these things reside in you and abound, they ensure that you will neither be useless nor unfruitful in the knowledge of our Lord Jesus Christ. [9]But the one who lacks these things is blind and shortsighted because he has forgotten that he was cleansed from his former sins" (1:5-9).

"And we have a more reliable word of prophecy, which you would do well to follow, as to a light that shines in a dark place, until the day dawns and the morning star arises in your hearts. [20]But know this first of all, that no prophecy of the Scripture is a matter of one's own interpretation. [21]For no prophecy at any time was produced by the will of man, but holy men moved by the Holy Spirit spoke from God" (1:19-21).

By having a strong prayer life, thus getting to know the Holy Spirit, gaining personal knowledge of Scripture for yourself, and staying in a strong church, we can stand strong against all deceptive tactics Satan would try to throw against us.

This writing was done by Peter without the help of Silvanus (Silas), and thus it has a different feel to the writing. Peter knew his time was short and wanted the church to hear his warnings before his departure. There are very similar warnings written in Jude that also appear in this writing. It is in 2 Peter that we get the famous quote that with God a day is as a thousand years, and a thousand years as a day (3:8).

A BASIC OUTLINE FOR 2 PETER:

1. Greetings. Chapter 1:1-2
2. Spiritual election and growth. Chapter 1:3-21
3. Exposing false teachers and their heretical doctrines. Chapter 2:1-22
4. The promise of the Lord's coming. Chapter 3:1-18

MEMORABLE SCRIPTURES IN 2 PETER:

2 Peter 1:16 "For we have not followed cleverly devised myths when we made known to you the power and coming of our Lord Jesus Christ, but we were eyewitnesses of His majesty. "

2 Peter 2:9 "The Lord knows how to rescue the godly from trial, and to keep the unrighteous under punishment for the Day of Judgment."

2 Peter 3:9 "The Lord is not slow concerning His promise, as some count slowness. But He is patient with us, because He does not want any to perish, but all to come to repentance."

2 Peter 3:17 "You therefore, beloved, since you know these things beforehand, beware lest you also fall from your own firm footing, being led away by the deception of the wicked."

1 JOHN

The apostle John wrote this letter. It is not stated, but there is sufficient evidence pointing to this within the writing itself. Comparing the Gospel of John with 1 John, we see John mention light (John 1:4-9; 1 John 1:5-6), darkness (John 1:5; 1 John 1:5-6), and in the beginning of both letters, John mentions the Word (John 1:1; 1 John 1:1). There is evidence that the apostle John moved to Ephesus and ministered there. It is possible these letters were written from Ephesus, which was a center of revival after Paul went there on his third missionary journey which is recorded in Acts 19. Scholars believe 1, 2, and 3 John to have been written in the same location around the same time, probably 92-93 AD. In 95 AD John was arrested by Roman authorities and banned to the Isle of Patmos where he wrote Revelation. Church tradition states after his release from Patmos, John returned to Ephesus, then later died and was buried there.

There is an interesting legend that as John lived in Ephesus, he became frustrated with the stubborn refusal of the people to abandon the idolatrous worship at the temple to Artemis (Diana). John challenges the priest and worshippers at their temple to pray to Artemis to kill him, if in fact Artemis was able to do so. Like Elijah of old, John then prays to the one true God, and legend has it that the altar to Artemis split in many pieces, the offerings on it fell to the floor, idols fell and shattered, and half the temple collapsed. As the temple was crumbling, the priest was killed as a pillar fell on him. If this legend is true, it could have been God's judgment at the way the city treated Paul years earlier (Acts 19:23-31), as their false god (idolatry) was being challenged by him.

John wrote this letter to deal with strange doctrines trying to creep into the church. Gnosticism was being presented to the congregants. Gnosticism is a belief that matter is evil and spirit is good. The solution to this problem is knowledge (or gnosis) from which man can rise from the mundane (of matter) into the spiritual. Philosophy was rampant in Greek culture. Therefore, knowledge was elevated above all. It seems that many centuries later, Hinduism (and later, Buddhism) began to pursue nirvana (perfect spiritual state) through meditation and yoga. This escape from the natural into the spiritual probably has roots that go back to Gnosticism.

John confronts this strange heresy along with the teaching that Jesus had been on the earth only in spirit, not in a physical body. This was being taught because physical matter was viewed as evil and spirit as good. John was an eyewitness to Jesus' physical body, and states that "every spirit that does not confess that Jesus Christ has come in the flesh is not from God. This is the spirit of the antichrist, which you have heard is coming and is already in the world" (4:3). This is why John makes statements like: "that which was from the beginning, which we have heard, which we have seen with our eyes, which we have looked upon, and our hands have touched, concerning the Word of life—[2]the life was revealed, and we have seen it and testify to it, and announce to you the eternal life, which was with the Father and was revealed to us—[3]we declare to you that which we have seen and heard, that you also may have fellowship with us. And our fellowship is with the Father and with His Son Jesus Christ" (1:1-3). Notice that John put a strong emphasis on "seen with our eyes, and hands have touched."

This letter was written in great love and compassion from John who is a spiritual father. It does not contain a greeting, or any identification of the author.

A BASIC OUTLINE FOR 1 JOHN:

1. Introduction. Chapter 1:1-4
2. God is light, therefore we must walk in the light. Chapters 1:5-2:29
3. Importance of walking in love. Chapters 3:1-4:21
4. Being an overcomer. Chapter 5:1-12

5. Purpose of the letter and final words. Chapter 5:13-21

SOME MEMORABLE SCRIPTURES IN 1 JOHN:

1 John 1:9-10 "If we confess our sins, He is faithful and just to forgive us our sins and cleanse us from all unrighteousness. [10]If we say that we have not sinned, we make Him a liar and His word is not in us."

1 John 4:7-8 "Beloved, let us love one another, for love is of God, and everyone who loves is born of God and knows God. [8]Anyone who does not love does not know God, for God is love."

1 John 5:13-15 "I have written these things to you who believe in the name of the Son of God, that you may know that you have eternal life, and that you may continue to believe in the name of the Son of God. [14]This is the confidence that we have in Him, that if we ask anything according to His will, He hears us. [15]So if we know that He hears whatever we ask, we know that we have whatever we asked of Him."

2 JOHN

John probably wrote this around the same time he wrote 1 John (92-93 AD). It seems that John was continuing to respond to the heresy creeping into the church that he confronted in his previous writing. John was the oldest living apostle of the original twelve Jesus chose. John refers to himself as an elder, which would be a reference to his age at this point. The elect lady John is writing to probably hosted a church in her home, and she was known by John as someone in the body of Christ who loved the truth. The elect lady and her children could have been an actual family, or could speak figuratively of the church. The Greek word for the elect "lady" is Kyria or Cyria. So it is possible that her actual name was Cyria as some have suggested.

Again, John is confronting Gnosticism which was stating Jesus was not physical, but only spiritual. One of the dangers in this false teaching was that if Jesus did not come in the flesh, he obviously could not have died on the physical cross for our sins. In this writing John calls Gnostics "deceivers and antichrists" (1:7). The churches of this time only met in houses. John was warning the leadership at this house church that if someone believing in the heresy of Gnosticism was to show up for church at their house, do not welcome them in or greet them (1:10). Also, it is very important to have discernment in supporting traveling ministries, lest someone unintentionally contribute to heretical teachers rather than the truth.

False teachers and dangerous doctrines abound today just as in John's time. We have to weigh all teachings by the Word of God, holding fast to that which is good (1 Thessalonians 5:21). We know that in the latter days some will be deceived by doctrines of demons of deceiving (seducing) spirits (1 Timothy 4:1).

This is one of only four books in the New Testament that have a single chapter. It is the shortest according to verse count since it only has thirteen verses.

A BASIC OUTLINE FOR 2 JOHN:

1. Greetings. Chapter 1:1-3
2. Truth and love. Chapter 1:4-11
3. Final words. Chapter 1:12-13

MEMORABLE SCRIPTURES IN 2 JOHN:

2 John 1:5 "And now I ask you, lady, not as though I wrote a new commandment to you, but that which we have had from the beginning, that we love one another."

2 John 1:6 "And this is love: that we walk according to His commandments. This is the commandment, that as you have heard from the beginning, you should walk in it."

2 John 1:9 "Whoever transgresses and does not remain in the teaching of Christ does not have God. Whoever remains in the teaching of Christ has both the Father and the Son."

3 JOHN

Tradition holds that the apostle John wrote this shortly after he wrote 1 and 2 John. John seems to express the importance of showing hospitality, in humility, to fellow believers. It is vital that we extend hospitality, give honor, and support those who travel for the Lord in ministry. The church needs to be willing to feed, give a place to stay, and support men and women of God with itinerate ministries since they depend on our support.

This letter was written to Gaius who receives praise from John (along with Demetrius) for his hospitality as the letter states: "Beloved, you are faithful in all you do for the brothers and for strangers, [6]who have testified of your love before the church. You will do well to send them along on their journey in a manner worthy of God. [7]For His name's sake they went out, receiving no help from the Gentiles. [8]Therefore we ought to receive such men, that we might be fellow workers for the truth" (1:5-8). The writer of Hebrews gives this interesting admonition regarding entertaining strangers: "Let brotherly love continue. [2]Do not forget to entertain strangers, for thereby some have entertained angels unknowingly" (see Hebrews 13:1-2). Gaius was most likely the pastor/elder of a local house church John was writing to.

In contrast John sternly rebukes Diotrephes for his arrogance, wanting preeminence, and refusing to show honor, hospitality, or give support to traveling ministers. Diotrephes also was rebellious and did not recognize John's apostolic authority over the church. John states that he will deal with these church problems in person when he arrives. Those who seek to be leaders in the church are required to be hospitable like we see in Titus chapter 1:

"For an overseer must be blameless, as a steward of God, not self-willed, not easily angered, not given to drunkenness, not violent, not greedy for dishonest gain, [8]but hospitable, a lover of what is good, self-controlled, just, holy, temperate, [9]holding firmly the trustworthy word that is in accordance with the teaching, that he may be able both to exhort with sound doctrine and to convince those who oppose it" (see Titus 1:7-9).

3 John 2 is a scripture used extensively to prove God's will that believers be in health and walk in prosperity. That certainly does not mean that we don't have trials or difficulties, but it does show God's heart to deliver us from trials and move into health and financial prosperity so we can be a blessing to others. It is also important to note that prosperity is far more than financial. Having God's presence in your life, and a loving family around you, are a greater level of prosperity than money could ever obtain. This was reiterated by John in his Gospel when he quoted Jesus: "The thief does not come, except to steal and kill and destroy. I came that they may have life, and that they may have it more abundantly" (see John 10:10).

The Scriptures clearly teach us that it is God's will for us to have healthy bodies (Exodus 15:26; Psalm 103:3; Isaiah 53:4-5; Isaiah 58:8; Matthew 8:17; 1 Peter 2:24; James 5:14-15), financial prosperity so we can be a blessing to the kingdom of God and others (Joshua 1:5-9; Job 36:11; Psalm 1:1-3; Matthew 7:7-11; John 15:7; Philippines 4:19), and prospering souls that are renewed and whole (Psalm 23:1-6; Acts 2:21; Romans 12:1-2).

A BASIC OUTLINE FOR 3 JOHN:

1. Greetings and Introduction. Chapter 1:1-4
2. Praise given to Gaius. Chapter 1:5-8
3. Warning for Diotrephes. Chapter 1:9-10
4. Commendation for Demetrius. Chapter 1:11-12
5. Final words. Chapter 1:13-15

MEMORABLE SCRIPTURES IN 3 JOHN:

3 John 2 "Beloved, I pray that all may go well with you and that you may be in good health, even as your soul is well."

3 John 11 "Beloved, do not imitate that which is evil, but that which is good."

JUDE

Jude (Hebrew Judah) was most likely the brother of James (Hebrew Jacob), who was an elder in the Jerusalem council (see Acts 15) and wrote the book of James. Both James and Jude were Jesus' half-brothers (see Mark 6:3). Jude could have been inspired to write this after Peter's second writing or vice versa. Both Jude and 2 Peter are very similar in many ways. This was probably written around 70 AD shortly after Peter wrote his second letter.

Jude shows his strong concern that we must contend for the faith, correct heresy, and not tolerate evil, divisive men in our midst.

Apparently false teachers were creeping in who were "grumblers, complainers, and walking after their own lusts," using God's grace as a license for their immorality, greed, and overall sinful lifestyles. Jude reminds the reader of Sodom and fallen angels that experienced God's wrath for their sexual immorality, Cain for his violence toward the righteous, Balaam for his lust for money, and Korah for his rebellion against authority. Jude speaks of how their presence brings a sense of defilement to the church services and that judgment would certainly come as Enoch prophesied. Satan diligently tries to sneak his infiltrators into the church. This is why intercessory prayer and leaders with true discernment are essential for the health of the local church. The Bible gives us warnings that not everyone who comes to church is a true believer:

1. Matthew 7:15-20 "Beware of false prophets who come to you in sheep's clothing, but inwardly they are ravenous wolves. [16]You will know them by their fruit. Do men gather grapes from

thorns, or figs from thistles? [17]Even so, every good tree bears good fruit. But a corrupt tree bears evil fruit. [18]A good tree cannot bear evil fruit, nor can a corrupt tree bear good fruit. [19]Every tree that does not bear good fruit is cut down and thrown into the fire. [20]Therefore, by their fruit you will know them."

2. Galatians 2:4 "This happened because false brothers were secretly brought in, who sneaked in to spy out our liberty, which we have in Christ Jesus, that they might bring us into bondage."
3. Acts 20:29-31 "For I know that after my departure, dreadful wolves will enter among you, not sparing the flock. [30]Even from among you men will arise speaking perverse things, to draw the disciples away after them. [31]Therefore watch, remembering that for three years night and day I did not cease to warn everyone with tears."
4. 2 Corinthians 11:13-15 "For such are false apostles and deceitful workers, disguising themselves as apostles of Christ. [14]And no wonder! For even Satan disguises himself as an angel of light. [15]Therefore it is no great thing if his ministers also disguise themselves as ministers of righteousness, whose end will be according to their works."
5. 1 Timothy 4:1-5 "Now the Spirit clearly says that in the last times some will depart from the faith and pay attention to seducing spirits and doctrines of devils, [2]speaking lies in hypocrisy, having their consciences seared with a hot iron, [3]forbidding to marry, and commanding to abstain from foods, which God has created to be received with thanksgiving by those who believe and know the truth. [4]For everything created by God is good, and not to be refused if it is received with thanksgiving, [5]for it is sanctified by the word of God and prayer."
6. 2 Timothy 3:13-17 "But evil men and seducers will grow worse and worse, deceiving and being deceived. [14]But continue in the

things that you have learned and have been assured of, knowing those from whom you have learned them, [15]and that since childhood you have known the Holy Scriptures, which are able to make you wise unto salvation through the faith that is in Christ Jesus. [16]All Scripture is inspired by God and is profitable for teaching, for reproof, for correction, and for instruction in righteousness, [17]that the man of God may be complete, thoroughly equipped for every good work."

True Christians will live a righteous life, reflect God's love, show compassion to the weak, and will help pull sinners "out of the fire" of God's judgment (see Jude 23).

This letter was not written to a specific church, but it was to be circulated to all the churches.

A BASIC OUTLINE FOR JUDE:

1. Greetings and introduction. Chapter 1:1-4
2. Warnings about evil men creeping in. Chapter 1:5-16
3. Final words. Chapter 1:17-25

MEMORABLE SCRIPTURES IN JUDE:

Jude 1:3 "Beloved, while I diligently tried to write to you of the salvation we have in common, I found it necessary to write and appeal to you to contend for the faith which was once delivered to the saints."

Jude 1:24 "Now to Him who is able to keep you from falling and to present you blameless before the presence of His glory with rejoicing."

REVELATION

The apostle John wrote book this while imprisoned on the Isle of Patmos around 95 AD under the Emperor Domitian. After the death of Domitian, John was released back to Ephesus where he made copies of this revelation he received on Patmos, and distributed it out to the churches. Patmos is a small rocky island located off the coast of modern-day Turkey. It was an area where prisoners were placed for hard labor as they worked off their sentence.

This is the last book of the Bible to be written by the last of the original twelve apostles still alive at this time. This is the revelation of Jesus Christ. An alternate title for this book of the Bible could be the Apocalyptic Prophecy. The book of Revelation shows the final work of God to judge evil in the world and reward the righteous for staying true to Him. It is interesting to see parallels to the rituals of the temple in Jerusalem as well as patterns connected to the seven major feasts of the Lord within the book of Revelation. Understanding the Hebrew roots of the faith would assist in understanding the book of Revelation.

You will need to refer to the Biblical symbolism section of this book to help you understand the symbolism of the book of Revelation. Also, you will need to understand the book of Daniel before fully understanding the book of Revelation.

In Revelation 1:1, John calls this book "the revelation of Jesus Christ." He then discusses how it was written to seven specific churches, even though there were many others at the time of this writing. With that said, this writing would have been duplicated and circulated to all the churches, which is why there is a warning at the end of Revelation to not add or take away from it (see 22:18-19).

Chapters 2-3 have an unfolding revelation of the two-thousand-year church age. If it were addressing any other churches, or the churches were in a different order, this revelation would not be accurate. Here is the understanding of the seven churches:

1. **Ephesus**: The first church planted by the apostles, born in fires of revival, operating in the gifts of the Spirit, and strong in the Word of God. This speaks of the beginning of the church age. The Apostolic Spirit filled church.
2. **Smyrna** "crushed myrrh": This speaks of the great persecution of ten emperors from 37-312 AD. The ten were emperors: **Nero**

37-68 AD (killed Peter and Paul), **Domitian** 81-96 AD (exiled John), **Trajan** 98-117 AD (Ignatius, the chief disciple of Peter, was thrown into a den of lions), **Marcus Aurelius** 161-180 AD (Polycarp and Justin and many others martyred), **Septimus Severus** 202-211 AD, **Maximum** 235-237 AD (massacred the Christians and had their bodies buried in lots of 50 and 60), **Decius** 249-253 AD (fiercely persecuted the church trying to destroy it), **Valerian** 257-260 AD, **Aurelian** 270-275 AD, and **Diocletian** 303-312 AD.

3. **Pergamum "Marriage":** 312 AD-590 AD Constantine rose to power and married the church with state and perverted Christianity. Pergamum represents the adulterous church that compromises and is worldly, which became known as the Roman Catholic Church. When suffering persecution, the early church was pure, but now the church becomes like a worldly idolatrous harlot. Pergamum had three major temples: 1. Emperor worship 2. Athena 3. Zeus is the throne of Satan referred to by Jesus. The Roman Catholic Church became an enemy of the true church, as they hunted down, burned at the stake, or imprisoned true Christians.

4. **Thyatira "Continued Sacrifice"** which is what Roman Catholic Mass symbolizes. Thyatira was a little city in Asia Minor. The chief industry was fabric dyeing and fortune telling, which was extremely prevalent in this city. The great rebuke of this church was tolerating Jezebel, also known as the Queen of Heaven. This church speaks of the period of 590-1517 AD, known as the dark ages because the light of the gospel had been snuffed out by religion. The worship of Mary is seen by Catholics as the worship of the "Queen of Heaven." It is interesting that one of the rebukes given in Revelation chapter 18 concerning the Whore of Babylon is that she "sits as a queen" (see 18:7).

5. **Sardis** means "those escaping." Prophetically this speaks of 1517-1750 AD. The church went through the Reformation, and a revival of sorts. The seven stars are God's faithful servants who would preach the truth and the seven Spirits refer to the fullness of the Holy Spirit God gives to those with a heart for restoration. Martin Luther stood firmly on one scripture, Ephesians 2:8-9, which states we are saved by grace through faith. Jesus commended those who believed the gospel and stated they would wear white.

6. **Philadelphia** means "brotherly love" and this church had a heart for God's presence and soul-winning. This church prophetically speaks of the years 1517-1905 AD. In the mid-1700s the Great Awakening through the Wesley brothers, Whitefield, and Edwards/Brainard took place. Then in 1801 the Great Cane Ridge revival took place. In the mid-1800s, Finney saw a great revival. In 1857 God poured out His Spirit again. Then around 1900 we saw the Welsh Revival and Azusa Street Revival. These revivals were used by God to restore the presence of God, the power of the Holy Spirit, and the operation of the gifts back to the church. This prophetically shows the latter-day outpouring of the Holy Spirit that will prepare a bride for the rapture of the remnant out of the earth, cause those seeking the Lord to continually dwell in God's presence like a pillar in the temple, and bring God's blessing upon our lives. This period in the church age could be referred to as revival and missions minded.

7. **Laodicea**: Laodicea was a city located 40 miles north of Ephesus. Laodicea was a large and very prosperous city on the banks of the river Lycus, a tributary of Meander. Laodicea lay between the hot springs of Hierapolis and the cold springs of Colossae. This city was famous for its medical school and eye salve, which supposedly had healing properties. This city was very wealthy and the people were entertainment based. There are remains

there to this day of a theater, gymnasium, and public baths. The people sought continual pleasure. **There was no commendation to this church. Prophetically this speaks of the last-day church we are living in. Laodicea means "right of laity,"** namely the church of people's rights. This speaks of a democracy in the church which is unscriptural. This is a time when laity have supposedly become more enlightened than the ministers, and when their political power is such that they can hire and fire a pastor at will if he doesn't do or preach what they want. So many churches only have a hireling who tells them what they want to hear, rather than a real man of God who will bring correction where it is needed. Hence, it is a spiritually corrupt age. The prophecy of 2 Timothy 4:3 that a time will come when men will not listen to sound doctrine, but gather teachers to themselves that only tell them what their itching ears want to hear, speaks of this age. This is a great warning to the last-day church. We will either be a Philadelphia church that is revival and missions minded (soul winners), or we will be a Laodicean church that is worldly, lukewarm, and selfish (see 2 Timothy 3:1-5).

After the catching away of the remnant bride of chapter 4, chapter 5 reveals the scroll. The scroll is the title deed to the earth. It was what Adam forfeited to Satan, but Jesus has purchased back as our kinsman redeemer. After the seals of the scroll are broken, chapter 11 shows us the two witnesses. Many believe these to be Moses and Elijah. Others believe them to be Enoch and Elijah. The woman of Revelation in chapter 12 is Israel and the Dragon is Satan. After the catching away of the remnant bride of the church in Revelation 4, the church isn't mentioned again until they return with Christ in the clouds. The focus becomes on the nation of Israel.

The two beasts are revealed in chapter 13. The beast out of the earth is the false prophet who will be a spiritual leader like a pope, while the Leviathan-type beast out of the sea is the Antichrist who will be a politician. The false prophet will be able to perform signs and wonders, will deceive the nations, and he will help the political rise of the Antichrist. The Antichrist will unite the world, having ten major nations with specific kings over them that consolidate his power. These ten kings are seen in Daniel as the ten toes on the statue, and the ten horns of the last beast. It is interesting to note that the focus now is on Israel. The seven-year tribulation will be the "days of Jacob's trouble" that Jeremiah prophesied about. The seven heads on the Leviathan beast symbolically speak of the seven major enemies of Israel through the ages: Egypt, Assyria, Babylon, Medo-Persia, Greece, Rome, and the final Babylon (or final Rome) of the Antichrist.

The judgments of God are poured out first in the seals, which could be pre-rapture judgments also called the "beginning of sorrows" by Jesus. The trumpet judgments take place during the first three-and-one-half years of the tribulation while Christians are being persecuted and martyred. These trumpet judgments are connected to the wrath of the Lamb based on how the earth is treating His followers. The bowl judgments are linked to the two witnesses and the last three-and-one-half years of the tribulation as the Antichrist is trying to kill the Jews. These last three-and-one-half years are also called the GREAT tribulation. Jesus stated if these days were not shortened, no flesh would survive (which could imply a nuclear war). The bowl judgments are God's response to how the world is treating the Jewish people and the land of Israel. So there are twenty-one specific judgments predicted to come.

Chapter 17 shows the whore of Babylon which is the Jezebel spirit (Queen of Heaven) associated with the false prophet and the one-world apostate church. Chapter 18 shows political Babylon overseen by the Antichrist in the realm of political power and economic control. This leads into chapter 19 which reveals the return of Jesus in His glory and power with the saints that were at the marriage supper of the Lamb. Jesus will destroy the Antichrist's world system and set up His eternal kingdom on the earth. This return of Christ was seen as the stone that struck the toes of the statue in Daniel 2:34. Chapter 20 reveals the thousand-year reign of Jesus as the King over all kings of the earth. Some believe the Antichrist will be a Muslim, while others believe the worldwide deception will be much bigger than just Islam.

The great white throne judgment is different than the judgment seat of Christ called the Bema seat. When a believer dies, they stand before Christ at the Bema judgment to receive their rewards. The white throne judgment is for the lost. At this time, the lost will be given back their bodies (a resurrection), the books opened to reveal why they are condemned, then they will be cast into the lake of fire for eternity. The final chapter of Revelation speaks of the new heaven, new earth, and the new Jerusalem. After the thousand-year reign of Christ, only those with glorified bodies will be on the earth. The earth will be changed into a heavenly place, in which the natural elements have been purged with God's fire (2 Peter 3:10). The Father will descend with the new Jerusalem, the heavenly city, on to the earth. Then God will dwell with man on the earth for all eternity.

The book of Revelation is an incredible book which reveals God's plan from the church age, into the final days, and into eternity future. It shows God's eternal plan unfolding until everything God has planned and purposed is finalized.

To better understand Bible prophecy, listen to Pastor Scott Boyd's teachings entitled The Spine of Prophecy, which are a very comprehensive study of end-time prophecy throughout all of scripture. To better understand the book of Revelation, listen to Pastor Scott Boyd's teachings entitled Revelation: The Final Days, which is a word-for-word study of the book of Revelation. These can be found on the media page of www.fnirevival.com under the playlist entitled End Time Prophecy. These are free to listen to, and they have corresponding notes.

A BASIC OUTLINE FOR REVELATION:

1. Introduction as Jesus appears to John. Chapter 1

2. The epistles of Jesus to the seven churches. Chapters 2-3

3. The judgments on the world:
    a. Rapture. Chapter 4:1-5:14
    b. Seven seals of the scroll. Chapters 6:1-8:5
    c. The seven trumpet judgments. Chapters 8:6-11:19
    d. The seven figures. Chapters 12:1-14:20
    e. The bowls of wrath. Chapters 15:1-16:21

4. Christ's judgments of Babylon
    a. Spiritual Babylon judged. Chapter 17
    b. Political Babylon judged. Chapters 18-19:10
    c. Beast and False prophet judged. Chapter 19:11-21
    d. Satan judged. Chapter 20:1-3

5. The reign of Christ
    a. Thousand-year reign. Chapter 20:4-6
    b. Final rebellion and judgment. Chapter 20:7-15
    c. New heaven, new earth, new Jerusalem. Chapters 21:1-22:5

MEMORABLE SCRIPTURES IN REVELATION:

Revelation 3:20 "Listen! I stand at the door and knock. If anyone hears My voice and opens the door, I will come in and dine with him, and he with Me."

Revelation 5:13 "Then I heard every creature which is in heaven and on the earth and under the earth and in the sea, and all that are in them, saying: To Him who sits on the throne and to the Lamb be blessing and honor and glory and power, forever and ever!"

Revelation 7:16-17 "'They shall neither hunger any more, nor shall they thirst any more; the sun shall not strike them,' nor any scorching heat; [17]for the Lamb who is in the midst of the throne will shepherd them and 'He will lead them to springs of living water.' 'And God will wipe away every tear from their eyes.'"

Revelation 12:11 "They overcame him by the blood of the Lamb and by the word of their testimony, and they loved not their lives unto the death."

Revelation 14:12 "Here is the patience of the saints; here are those who keep the commandments of God and the faith of Jesus."

Revelation 19:6-8 "Then I heard something like the sound like a
great multitude, as the sound of many waters and as the sound of
mighty thunderings, saying: 'Alleluia! For the Lord God Omnipotent
reigns! 7Let us be glad and rejoice and give Him glory, for the marriage of the Lamb has come, and His wife has made herself ready.
8It was granted her to be arrayed in fine linen, clean and white.' Fine
linen is the righteous deeds of the saints."

Revelation 21:2 "I, John, saw the Holy City, the New Jerusalem, coming down out of heaven from God, prepared as a bride adorned for her husband."

Section Seven: The Bride Made Ready

Be sure and get in the middle of this last-day outpouring of the Holy Spirit. This end-time revival is God's grace to give us strength for the days ahead.

FINAL THOUGHTS

"Now, brothers, concerning the coming of our Lord Jesus Christ, and concerning our gathering together unto Him, we ask you [2]not to let your mind be quickly shaken or be troubled, neither in spirit nor by word, nor by letter coming as though from us, as if the day of Christ is already here. [3]Do not let anyone deceive you in any way. For that Day will not come **unless a falling away comes first,** and the man of sin is revealed, the son of destruction, [4]who opposes and exalts himself above all that is called God or is worshipped, so that he sits as God in the temple of God, showing himself as God.

[5]Do you not remember that when I was still with you, I told you these things? [6]Now you know what restrains him that he might be revealed in his time. [7]For the mystery of lawlessness is already working. Only He who is now restraining him will do so until He is taken out of the way. [8]Then the lawless one will be revealed, whom the Lord will consume with the breath of His mouth, and destroy with the bright-

ness of His presence, [9]**even him, whose coming is in accordance with the working of Satan with all power and signs and false wonders,** [10]and with all deception of unrighteousness among those who perish, **because they did not receive the love for the truth that they might be saved. [11]Therefore God will send them a strong delusion, that they should believe the lie**: [12]that they all might be condemned who did not believe the truth but had pleasure in unrighteousness" (2 Thessalonians 2:1-12, emphasis mine).

I want you to take notice of a few concerning predictions made by the apostle Paul in this passage. First, he predicts that there will be a great falling away. The Greek word used here is *apostasia*, and it is literally translated apostasy. An apostate is someone who walked with the Lord, but later on turned their back on him. The word *apostasia* is also translated as "rebellion" in some translations. What could possibly cause someone to fall away from the faith? In other places the Bible predicts great deception. The simple answer is that they become deceived. The first warning Jesus gave in Matthew 24 in regard to His coming is to "watch out that no one deceives you" (verse 4).

We also read in 1 Timothy 4:1-2, "Now the Spirit clearly says that in the last times some will depart from the faith and pay attention to seducing [deceiving] spirits and doctrines of devils, [2]speaking lies in hypocrisy, having their **consciences seared** with a hot iron (emphasis mine)."

A seared conscience is a conscience that has been hardened and desensitized to the truth of the Bible and the conviction of the Holy Spirit. We see Paul predicts in 2 Thessalonians 2:10, **"Because they did not receive the love for the truth that they might be saved. [11]Therefore God will send them a strong delusion, that they should believe the lie** (emphasis mine)." When people don't love the truth, they are vulnerable to deceiving demons, and the false teachings that lead them away from Christ.

The Bible goes on to warn that there would be false teachers that lead people astray. 2 Timothy 4:3 states, "For the time will come when people will not endure sound doctrine, but they will gather to themselves **teachers in accordance with their own desires**, having itching ears, [4]and they will turn their ears away from the truth and turn to myths (emphasis mine)." This scripture predicts that people will gather unto themselves teachers that tell them only what they want to hear.

We must have such a love for the truth, that we want to feel the conviction of the Holy Spirit when we are wrong. We love the correction of the Lord! We love the Holy Spirit speaking directly to us through anointed preachers calling us unto repentance.

The Bible continues to warn that there would be false teachers, false prophets, false apostles, and infiltrators in our midst.

Acts 20:28-31 "Therefore take heed to yourselves and to the entire flock, over which the Holy Spirit has made you overseers, to shepherd the church of God which He purchased with His own blood. [29]For I know that after my departure, dreadful wolves will enter among you, not sparing the flock. [30]Even from among you men will arise speaking perverse things, to draw the disciples away after them. [31]Therefore watch, remembering that for three years night and day I did not cease to warn everyone with tears."

1 Corinthians 11:13-15 "For such are false apostles and deceitful workers, disguising themselves as apostles of Christ. [14]And no wonder! For even Satan disguises himself as an angel of light. [15]Therefore it is no great thing if his ministers also disguise themselves as ministers of righteousness, whose end will be according to their works."

Another portion of Scripture that is of great concern is the false signs and wonders. God has always moved in great miracles all throughout history, but Satan loves to counterfeit and deceive through false signs and wonders. That is why 2 Thessalonians 2:9 speaks of **"even him, whose coming is in accordance with the working of Satan with all power and signs and false wonders** (emphasis mine)." We see in 2 Timothy 3:7-9 Paul mentions Jannes and Jambres who were the magicians in Pharaoh's court who opposed Moses. The scripture states some are "always learning, but never able to come to the knowledge of the truth. [8]Now as Jannes and Jambres resisted Moses, so these also resist the truth, men of corrupt minds and worthless concerning the faith. [9]But they shall proceed no further, for their folly will be revealed to everyone, as theirs also was."

Revelation 13:14-15 "He deceives those who dwell on the earth by the **signs which he was granted to do in the presence of the beast [Antichrist]**, telling those who dwell on the earth to make an image to the beast who was wounded by a sword and lived. [15]He was allowed to **give breath to the image of the beast**, that the image of the beast should both speak and cause as many as would not worship the image of the beast to be killed (emphasis mine)." We see here the False Prophet will be able to perform satanic signs and wonders to deceive the entire world. This includes (but is not limited to) calling down fire from heaven in full view of men, and giving a statue the ability to speak.

Paul continues to warn us in 2 Timothy 3:13-15 "But evil men and **seducers** will grow worse and worse, deceiving and being deceived. **[14]But continue in the things that you have learned and have been assured of, knowing those from whom you have learned them, [15]and that since childhood you have known the Holy Scriptures, which are able to make you wise unto salvation through the faith that is in Christ Jesus** (emphasis mine)." The word "seducers" is the same word for wizard and imposter.

THE HOLY BIBLE

Notice that Paul tells us in light of all the deception, imposters, false ministers, doctrines of demons, and counterfeit signs and wonders, we must know the Holy Scriptures. If we will truly study the Word of God for ourselves, we will be wise unto salvation and not easily deceived.

Acts 17:10-12 "The brothers immediately sent Paul and Silas away by night to Berea. When they arrived, they went into the synagogue of the Jews. [11]These were more noble than those in Thessalonica, for they received the word with all eagerness, **daily examining the Scriptures, to find out if these things were so.** [12]Therefore many of them believed, including honorable Greek women and many Greek men (emphasis mine)." Notice that the Bereans carefully examined the Scriptures to make sure everything was true.

If we will study the Word and truly know it, we will be kept from deception. We must have a deep love for the truth of God's Word to not fall away. The reason I wrote this book was to impart knowledge of the Word of God in these last days.

As we also see from these scriptures above, we must examine the fruit of people's lives. Don't just accept everyone at face value. There will be false ministers and counterfeit Christians. Jesus taught us we will know them by their fruit. They may look good and know what to say, but the fruit of their lives will reveal what they really are.

KNOW THE HOLY SPIRIT AND TEST THE SPIRITS

1 John 4:1 "Beloved, do not believe every spirit, but test the spirits to see whether they are from God, because many false prophets have gone out into the world."

Acts 16:16-18 "On one occasion, as we went to the place of prayer, a servant girl possessed with a spirit of divination met us, who brought her masters much profit by fortune-telling. [17]She followed Paul and us, shouting, 'These men are servants of the Most High God, who proclaim to us the way of salvation.' [18]She did this for many days. But becoming greatly troubled, Paul turned to the spirit and said, 'I command you in the name of Jesus Christ to come out of her.' And it came out at that moment."

This particular demon of divination was trying to pretend to be the Holy Spirit by stating "These men are servants of the Most High God, who proclaim to us the way of salvation." The apostle Paul discerned in his spirit that it was not the Holy Spirit, but it was a demon that needed to be cast out. Demons can mimic the Holy Spirit with counterfeit gifts of the Holy Spirit and lying signs and wonders. This accomplishes much by spreading deception. Also, those exposed to the counterfeit will usually never accept the real move of the Holy Spirit because of what they experienced with the counterfeit. So this is a very effective tool in Satan's arsenal.

WE MUST DEVELOP A RELATIONSHIP WITH THE HOLY SPIRIT.

Jesus taught us:

John 14:15-17 "If you love Me, keep My commandments. [16]I will pray the Father, and He will give you another Counselor, that He may be with you forever: [17]the Spirit of truth, whom the world cannot receive, for it does not see Him, neither does it know Him. But you know Him, for He lives with you, and will be in you."

John 16:4-15 "I did not tell you these things at the beginning, because I was with you. [5]But now I am going to Him who sent Me, and none of you asks Me, 'Where are You going?' [6]Rather, sorrow has filled your heart because I have told you these things. [7]Nevertheless I tell you the truth: It is expedient for you that I go away. For if I do not go away, the Counselor will not come to you. But if I go, I will send Him to you. [8]When He comes, He will convict the world of sin and of righteousness and of judgment: [9]of sin, because they do not believe in Me; [10]of righteousness, because I am going to My Father, and you will see Me no more; [11]and of judgment, because the ruler of this world stands condemned. [12]"I have yet many things to tell you, but you cannot bear them now. [13]But when the Spirit of truth comes, He will guide you into all truth. For He will not speak on His own authority. But He will speak whatever He hears, and He will tell you things that are to come. [14]He will glorify Me, for He will receive from Me and will declare it to you. [15]All that the Father has is Mine. Therefore I said that He will take what is Mine and will declare it to you."

We see that Jesus was teaching that we must develop a relationship with the Holy Spirit who will lead us into truth. The apostle Paul also taught us:

Romans 8:14-17 "For as many as are led by the Spirit of God, these are the sons of God. [15]For you have not received the spirit of slavery again to fear. But you have received the Spirit of adoption, by whom we cry, 'Abba, Father.' [16]The Spirit Himself bears witness with our spirits that we are the children of God, [17]and if children, then heirs: heirs of God and joint-heirs with Christ, if indeed we suffer with Him, that we may also be glorified with Him."

2 Corinthians 13:14 "The grace of the Lord Jesus Christ, and the love of God, and the **communion** of the Holy Spirit be with you all. Amen (emphasis mine)."

Being "led" by the Holy Spirit is from a relationship. It also implies coming to maturity. Jesus taught us, "My sheep hear My voice." This is accomplished by the Holy Spirit. The Greek word for "communion" with the Holy Spirit is *koinonia*, and it implies "intimate fellowship." So we can see that as we are coming to maturity, we will learn to know the Holy Spirit and be led by Him.

Bank tellers are taught to get so accustomed to the real, in handling money, when a counterfeit comes, they can spot it quickly. If we truly know the Bible for ourselves, and through a powerful personal prayer life, we have developed a deep meaningful intimate relationship with the Holy Spirit, we will know the counterfeit when it comes. The counterfeits will certainly come, but we can walk closely with the Lord and discern it.

As we pray in the presence of the Holy Spirit, we should get so accustomed to His presence, His voice, and His leading, that when another spirit is at work, we can tell it isn't the Holy Spirit immediately.

THE BIBLE WARNS US THERE ARE COUNTERFEIT:

- Christians (Matthew 7:21-23)

- Ministers (2 Peter 2)
- Spirits (2 Corinthians 11:4)
- Gospels (2 Corinthians 11:4)
- Christs (2 Corinthians 11:4)
- Signs and wonders (2 Thessalonians 2:9)
- Teachings (1 Timothy 4:1)

From the parables of Jesus we can conclude the end of the age is the harvest (Matthew 13:39). With that said, the harvest field had both wheat and tares in it (Matthew 13:24-30). It took the activity of angels to remove the tares from among the wheat. This gives us revelation on how we should pray. The angels will be effective in the removal of the tares from our midst.

Finally, Matthew 25:1-13 teaches us that only half of God's people (virgins) were ready when He comes. The only difference was who had extra oil and who didn't. The extra oil is the Holy Spirit. We won't get enough oil by trying to ride someone else's prayer life or personal revival. We must cultivate a strong prayer life for ourselves. The Lord will continue to pour out His Spirit in these last days, and we need to get in the move of the Spirit, but don't make the mistake of replacing the move of God for your own personal prayer life.

CLOSING

There has been a deceptive hybrid false "Christianity" that has been emerging for years. This group does not require a new birth, or repentance of sins. They do not believe the Bible is infallible, and do not accept the activity of the Holy Spirit. They do, however, embrace the deconstruction movement, support abortion, are for LGBTQ movements, and will be one of the greatest persecutors of God's elect in these last days. You can see them represented in the cross of the COEXIST bumper stickers out there. These fake Christians attend large gatherings that are just a social club full of programs and entertainment. Eventually, they will align themselves with the False Prophet and the Antichrist. This will be a one-world ecumenical global religion the Bible calls the harlot church of Babylon (Revelation 17). The whore of Babylon will sit over this group like a queen as they give their allegiance to the Antichrist.

Hebrews 5:14 "Solid food belongs to those who are mature, for those who through practice have powers of discernment that are trained to distinguish good from evil."

As we spend time daily in prayer, and in the Word, we will develop our inner man to distinguish between good and evil.

We must be ready for these days ahead. Begin now to develop a powerful personal prayer life. Start attending an anointed church where the truth is preached, and the power of the Holy Spirit is actively at work. Begin to deeply study the Bible for yourself. Stay away from the critics of revivals as they are also Satan's servants. They are modern-day Pharisees who persecute the move of God and power of the Holy Spirit. Develop a deep intimate relationship with the Holy Spirit. Ask the Lord for wisdom and discernment, and be accountable to a local fellowship. Make sure to be found faithful when the Lord comes by doing what He has called you to do, living a righteous life, faithfully tithing, faithfully attending church, and being faithful to your spouse and family.

If you will use this book to its potential, I believe it will help you have a powerful prayer life, know the Bible for yourself, and be an effective witness for the Lord.

For twenty years, Sandy Boyd was trapped in the dark and evil world of Satanism, witchcraft, and the occult.

Her father dedicated her to Satan and used her in satanic rituals from childhood. With over twenty years of ministry experience and countless lives set free, Scott and Sandy Boyd release this book in the hope of seeing many set free. This book gives the in-depth look into Sandy Boyd's powerful story, and teaching, that will equip you to be free and see many others set free.

www.fnirevival.com